Walter Dick *Florida State University*
Lou Carey *Florida State University*

The Systematic Design of Instruction

Scott, Foresman and Company   Glenview, Illinois
Dallas, Tex.   Oakland, N.J.   Palo Alto, Cal.   Tucker, Ga.   London, England

Dedicated to the Memory of
    Dr. Robert M. Kibler

In his brief life
He showed us how to learn,
How to communicate,
    and most of all
How to act on what seems right.

Library of Congress Cataloging in Publication Data

Dick, Walter, 1937-
    The systematic design of instruction.

    Includes bibliographies and index.
    1. Individualized instruction.   2. Lesson planning.   3. Teaching—Aids and devices.
I. Carey, Lou, joint author.   II. Title.
LB1031.D5   371.39′4   77-14138
ISBN 0-673-15122-0   678910-MPC-8584

Preface

In the past fifteen years there has been a significant trend toward the careful design of instructional systems at all levels and in all types of educational institutions. While "systematic instruction" has many definitions, it almost always conveys the idea of greater reliance on instructional materials for the presentation of content and on teachers for testing and personal guidance of students.

This book is intended for those who wish to develop skills for designing instructional materials, or who want to gain knowledge about the instructional process. This audience includes undergraduate teacher-education students; classroom instructors; instructional designers working for professional schools such as medicine, law, or allied health sciences; materials designers for adult and vocational education; and instructional designers involved with military or industrial training.

The systems approach model used in this book was first taught in a course at Florida State University in 1968. Since that time hundreds of students have taken the course and have developed instructional materials which have had demonstrated effectiveness with learners. The systems approach model is not a simplistic model, nor is it so highly complex that users could not use it practically in their work. The model has been most heavily influenced by the work of Robert Gagné, Leslie Briggs, Robert Mager, Robert Glaser, and Lee Cronbach. It is a behaviorally oriented model which stresses the identification of skills students need to learn, and the collection of data from students to revise instruction.

During the nine years we have taught the instructional design course, we have had the valuable opportunity to observe our students' work and thus to refine our presentation of the concepts and procedures associated with each step in the model. This book is the culmination of a carefully conceived instructional strategy and of the many years of practical experience in teaching it. The first chapter describes the growth of individualized instruction and the use of systematic design procedures. Each of the next ten chapters is devoted to a component of the model.

Perhaps the most important feature of this book is the regular linking of the theoretical descriptions of the concepts with numerous illustrations of their application. The examples have been carefully selected to represent a wide range of content in order to appeal to the largest audience. The examples and practice exercises have been designed to lead the reader from an initial understanding of concepts to their practical application, resulting in his or her own instructional design project. We have kept our examples purposefully simple in content because the purpose of this book is to teach process. When content is purposefully simple, the reader can concentrate on process.

The authors wish to acknowledge the patience and criticism of the students who used the text during its formative stages. Their individual suggestions as well as their test performances provided an invaluable data base for subsequent revisions. The authors retain the responsibility for any errors, either of omission or commission, which still remain.

The reader will find that each of the chapters following the introduction is structured in a similar manner. We hope this structure will facilitate the learning of the concepts and procedures associated with the instructional design model. The description of the model's components in each of the chapters is outlined in the following paragraphs.

Objectives. The major objectives are listed for each chapter. They describe what the reader should be able to do after completing the unit. They are stated in relatively general terms.

Background. This portion of each chapter provides the reader with a brief statement of the background, research and development, and/or problems which have led to the development of the procedures associated with each particular component of the model.

Concepts. This section includes both definitions of critical concepts associated with the component as well as a description of "how to do it." It indicates how to carry out the procedures associated with each particular component.

Examples. In each unit we provide examples of ways the processes described for each component can be applied. We use a variety of examples so that the reader will be able to apply each procedure to the particular content area in which he or she is interested.

Practice and Feedback. We also provide a series of practice activities in which the reader is required to apply the process to a variety of examples. Students will receive feedback on their responses in order to determine if they have understood the principles involved in the chapter and to correct any difficulties they may be having. The examples used to illustrate procedures in the book have been purposefully kept simple. The reader should not have to learn the content related to an example to understand the procedure, which is the main focus.

Implementation. This section is specifically provided for those readers who will be developing instructional materials as they study these chapters. It organizes the concepts and procedures discussed in each chapter into an input, process, and output framework. By presenting the material in this manner, we hope to illustrate the interrelatedness of the various components of the model.

References. A brief listing of the most relevant references appears at the end of each chapter. These are annotated to direct the reader to those resources which may help to amplify points made in the chapter.

Contents

1 Origins of Systematically Designed Instruction

We educators are sometimes the last persons to recognize the magnitude of changes that are taking place in our own profession. Perhaps it is because we are so close to the trees that we cannot see the forest. If we consider for a moment what has happened in public education during the past decade, however, we can see that there has been a tremendous broadening of the content included in the academic curriculum as new subject matter is added. Career education and environmental education have emerged as separate instructional areas or have been integrated into existing courses. In addition, advanced placement courses have been added for talented high-school students, and colleges and universities are granting advanced placement in their own programs to these students. There has also been a steady increase in the amount and type of in-service training provided for persons already on the job.

Vocational/technical schools have been growing at increasing rates and are providing instructional opportunities which have been unavailable to many students in the past. In addition, schools have added more work-study programs which have permitted students to stay in school and complete their formal programs while working at part-time employment.

More dramatic types of changes have occurred in the establishment of both public and private alternative schools. These schools attempt to use radically different procedures to reach the specially talented, or the less capable student.

There have been other types of changes in the last decade such as the consolidation of rural schools in order to maximize the use of resources and the employment of business management techniques in schools to get the most from the available resources. Likewise, teachers in more and more school districts are becoming organized as unions begin to play a role in public education.

During this time, students have become freer in their expression of their feelings about what is right and what is wrong in the culture and in the schools. It appears they have established a different type of relationship with their peers and with school personnel. Young people have defined for themselves what they will consider success and nonsuccess in their culture. No longer will they accept the traditional value that everyone must go to college to succeed. They, too, are looking for alternatives.

Nowhere is there more evidence of an effort to try to serve the needs of students than in the trend toward systematically designed instruction in education. In the past, teachers have been taught that they should attend to the needs of each and every individual student. But, teachers were employed in classrooms where their only alternative was to treat the students as a group and proceed in a lockstep manner to try to provide the best instruction for the total group. In essence they were not provided with the methodology required to attend to individual student needs. Systematically designed instruction provides teachers with statements of exact skills to be learned. These statements can be used to determine each student's instructional needs in order to tailor instruction to each student as much as possible.

MAJOR APPROACHES TO INSTRUCTION

If asked, each reader could probably provide a definition of individualized instruction and believe it was fairly accurate and reflective of the current thinking of most educators about individualization. If these definitions were shared, however, one might find almost as many definitions of individualized instruction as there are persons using the term. Current definitions vary from those that say students will proceed at their own rate through a prescribed set of materials to reach a predetermined set of objectives, to definitions that say students will be free to select their own means of achieving their own objectives. These two types of definitions reflect in part the two traditions which have contributed the most to the growth of systematically designed instruction. These two approaches may be characterized as the *humanistic approach* and the *behavioral science or systems approach* to instruction.

Educators who consider themselves in the humanistic camp have a genuine interest in the total development of individual children. They recognize the importance of individual differences and believe that the essence of an outstanding education is to show genuine care and concern for students as they attempt to define those areas of learning which are important and relevant to them. There is a strong focus on the personal growth and development of the individual student. This emphasis on individual personal development and human relationships is an attempt to counteract the increasing alienation which students encounter in their society and perhaps in their own homes. The rapid growth of the book sales in personal development and in the establishment of various personal development groups reflects society's interest in these same problems.

It is probably no overstatement to say that most teachers view themselves as humanists. Surveys indicate that many select the teaching profession because of their interest in helping students. Teachers are almost always concerned about the feelings, attitudes, beliefs, and values of students, that is, about those things which make an individual distinctly human. Many teacher-training programs can also be viewed as humanistic, since they focus upon the importance of the interactive relationship between the teacher and the student and emphasize such aspects of the educational process as flexibility and adaptability, methods of learning, self-actualization, discovery methods, and promotion of each student's individuality. In essence, humanistically oriented teachers believe that there is no best way to manage a classroom or to organize a learning experience. They believe there is no single formula for good teaching, but rather a number of approaches, one or more being appropriate for the needs of a particular student.

Some teachers prefer a behavioral approach to teaching. These individuals tend to view the teacher as one responsible for instruction in cultural heritage, social responsibilities, and specific subject matter. They believe that these matters can not be left to the individual interests of students alone. This type of teacher emphasizes a carefully prepared lesson plan, logically organized material, and specific educational objectives and tends to emphasize "getting the correct answer." In essence, these teachers prefer a systematic approach which utilizes research knowledge on the conditions of learning required for students to achieve clearly defined outcomes. Much of the knowledge already gained through research is now used in the development of instructional materials, but little has been incorporated into teacher-training programs.

The systematic approach to instruction had its initial impact on the development of programmed instruction. This medium of instruction emphasizes the importance of a precise definition of what it is that the student will learn and the importance of careful structuring of instructional materials. Programmed instruction requires the active participation of students in instruction to facilitate achievement of given objectives. Many of the teaching principles of programmed instruction are applied today in the systematic design of instructional materials, although programmed instruction per se is not in great use.

Both of these instructional approaches—the humanistic and the behavioral—emphasize the significance of individual differences and the necessity for providing appropriate instruction to the student. More and more teachers, especially at the elementary-school level, have begun to individualize their instruction in the classroom. They have either designed their own systems and modified materials for their students, or they have adopted one of the national individualized instruction systems such as Individually Prescribed Instruction (IPI), Plan for Learning According to Needs (PLAN), or Individually Guided Education (IGE). These national programs provide schools with descriptions of procedures as well as materials and teacher-training aids to implement individualized instruction. As a result of these efforts, there has been more and more interest shown in the development of new and effective instructional techniques for individualized instruction.

It should be noted that while in academic circles representatives of humanism and behaviorism debate the merits of their approaches, there is little evidence of this conflict when one views individualized instruction in use in classrooms. Recent studies by Fox and DeVault (1974) indicate that the best examples of individualized instruction are those that blend the best of both the humanistic and the systems approaches to instruction. Though this book will stress the behavioral science approach to designing, developing, and evaluating instruction, the authors are in full accord with Fox and DeVault's position that the humanistic and systems approaches must be integrated in the classroom to provide the best atmosphere for effective student learning.

THE ROLE OF THE TEACHER

If the trend in education is toward a genuine integration of humanism and behaviorism, then how will this affect the role of the teacher? It is our thesis that the primary role of the teacher is that of designer of instruction, with accompanying roles of implementor and evaluator of instruction. This is a critical statement to consider. If education is to meet the needs of individual students through provision of appropriate knowledge and training in important skills, there must be increased dependence upon well-designed, effective instruction. Teacher-dependent, group-paced instruction can no longer serve as the primary model for the teacher. Conversely, teachers have been, are, and will continue to be designers of at least some of their own instructional materials. Some of the best teachers have been doing this intuitively for years. However, it will become more important for teachers to have technical skills that will enable them to design *and* implement instruction in the classroom. In addition, they must be prepared to make wise decisions about the selection of materials developed elsewhere. Knowledge of instructional design techniques will greatly enhance each teacher's ability to select such materials wisely. Certainly, not all instruction will (or should) be based totally on the use of instructional materials. Interactive classroom instruction will continue, and such instruction should be planned and designed with the same precision as that used in designing instructional materials.

The integration of the humanistic and behaviorist approaches means a change in the teacher's role. There is a reduced need for the teacher to disseminate information. Obviously, the teacher must be concerned with the act of teaching. The expanded role includes monitoring the progress of students using individualized materials, tutoring and counseling students, conducting small-group discussions, assisting with special projects, and, when necessary, presenting major topics to an entire class. The teacher must also act as evaluator—not only of student success in the learning process, but also of the instructional process itself. Did the instruction work? For which students, and to what extent? What components of the instruction failed? What aspects could be improved? Teachers should answer these questions systematically and use their answers to redesign the instruction for future use.

While the skills of implementation and evaluation of instruction are crucial to the teacher, an equally critical skill is that of instructional design.

Principles that have been successfully applied by professional instructional designers can prove equally valuable to the instructor. One can apply them to the design of instruction or to the selection or modification of existing materials. One can also use them in the design of a strategy that incorporates a collection of varying instructional modes, including interactive instruction and group activities in the classroom. This text is designed primarily to teach the skills associated with instructional design and evaluation processes, with considerable emphasis also given to the application of these skills to the selection of instructional materials, the development of lesson strategies, and the implementation of instruction in the classroom.

The authors recognize that, in the "real world," teachers are unable to design materials for all their own instruction. On the other hand, it is important that teachers obtain the required skills to design materials because of the applicability of such skills to other parts of the instructional process. Because of this emphasis on instructional design skills, for the remainder of this text the teacher will be referred to interchangeably as the instructor or the instructional designer. It should be understood that these references are not made to professionals who have a full-time responsibility for designing instructional materials, but rather to the teacher who has the ongoing responsibility for teaching specific content to a specific group of learners. Having considered this evolving role of the instructor, we now examine the nature of the instructional materials used in individualized instructional programs. The paragraphs that follow describe these materials.

CHARACTERISTICS OF INSTRUCTIONAL MATERIALS

The types of instructional materials which are typically used in systematically designed instruction have come to be referred to as modules. Just as there is no universally accepted definition of individualized instruction, similarly there is no general definition of a module. An analogy may help in this explanation. Consider the technique known in the building industry as *modular construction.* Various components of a building are built and assembled in a factory and shipped to the construction site. These components, or modules, are then assembled in a particular configuration that results in the construction of a new building. Workers are still required to drive the nails and place the screws and bolts which hold the entire structure together. They also pour the foundation and add the finishing touches that make it a sound and secure building.

One may consider modular instruction in much the same way. A module is a self-contained or self-instructional unit of instruction that has an integrated theme, provides students with information needed to acquire specified knowledge and skills, and serves as one component of a total curriculum.

Most instructors would agree with the definition given above. However, they would differ on a number of the specific characteristics of modules. For example, the length of time required for students to study a module may vary from one to fifteen hours. Even less time may be required for very young children. Some designers will insist that a module of instruction should include at least two alternative conceptual presentations of the instructional materials and preferably two or more modes of presentation to accommodate individual differences. Other designers would not agree that all these alternatives are necessary.

In addition, some instructors would argue that a module should be strictly self-contained. That is, a student should be able to achieve all the objectives which are stated in the module without interacting with the teacher or other individuals. Other instructors will specifically include in the design of the module the participation of peers, teachers, and outsiders in order to involve the student in a variety of interactive activities.

Many instructors even differ on whether students should be informed of the major objectives for a module. Some insist that students should receive precise statements of the objectives for a module, while others argue that objectives may be reworded at a level more appropriate for the student, or that objectives may be omitted all together.

Regardless of the issues listed above, most modules require the students to interact actively with the instructional materials rather than simply allowing the students to read the materials passively. The students are asked to perform various types of learning tasks and receive feedback on that performance. There is some type of testing strategy that tells the students if they achieved mastery of the content and what they should do if they did not.

Based upon the description in prior paragraphs, how would you recognize a module if you saw one? In its most simple form, a module might be a typewritten statement to students that says what it is they are about to learn and how they will be tested. It would provide printed or typed instructional materials as well as some practice test items. A self-test which might be used prior to taking a terminal test could also be included.

The most complex module might contain all of the items listed above, but might also incorporate a number of alternative sets of materials from which the student could choose the most appropriate one for him or herself. Alternative media forms such as audiotapes or filmstrips could also be included. In addition, the student might go to a laboratory to conduct an experiment or go outside the school to gather information.

Regardless of the complexity of a module, it should be validated; that is, it should be demonstrated that students learn from it—that they can perform the skills as described in the objectives for the module. Methods have been developed which are used to obtain information from students as a module is being developed to improve its quality. After the module has been completed, data are collected which are used to demonstrate the extent to which the module is effective in bringing about anticipated changes in student behavior.

This empirical approach to the development of instruction most distinctly differentiates the systems approach from prior approaches to designing instruction. In the next section, the general systems approach to designing instruction will be presented. The importance of empirical evaluations and revisions of instruction will become more apparent in later chapters.

A SYSTEMS APPROACH MODEL FOR INSTRUCTIONAL DESIGN

Given the need to develop instructional materials, what is the best method to accomplish the task? One seemingly reasonable approach is to use an existing module as a model. There are several problems associated with this approach. Any given module is designed to teach a particular type of learning to a particular type of student. What is needed is a more generalized model—one which will describe the procedures for developing a module regardless of the type of learner or the type of learning which is to occur.

One general model for designing instructional materials is referred to as the *systems approach model*. We emphasize, however, that there is no single systems-approach model for designing instruction. There are a number of models which bear the label "systems approach," and all of them share most of the same basic components. The systems approach model, which will be presented in this book, includes the major components that are included in other models, but this model is perhaps less complex than some.

The systems approach models are an outgrowth of over twenty years of research into the learning process. Each component of the model is based upon theoretical or research outcomes which demonstrate the effectiveness of that component. The model brings together in one coherent whole many of the concepts that you may have already encountered in a variety of educational situations. For example, you undoubtedly have heard of behavioral objectives and may have already developed some yourself. Such terms as *criterion-referenced testing* and *formative evaluation* may also be familiar. The model will show how these terms, and the processes associated with them, are interrelated and how these procedures can be used to produce instructional materials that work.

The model, as it is presented here, is based upon both research and a considerable amount of practical experience in its application. We suggest that the novice instructional designer use the model principally in the sequence and manner that we present it in this chapter. Hundreds of students who have done so have produced effective instructional materials. On the other hand, we acknowledge that in particular circumstances and with increased experience with a model, you may change the model in order to meet those particular circumstances. Also, we expect that more research and experience will help to amplify the procedures associated with each component of the model.

In the section that follows, we will present the general systems approach model (and you can read it) in much the same way as a cookbook recipe—you do this and then that and you have a pie. When you begin to use a recipe in your own kitchen, however, it takes on greater meaning, just as the model will when you begin to involve your own interests with the topic you have selected: you develop your own instructional resources, you select your own set of learners, and so on. Your perspective on the model will probably change greatly. In essence, your use of your own kitchen, your own ingredients, and your own personal touch will result in a unique product.

This discussion is a roundabout way of saying that there are two levels at which this book may be used by the reader. The first is at an academic, cognitive level at which you learn new terminology, concepts, and how they may be integrated as an approach to designing instructional materials. The second level is at a productive or developmental level, and it sharply differs from the first. It involves the production of your own module at the same time that you study these units. This combination of the conceptual and productive study of a systems approach model seems to provide a depth of perspective on these techniques which is nearly impossible to obtain by studying only the cognitive information.

The model which will be described in detail in succeeding chapters is graphically presented in Figure 1.1. The model includes eight interconnected boxes and a major line that shows feedback from the last box to the earlier boxes. The boxes refer to sets of procedures and techniques which are employed by the instructional designer to design, produce, evaluate, and revise an instructional module. The steps will be briefly described in sequence. Each will be described in much greater detail in later chapters.

Components of the Systems Approach Model

Identifying an instructional goal. The first step in the model is to determine what it is that you want students to be able to do when they have completed your instruction. The definition of the instructional goal may be derived from a statement of goals, from a needs assessment with regard to a particular curriculum, or from practical experience with learning difficulties of students in the classroom.

Conducting an instructional analysis. After you identify the instructional goal, you will analyze it in order to identify the subordinate skills that a student must learn in order to achieve that goal. This process may result in the identification of concepts, rules, and information which a student needs, or the identification of steps in a procedural sequence which must be followed to perform a particular process.

Identifying entry behaviors and characteristics. In addition to identifying the substance of the content which must be included in the instruction, it will be necessary to identify the specific skills that students must have prior to beginning instruction. You need to determine not only the specific knowledge and skills students must have in order to be ready to use the module, but also the general characteristics of the learners which may be important to the design of the instruction. These characteristics might include special interests, maturation level, attention span, and so on.

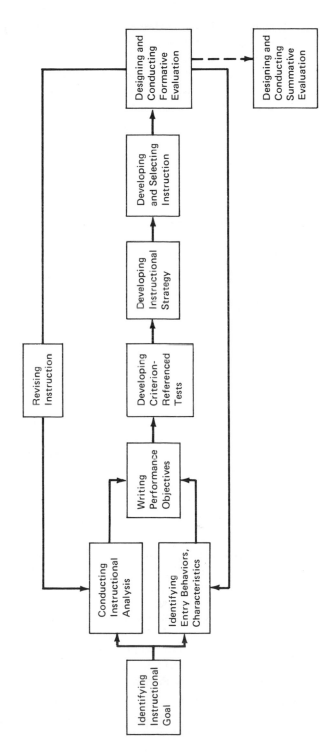

Figure 1.1   Systems Approach Model for Designing Instruction

Writing performance objectives. Based on the instructional analysis and the statement of entry behaviors and characteristics, you will write specific statements of what it is the students will be able to do when they complete your module. These statements, which are derived from the skills identified in the instructional analysis, will identify the skills students will learn, the conditions under which they must perform these skills, and the criteria for successful performance.

Developing criterion-referenced tests. Based on the objectives you have written, you then develop assessment instruments which are parallel to and measure the student's ability to achieve what you described in the objectives. Major emphasis is placed on relating the kind of behavior described in the objectives to that which is required in the assessment instruments.

Developing an instructional strategy. Given information from the five preceding steps, you will now begin to identify the strategy which you will use in the instructional module to reach the terminal objective. The strategy will include sections on preinstructional activities, presentation of information, practice and feedback, testing, and follow-through activities. The strategy will be based upon current outcomes of learning research, current knowledge of the learning process, content to be taught, and the characteristics of the students who will use the materials. These same features can be used to select materials and to develop a strategy for interactive classroom instruction.

Developing and selecting instruction. In this step you will utilize your instructional strategy to produce the instructional module. The module will include a student manual, instructional materials, tests, and a teacher's guide. Whether you develop original materials for the module will depend upon the type of learning to be taught, the availability of existing relevant materials, and developmental resources available to you. Criteria for selecting from among existing materials will be provided.

Designing and conducting the formative evaluation. Following the completion of a draft of the module, a series of evaluations are conducted to determine how effectively the module works and to collect data which may be used to identify how to improve the module. The three types of formative evaluation are referred to as one-on-one evaluation, small-group evaluation, and field evaluation. Each type of evaluation provides the designer with a different type of information which can be used to improve the instructional module. Similar techniques can be applied to the formative evaluation of selected materials or a strategy for classroom instruction.

Revising instruction. The final step (and the first step in a repeat cycle) is revising the instruction. Data are summarized from various formative evaluations and interpreted in such a way as to attempt to identify difficulties experienced by learners in achieving the objectives of the module, and to relate these difficulties to specific deficiencies in the module. The line in Figure 1.1 labeled "Revising Instruction" indicates that the data from a formative evaluation is not simply used to revise the module itself, but is used to help reexamine the validity of the instructional analysis and the assumptions about the entry behaviors of students. It is necessary to re-examine statements of performance objectives and test items in the light of collected data. The instructional strategy is reviewed and finally all this is incorporated into revisions of the module to make it a more effective instructional tool.

Conducting summative evaluation. The dotted line in Figure 1.1 indicates that although summative evaluation is the culminating evaluation of the effectiveness of instruction, it is not a part of the design process. It occurs only after the instruction has been formatively evaluated and sufficiently revised to meet the standards of the designer. Since the summative evaluation usually does not involve the designer of the instruction (but rather an independent evaluator), this component is not considered an integral component of the instructional design process, per se. However, there are direct implications from this step for the process of grading students, and this relationship is described in some depth in the text.

The nine basic steps represent the procedures which one employs when one uses the systems approach to designing instructional materials. The reason this set of procedures is referred to as a systems approach model is that it is made up of interacting components, each having its own input and output, which together produce predetermined products. A system also collects information which is fed back into the system so that the final product reaches the desired level of effectiveness.

The instructional design model described here is considered a systems approach model because there is a specific input, process, and output for each component. When instructional materials are being developed, data are collected and the module is reexamined in light of these data to make it as effective and efficient as possible.

Before concluding our discussion of the systems approach model, those things for which the model is not a solution should be made clear. As it stands, it is not a curriculum design model. In order to design a curriculum many more steps would be required prior to the identification of the instructional goals. Some of these techniques are known as goal identification analysis, needs assessment, and curriculum analysis. The model described here is intended to be used at that point when the instructor is able to identify a specific instructional goal. The model can and is being used in curriculum development projects after the instructional goals have been derived.

REFERENCES

Banathy, B. *Instructional systems.* Belmont, Calif.: Fearon Publishers, 1968.
   This small book for educators describes the nature of systems and
   how systems techniques can be applied to the design of instructional
   materials.

Fox, G. T., & DeVault, M. V. Technology and humanism in the classroom:
   Frontiers of educational practice. *Educational Technology,* 1974, *XIV*
   (10), 7-13.
   This is an excellent discussion of the realities of the classroom and the
   importance of the blending of humanism and technology.

Kolesnik, W. B. *Humanism and/or behaviorism in education.* Boston: Allyn
   and Bacon, Inc., 1975.
   This book provides a very readable and enjoyable comparison between
   humanism and behaviorism, and points out the necessity for integrating
   these two approaches.

Talmage, H. (Ed.). *Systems of individualizing instruction.* Berkeley, Calif.:
   McCutcheon Publishers, Inc., 1975.
   This book provides chapters on the theoretical bases for the individ-
   ualization of instruction.

Weisgeber, R. A. *Developmental efforts in individualizing learning.* Itasca, Ill.:
   F. E. Peacock Publishers, Inc., 1971.
   This book contains descriptions of various materials and individualized
   instruction systems such as IPI, PLAN and IGE, as well as some locally
   developed programs.

Note: The journal, *Educational Technology,* carries many articles which
   are of interest to the instructional designer. Numerous applications of
   systematic design procedures are described. Empirical research and
   theory articles are also included.

2 Identifying an Instructional Goal

OBJECTIVES

1. *You will be able to identify an instructional goal that meets the criteria for initiating the design of effective instruction.*

2. *You will be able to write an instructional goal for instruction of your own choosing. The instructional goal will meet the major criteria required for initiating the development of instructional materials.*

BACKGROUND

Any module must have a starting point, and for the instructional designer the job begins with identifying an instructional goal for the module. Instructional goals come from sources that need to be identified and then considered in some detail.

If you are designing modular instruction for use in public schools, the instructional goal which you select may result from previous decisions made at various administrative levels above you. For example, many states have general educational goals stated for their programs. These goal statements are so general that it is almost impossible to design instruction to meet the goals. It is often necessary for a particular school or school district to develop its own statement of educational philosophy and goals which is specific to the students in that particular school or district. However, often these statements are also too general for the designer.

School goals are often converted into curriculum guides which will, if properly used, result in student learning consistent with goals. The curriculum guides become the general outline for a course of instruction. They may or may not include lists of specific competencies students should achieve from the course. At this level, however, the designer can begin to derive (if not directly identify) specific kinds of behaviors which students should be able to accomplish as a result of the instructional program.

In recent years statements of school district goals have been supplemented by needs assessment studies. These studies have attempted to identify not only the goals of the district but also to determine if they have been met. The discrepancy between the present status and the desired goals becomes an identified need. This need may be directly convertible to instructional goals for the instructional program.

Another source of instructional goals is that of expert opinion. In a number of content areas, subject-matter experts have been employed to identify the critical topics in a defined discipline. Experts use their opinions in the writing of textbooks, which in turn establish a tradition of content inclusion and exclusion in a particular discipline. While the use of this source for identifying instructional goals has certain limitations, it is one of the more influential determiners of content in instructional programs.

Those instructors who work in such areas as technical training or adult education programs often identify their instructional goals in a very different way. For example, a process known as *job analysis* is frequently employed to identify critical skills required of a person in a particular occupation. Experts in an occupation are observed as they perform skills required for the job. These skills are noted and analyzed to identify critical skills which should be included in the curriculum. These critical skills become the source of the instructional goals.

Instructors who work in adult continuing education programs may need to depend upon interest surveys to identify skills and knowledge which adults wish to learn in nonformal or continuing education. Topics identified under these circumstances are often ones which are excluded from traditional instructional programs or are related to the vocational interests of adults.

In this chapter we will not attempt to teach processes such as needs assessment or job analysis. It is enough to know that these techniques do exist and are used as sources for identifying the content of instructional programs. References to these techniques are listed at the end of the chapter. The major emphasis of this chapter will be to help you identify a specific instructional goal which will then be the focus for your instructional development effort.

CONCEPTS

There is one major concept associated with this chapter, namely the *instructional goal*. The instructional goal is a statement that describes what it is that students will be able to do after they have completed instruction. The goal should describe the major culminating or synthesizing behavior which results from studying the unit. One should not infer that this is the only behavior the learner will know or be able to perform as a result of studying the module, but that he or she will at least be able to perform *this* skill. Instructional goals describe what students will be able to do after studying the unit, not what teachers will do during the unit.

Since a module is only one component of a total curriculum, it is clear that an instructional goal only describes the terminal skill with regard to a particular module. The instructional goal for one module may describe the skills a student must perform as the curriculum builds toward higher levels of knowledge, skills, and understanding. This building process can be achieved through integrating several modules, using instructional goals to interrelate various modules one to another.

Your first concern in identifying an instructional goal is to determine whether there is an actual need for instruction in a particular area. The importance of this factor is not to simply avoid reinventing the wheel; there is also a psychological consideration. As a module developer you will invest a great deal of your own time, energy, and creative talents in your materials. The product you develop will, we hope, find a home in an ongoing instructional program. The need for a particular instructional package can be highly motivating to the designer, and when the going gets rough in the design process, this motivation becomes important.

A second concern for you to take into account is your expertise in the content area which you identify. Proficient instructional designers work in interdisciplinary teams with content experts, media specialists, and instructional systems specialists. They integrate their skills to produce effective products. However, beginning designers often find they must be both designer and subject-matter expert. If this is the case, it is critically important that the designer have a thorough knowledge of the content which is to be taught. If the instructor lacks necessary subject-matter expertise it invariably leads to frustration and loss of time on the project while required expertise is gained or product quality is lost. Instructors often need to design classroom materials and activities covering subject matter in which they are not experts. In this situation they should consult a source of information accepted as expert. Such opinion can help the instructor plan the instructional goal statement and analyze the related content, or to confirm the appropriateness, accuracy, and completeness of a designated goal.

Specialized help is available for instructors at all levels of education. Those teaching in colleges and universities usually have colleagues who are considered specialists in certain content areas. Public-school personnel located close to higher education institutions can request expert help from university resource personnel. In addition to the university, help in content is often available at the public-school level. Colleagues who majored in the content area in college can also offer expertise. Most schools have curriculum study teams with members who may be willing to serve as content specialists for a given development project. Textbooks and journal articles written by specialists can provide excellent guidance in planning or validating an instructional goal and analysis. An instructor who is not a content specialist should seek expert help in planning and validating the instructional goal and content analysis.

A third concern when identifying an instructional goal is directly related to the content itself. Will the content remain relatively stable over a period of several years? Does it have a somewhat logical structure to ease the task of developing instruction? Is the content of a reasonable length? One way of answering these questions is to determine the usual length of time required to teach a particular topic using traditional classroom methods. We recommend that the behavior described in your instructional goal require less than fifteen hours of classroom instruction, and that the novice designer select content or skills which require much less than fifteen hours of instruction time in a normal classroom.

Two other factors should be taken into consideration after identifying the instructional goal. The first is to examine the objective to identify precisely the type of behavior the students will be engaged in when they demonstrate achievement of your goal. You may find, for example, that they are primarily writing information which they have memorized from the instructional materials. On the other hand, they may be solving a complex problem based upon concepts and principles which they learned in the module. The nature of what the students will be doing is determined primarily by the verb in the instructional goal statement. Examine the verb in the objective and ask yourself whether that is really an important behavior; does that behavior merit the hours required to develop instruction for students to perform the objective? You may find that while your instructional goal meets many of the criteria listed above, it simply does not appear to be an important behavior for students to learn. Don't throw out the goal—start again. Reexamine it and determine whether through rewording, particularly the verb, you have a more valuable learning outcome.

Another consideration is to determine whether the instructional goal describes two or more related or separate kinds of behavior. This is certainly acceptable and in no way should result in stating a new goal. The first step in the design of the module will probably be to separate these behaviors into separate sets of skills before proceeding to design the instruction. You should be aware, however, that a goal such as this may describe behaviors which are too large and too complex for an initial attempt at module development.

Another area of concern in identifying an instructional goal is the availability of students. Will there be enough students available to you who can study your module and provide you with feedback concerning its effectiveness? If such students are unavailable, you will miss one of the most important features of the design process, namely trying out materials with students and revising those materials based on student performances to reach your prestated goals.

A final concern of matching the instructional goal to students is identifying areas where they have had difficulty learning in the past. Experienced instructors can identify particular concepts, principles, and problem-solving tasks which almost always prove to be difficult for students. If the module designer has content expertise in such areas, these difficult topics may be ideally suited for a module.

All the factors listed above are important in selecting an instructional goal for a module. Experience indicates that three of these factors are of extreme importance to the person who is developing a first module: magnitude of content to be covered, subject-matter expertise, and availability of students. If the instructional goal represents a large area of instruction, the novice designer will soon become discouraged by the magnitude of the tasks involved in subsequent steps in the model. We recommend that a first attempt at instructional design involve no more than three hours of instruction. Without expertise in the content, you will spend more time learning it than you will in teaching it to others. Without students, the designer has no way of evaluating instruction.

If you have chosen (or are required) to design an instructional package as you work through these chapters, you will undertake a process that will consume many hours of your time. You will find your ego involvement mounting as you complete each additional component of the model.

Before you select or identify an instructional goal for your set of materials, read through the suggestions listed in this chapter. It is particularly important (1) that you have the expertise to deal with the subject matter, (2) that students are available to you to test and revise the instructional materials, and (3) that you have selected content which can be taught in a reasonable amount of time. With regard to the third condition, if you are designing instruction for young children in preschool, kindergarten or first grade, you may wish to design activities which require no more than twenty to thirty minutes of the children's time.

In order to assure yourself that the instructional goal does reflect a meaningful statement of what a student will be doing, ask a colleague to describe what the student will be doing to fulfill the instructional goal. These descriptions should tell you how clear your statement is. You may find that you have obtained a much more detailed description than you anticipated. This is not a problem, however, unless behaviors are described which you have not anticipated or cannot accept. If the latter is the case, then it is important that you reword the instructional goal to reflect exactly what it is that you want the student to be able to do.

EXAMPLES

Some examples of instructional goals may help you formulate or evaluate your own goals. Three characteristics of instructional goals should be considered. They are (1) whether the goal is behavioral or nonbehavioral; that is, it describes what the student will do; (2) whether the goal is too large, too small, or just right for your purpose and your students' needs; and (3) whether the goal you have chosen is "fuzzy" or clear. Examples of goals that illustrate these three characteristics follow.

In general, goal statements should describe behaviors that someone could observe a student doing. Behavioral goals have as their outcome a behavior which can be directly observed and measured as evidence of whether the behavior has been acquired. An example of a behaviorally expressed instructional goal is objective 1 from this chapter: "You will be able to identify an instructional goal that meets the criteria for initiating the design of effective instruction." This is classified as behavioral because your response will be observable. Your statements about the goals, either oral or written, can be evaluated, and a decision can be made about your present capability of applying suggested criteria to identify plausible instructional goals.

Nonbehavioral goal statements describe outcomes that are not directly observable and therefore are hard to measure and should be avoided if possible. An example of a nonbehavioral goal statement would be: "Students will appreciate watercolor paintings." This may be a desired outcome of a unit in art, but appreciation is difficult to measure. Students' ability to identify paintings made with watercolors, to name famous watercolor paintings, to mix watercolors, or to paint with watercolors can be observed—these are all behavioral outcomes. The degree to which students learn to *appreciate* watercolor paintings, however, cannot be directly observed or measured.

Nonbehavioral goal statements can sometimes be indirectly measured by making inferences about the meaning of a person's behavior. For example, if a person always chose watercolors from a wide variety of painting mediums, then it may be inferred that this person appreciates watercolors. If a person chooses to visit the watercolor sections of art galleries, then it might be inferred that he or she appreciates watercolor paintings. These are inferences about, and not measures of, appreciation.

The amount of time required for the instructor to write instruction for a goal and the amount of time required for a student to complete the instruction and achieve the instructional goal are both considerations for determining whether you have selected a goal that is too large, too small, or just right. Selecting the appropriate amount of instruction for a unit can make the content seem easier and learning more pleasant for the student. If, however, students are usually required to do more work than time allows or more than will hold their interest, the subject matter will tend to seem more difficult to them. If they are required to do too little work, then motivation and interest can become a problem.

Many considerations must be made to determine whether a piece of instruction will be too large, too small, or just right for intended students. Factors relating to the length of time available for instructional activities and practice, the logical sectioning of content, the type of learning activity, and the characteristics of learners such as age, attention span, and motivation must all be considered before judgments about the correct size of instructional "chunk" can be made. A goal that seems appropriate for one student group may be inadequate for another.

Consider the following goals:

1. The student will be able to write a paper which illustrates the application of scientific investigation techniques to the identification, investigation, and discussion of a problem.
2. The student will be able to formulate and write a statement of null hypothesis and logical alternative hypotheses for given problem situations.
3. Given several hypotheses, the student will be able to rewrite the hypotheses using the following notation system: Ho: $G_1 = G_2$, Ha: $G_1 \neq G_2$; Ho: $G_1 = G_2$, Ha: $G_1 > G_2$; Ho: $G_1 = G_2$, Ha: $G_1 < G_2$.

Though these three goals are related, they are concerned with different-sized "chunks" of instruction, all of which concern scientific investigation techniques. If a designer wishes to write instruction that requires one hour for secondary-school students to complete, the first goal statement would be much too large. Of course, this may be the ultimate objective of a unit, but it would require many hours of instruction which would include varied information, skills, and activities. This goal may be reduced to fit into one hour of instruction if the verb or behavior required of the student is changed to "to know about" scientific investigation techniques rather than "to perform" them and write a summary paper. Instruction for the goal could be fit into one hour if the goal were restated thusly: "The student will be able to describe in his or her own words the five main activities related to scientific investigation and the purpose for each activity." This type of information goal may serve as an overview to instruction on scientific methods and may serve as an organizer for students' thoughts; however, it will not teach students to carry out scientific investigations.

The second goal is about the right-sized "chunk" for one hour of instruction. One hour would enable students to consider information that must be presented, to complete practice and review activities, and to receive feedback on their own hypotheses statements.

Although the third goal is too small for one hour of instruction, it nonetheless is an important objective in scientific notation for hypothesis writing. Given appropriate entry behaviors for this objective, students could accurately perform the instructional goal long before the hour is over. Several smaller subobjectives such as this may be clustered to fill an hour of instruction.

The intent related to an instructional goal should be clear, not fuzzy. Clear topics are logical and the content, as well as the associated skills, are well defined. There is agreement among experts about the needs for instruction and the content which should be included. Examples of clear topics might include mathematics or history. There is a general understanding of the content, skills, and behavior required for a student to add numbers, and an instructional goal about addition can be clearly stated. The content and learning required for a student to "discuss events leading up to World War II" is also easily agreed upon. However, many topics desirable for instruction are not that clear and easy.

An instructional goal on leadership can illustrate a fuzzy topic. Teaching leadership is often the objective of both school systems and management training programs; exactly how leadership is taught, however, is usually a subject for debate. Teaching about leadership or skills to enhance leadership and affording opportunities to practice leadership do not necessarily produce students who will become leaders. Not all instructional goals on leadership convey the same ideas, skills, content, or activities to instructional writers. If your instructional goal is "fuzzy," perhaps additional work in stating the goal would be beneficial. Sometimes collaboration with others to determine behaviors which are desirable for leaders would be beneficial. The instructional goal might be subdivided into identified behaviors which can be used to develop a clear framework on which to build instruction. In order to build such a framework, make sure you have the competence required to clarify an instructional goal in a particular area and to analyze it for identification of knowledge and skills required of the student.

PRACTICE AND FEEDBACK

Practice

I. The first step in building a module of instruction is to state the instructional goal. Several criteria can be used to help you select a suitable topic.

1. Below is a list of possible considerations for selection of an instructional goal. Identify those which are relevant to a designer's selection of an instructional goal.

   _____ a. personal knowledge and skills in content area
   _____ b. stable content area
   _____ c. time required for writing instruction versus the importance of students' possessing that knowledge or skill
   _____ d. students available to try out materials for clarity and revision purposes
   _____ e. area in which students have difficulty learning
   _____ f. few materials available on the topic though instruction is considered important
   _____ g. content area is fairly logical
   _____ h. topic can be sectioned to the time available for both writing the module and students using the module

2. Make a tentative topic selection for an instructional module which you would be interested in writing. To determine whether you have the topic clearly in mind, write the instructional goal on paper.

II. Now that you have identified an instructional goal that meets the selection criteria, you need to state it as clearly as possible. Below is a list of considerations for writing instructional goals. Select those which are important considerations for writing instructional goals.

1. Behavioral Versus Nonbehavioral

_____✓__ a. Goal is behaviorally stated.
_____✓__ b. Behavior required of the student is obvious in the goal.
_____✓__ c. Behavior in the goal can be observed.
_____✓__ d. Behavior in the goal can be measured to determine whether students have reached the goal.

2. Clear Versus Fuzzy Goals

_____✓__ a. Instructional goal is stated clearly with a topic, intended behavior, and any limitations stated which will be imposed on the behavior of the topic.

3. Time

_____✓__ a. Approximate instructional time required for students to reach the goal.
_____✓__ b. Approximate writing time you can devote to writing and revising instruction.

Feedback

I. 1. If you answered yes to all of the previous criteria, you are correct. Each of these criteria is an important consideration in developing an instructional goal.

2. With the goal written on paper, refer back to question 1 in the same section. Evaluate your topic using each criterion statement.

a. Does your goal meet each criterion? yes
b. If it does not meet some criterion, can it be revised to do so?
c. If it does not meet a particular criterion and cannot be revised to do so, you may want to write another instructional goal and try again.

You may need help determining whether your goal meets some of the criteria for topic selection such as need or interest. You might discuss these issues relative to your goal with colleagues and target students. Libraries are another good source for determining whether materials on your topic are available and the nature of available materials. Revise and rewrite your instructional goal as needed to meet the above criteria.

II. If you believe that all the considerations in section II of Practice are important, you are correct.

You may check the clarity of your goal by asking colleagues and intended students to verbally interpret the instructional goal you have written. Do they interpret the goal and the required behavior exactly as you intended? You may need to revise.

If your goal is too big for the instructional time available (thirty minutes, one hour, two hours, etc.) you may want to divide the goal into its logical major parts, reword each part as an instructional goal, and then select the part most suited to your needs and time constraints as the instructional goal for your materials.

If your goal is too small for the amount of time you desire, consider the skills the student will need to enter your module and the skills the student will be ready to learn as a result of completing it. By considering skills related to your goal in this fashion, you can identify the appropriate instruction to include in a module for a specified period of time. Of course you will want to revise your instructional goal to include more skills or information as required.

Rewrite your instructional goal if necessary, and begin chapter 3 after you have developed a clear, behaviorally stated instructional goal that you estimate will require the desired amount of instructional time.

IMPLEMENTATION

To implement the process of identifying an instructional goal, consider what has been presented in this chapter in terms of a systematic input, process, and output analysis.

Input

The input required to identify an instructional goal was stated as (a) the identification of sources for instructional goals; and (b) an examination of the behavior required of the target student, the need for that particular behavior, your expertise in the area identified, the nature and magnitude of the content, and the availability of students to test the materials.

Process

During the process phase, you should identify the topic area you want to work in and then select and write an instructional goal based on the information you gathered during the input phase. Once you have written the instructional goal, you should:

1. Examine the goal to identify the exact behavior(s) required to meet the goals.

2. Evaluate the goal in light of the considerations/constraints which have been discussed for selection of an instructional goal.
3. Evaluate the need for and the clarity of the goal by discussing it with colleagues and target students and by consulting the reference section of the library.
4. If necessary, revise the goal you have selected until it meets the criteria for goal selection which were presented in this chapter.

Output

The output for this component is a clearly stated instructional goal. This goal statement becomes the input for the next component of the instructional design model, conducting an instructional analysis. Without a clearly identified goal as input, the instructional analysis process cannot begin.

REFERENCES

Gagné, R. M., & Briggs, L. J. *Principles of instructional design.* New York: Holt, Rinehart, and Winston, 1974, 19-34.
    Education goals are related to instructional outcomes, especially as they relate to different categories of learning.
Lysaught, J. P., & Williams, C. M. *A guide to programmed instruction.* New York: John Wiley and Sons, 1963, 29-41.
    The same principles which are applied to the selection of a topic to be programmed may be applied to the identification of an instructional goal for modular instruction.
Mager, R. F. *Goal analysis.* Belmont, Calif.: Fearon Publishers, 1972.
    This brief book describes a process used by the author to help groups clearly identify goals for their instruction.
Miller, R. B. Task description and analysis, in R. M. Gagné (Ed.), *Psychological principles in system development.* New York: Holt, Rinehart, and Winston, 1962, 187-230.
    This chapter is an early effort in relating job-analysis techniques to the development of training systems.

3 Conducting an Instructional Analysis

OBJECTIVES

1. *You will be able to identify and describe procedural, hierarchical, and combination approaches to instructional analysis.*

2. *You will be able to describe the relationship among the subskills which are identified through an instructional analysis.*

3. *You will be able to apply instructional analysis techniques to identify subskills required to reach an instructional goal.*

BACKGROUND

As we said earlier, it has been traditional for the content of instructional materials, typically textbooks, to be defined by experts who have developed a structure for knowledge which makes up a particular discipline. Experienced teachers, using these textbooks, often have varied the instructional approach, sequence, or content as they proceeded to teach students on a somewhat trial and error basis.

In recent years, researchers have tried to identify more effective procedures for identifying the precise skills and knowledge which should be included in instructional materials for students to efficiently and effectively achieve an instructional goal. For example, rather than defining a course on Shakespeare in terms of ten or fifteen plays which a student might need to read, there has been an effort by instructional designers to identify precisely what it is that students will be able to do when they complete their course on Shakespeare. The next step is to identify the subordinate skills which are required for the student to achieve the instructional goal. Several procedures have been developed for identifying major subordinate skills. This unit will present several such approaches.

The particular approaches chosen for an instructional analysis will depend upon the kind of learning required in the instructional goal. One of the approaches is straightforward; the other two are somewhat more complex. It should be stressed that while researchers do not claim that the instructional analysis approach is the only way to identify content which should be included in a set of instructional materials, their data suggest that the use of these approaches results in the identification of skills which efficiently lead to the achievement of the instructional goal.

CONCEPTS

An instructional analysis is a procedure that, when applied to an instructional goal, results in the identification of the relevant subordinate skills which are required for a student to achieve the goal. A subordinate skill is a skill that, while perhaps not important in and of itself as a learning outcome, must be achieved in order to learn some higher or superordinate skill. The acquisition of the subordinate skill facilitates or provides positive transfer for the learning of superordinate skills.

When using the systems approach to design instruction, the content that will be included in instructional materials cannot necessarily be identified either by reverting to a typical textbook which describes what is always included in this topic or by utilizing the topics which always seem to be included when this topic is taught. We hope you will be convinced that instructional analysis procedures help identify skills that should be included in instruction for students to achieve the instructional goal efficiently.

Two somewhat different approaches to instructional analysis will be described first: the procedural approach and the hierarchical approach. We will also describe a third technique which is, in fact, a combination of these two. The method used depends entirely upon the type of behavior described in the instructional goal. None of the three methods should be considered as the "best" for any instructional goal, but rather the method should match the behavior described in the goal.

The Procedural Approach

Let us begin by looking at the simplest of the three instructional analysis approaches, the procedural approach. This approach is used when the behavior to be taught is essentially a series of behaviors which must be performed in sequence to achieve the instructional goal.

If you were teaching individuals how to direct dial a long-distance telephone call, you would teach them a step-by-step procedure which they could follow to make a call correctly. Figure 3.1 presents the sequence of steps required to place a call.

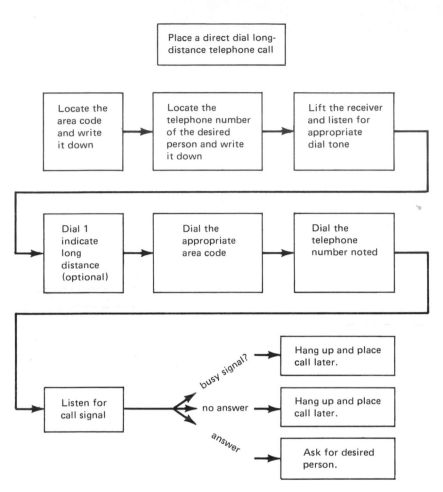

Figure 3.1 A Procedural Analysis for Long-Distance Telephone Calls

Several things can be seen from this example. First, a student must go through the steps in sequence (although the first two could be reversed). Second, each step could be taught separately and independently of any other step. Third, the output of each step usually serves as the input for the next step.

Let's look at another simple procedure from the psychomotor domain of learning. Think back to the time when lift lids were placed on vacuum-pack cans. If you were teaching someone to open a new can, you might use the following steps.

1. Grasp the ring with your index finger and lift it up from the lid.
2. Pull the ring toward the far rim of the can.

3. Twist the ring in the opposite direction in order to remove the lid from the can. These procedures can be described in a procedural approach as shown in the diagram:

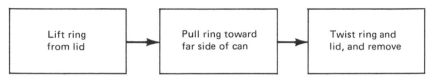

You can see that this is a set of procedures which result in a final performance of removing the lid from the can. Each step is independent, and the steps could be taught separately from one another. The result of executing each step is an input for executing the next step. In other words, the ring is first lifted, then, while in this position, pulled toward the rim, and then twisted in the opposite direction.

In order to perform a procedural instructional analysis, we recommend that you mentally "walk through" all the steps required to perform the task noting (a) each step in sequence and (b) the input, process, and output required for each step. For the can-opening example, you could use the following analysis procedures to "walk through" opening the can.

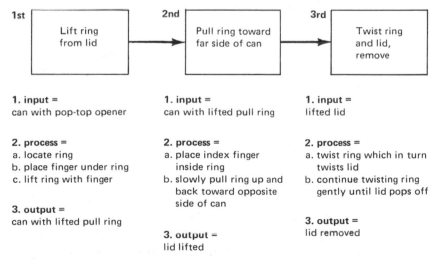

The Hierarchical Approach

It has been found useful to identify the type or level of learning which is being required in an instructional goal and to use hierarchical techniques to identify subordinate skills which must be achieved prior to achieving the goal.

As an example, consider an instructional goal which requires the student to recommend and to justify a decision as to whether a particular piece of real estate should be purchased at a particular time. It would be necessary for the student to learn a number of rules and concepts related to the assessment of property values, the effect of inflation on property values, the financial status of the buyer, and the buyer's short- and long-term investment needs. The skills in each of these areas would depend upon an understanding of the basic concepts used in the financial and real estate profession. In this example, it would be extremely important to identify and teach each of the critical rules and concepts to students prior to teaching them to utilize these skills to analyze a particular case and make a recommendation.

How does the designer go about identifying the critical subordinate skills a student must learn in order to achieve a higher level intellectual skill? The process suggested by Gagné is one of asking the question, "What does the student have to already know how to do, so that with a minimal amount of instruction this task can be learned?" By asking this question, the designer can identify, as has been done above, one or more critical subordinate skills which will be required of the learner prior to attempting instruction on the final task. After these subordinate skills have been identified, the designer then asks the same question with regard to each of these skills, namely, "What is it the student must already know how to do, the absence of which would make it impossible to learn the given task?" This will result in the identification of one or more additional subordinate skills. If this process is continued, one quickly reaches a very basic level of performance such as being able to recognize whole numbers or being able to recognize letters.

An example of the result of using the hierarchical instructional analysis technique appears in Figure 3.2. In the diagram it can be seen that the instructional goal requires the student to estimate to the nearest one-hundredth, plus or minus one-hundredth, a designated point on a linear scale which is marked only in tenths. Given this goal, three subordinate skills have been identified. These are related to estimating a point to the nearest tenth on a scale marked only in whole units, dividing a scale into subunits, and identifying a designated point on a particular scale. Each of these skills has subordinate skills which are identified.

It should be noted that this particular hierarchical analysis was not devised on the basis of one attempt at the process, or even two or three. It takes a number of attempts at identifying the vertical subordinate skills and their interrelationships before you can be satisfied that you have identified all the relevant skills and have stated them appropriately.

Unlike the procedural analysis, it is almost impossible to know when an appropriate and valid hierarchical analysis of an instructional goal has been achieved. We will make several suggestions for testing the hierarchy at this point in the instructional development process. While somewhat time consuming to validate, the hierarchical approach is the best possible process for identifying skills which should be included in an instructional program for intellectual skills.

Once you are satisfied that you have identified all the subskills required for students to master your instructional goal, you will want to rethink and

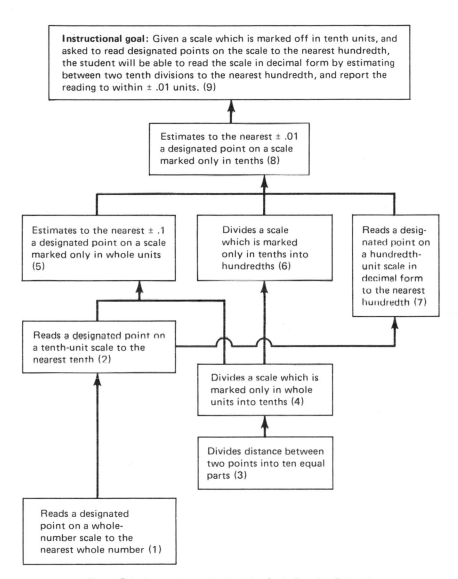

Instructional goal: Given a scale which is marked off in tenth units, and asked to read designated points on the scale to the nearest hundredth, the student will be able to read the scale in decimal form by estimating between two tenth divisions to the nearest hundredth, and report the reading to within ± .01 units. (9)

Estimates to the nearest ± .01 a designated point on a scale marked only in tenths (8)

Estimates to the nearest ± .1 a designated point on a scale marked only in whole units (5)

Divides a scale which is marked only in tenths into hundredths (6)

Reads a designated point on a hundredth-unit scale in decimal form to the nearest hundredth (7)

Reads a designated point on a tenth-unit scale to the nearest tenth (2)

Divides a scale which is marked only in whole units into tenths (4)

Divides distance between two points into ten equal parts (3)

Reads a designated point on a whole-number scale to the nearest whole number (1)

Figure 3.2 Instructional Analysis for Scale-Reading Example

evaluate your analysis before you do any further developmental work. This first step in the evaluation considers the behavior required by students. Does the goal imply that students must discuss an issue, state definitions, relate important events, follow directions to complete a procedure, solve problems, and so forth? You must consider whether subskills are included in your analysis that will enable students to perform your instructional goal according to your expectations. The following questions can be used to evaluate your instructional analysis.

1. Do you have a clear picture of the behavior (verb) students will have to perform to demonstrate mastery of each subskill and of the instructional goal?
2. At the lowest level of the hierarchy, are there stimulus or object differences that learners may not yet have acquired? (Example: Is a square still indistinguishable from a rectangle, or a "d" from a "b"?)
3. Are there subskills that relate to the identification of basic concepts, such as objects or object qualities? (Example: Can a tetrahedron be identified?)
4. Have you included subskills that enable students to identify abstractions by means of a definition? (Example: Can the student explain what a city is, or show what an emulsion is?)
5. Have you included subskills that will enable students to apply rules? (Example: Making sentence verbs agree with subjects; simplifying mixed fractions.)
6. Have you included subskills in your analysis that will enable students to learn how to solve problems required to demonstrate mastery of your instructional goal?

You may be able to identify subskills you have omitted by using these questions to evaluate your instructional goal and your instructional analysis. It is important to review your analysis several times, making sure that you have identified all the subskills required for students to master the instructional goal. At this point you should again use the backward-stepping procedure, from the highest, most complex skill in your hierarchy to the lowest, simplest skills required by your target population. This will allow you to determine whether you have included all the necessary subskills. It may be possible to check the adequacy of your back-stepping analysis, by starting with the simplest skills in your hierarchy, and working forward through the subskills to the most complex skills. Carefully evaluate your own analysis prior to having content experts or colleagues evaluate it for you. Adequate evaluation and revision of your analysis at this stage will save you considerable time in the future. The best behavioral objectives, when written for an inadequate instructional analysis, will be inadequate for your development project.

Various difficulties will arise in the application of the hierarchical instructional analysis procedures. If you are not making progress with a particular skill you might ask an additional question, "How might students make a mistake or go wrong if they were doing this task?" This can often help identify subordinate skills which are critical to that task through examining the kinds of errors students might make if they were attempting to carry it out. After you have made your first draft of the instructional analysis, you should determine if you have placed a verb in the description of each subordinate skill. This is very important both for your own understanding of what it is you expect the student to be able to do and for describing this task for other people. We suggest that you explain your hierarchy to a colleague to point out how subordinate skills are interrelated and how they support learning of the superordinate skills. If the explanation does not sound convincing to you or your colleague, more work needs to be done.

The Combination Approach

There is a third approach to the instructional analysis process which is a combination of both the procedural and hierarchical approaches. This combination process can be seen most clearly when applied to a complex psychomotor skill or a relatively complex linear chain of cognitive tasks. Let us take the psychomotor example first.

Assume that you were going to teach a person to parallel park a car. This is a task which requires several intellectual skills, including various judgments as well as a set of motor skills for actually moving the automobile into several specific locations. This task is represented in Figure 3.3.

You can see that the process has been broken down into four basic components. The instructional goal is to parallel park a car in a particular position on a street. Since positioning the car in that position represents a sequence of movements which must be executed in sequence, it would appear that the appropriate analysis is the procedural approach. However, it should be noted that for each step in the procedure, there is an intellectual skill as well as a physical skill which must be learned. Therefore, the hierarchical approach has been applied to identify the subordinate skills associated with each of the major skills. In this example, students would have to learn the intellectual skill of positioning the front bumper of their cars with regard to the car on the right. They would also have to learn the motor skill of bringing the car into that position. A similar type of analysis could be made for each of the other steps.

Let us consider an example that does not fall in the psychomotor domain but has heavy emphasis on cognitive skills. If we were to look at the systems-approach instructional design model as a sequence of intellectual skills which the designer must learn in order to produce effective instructional materials, then the model is very similar to a procedural analysis. We are in fact moving from left to right in sequence, teaching each component in turn. The output of one step is the input for the next step. It is not assumed, however, that the learner has already achieved each of the skills described in the boxes. Therefore, we are not simply integrating the skills. Each box in the model contains a major principle about how a task is carried out, and beneath it are sets of rules and concepts which are being taught and combined so that the student can execute the model.

The Analysis of Attitudes

Thus far we have discussed how procedural skills, intellectual skills, and psychomotor skills might be analyzed to identify relevant skills required to

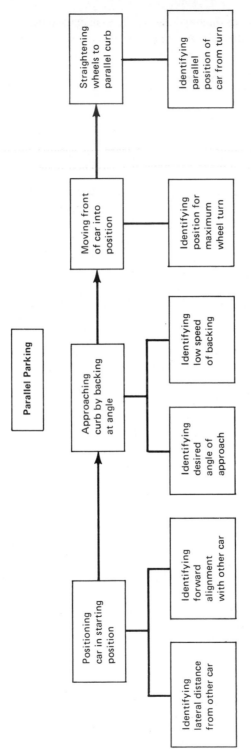

Figure 3.3 Combination Instructional Analysis for Parallel Parking
(Adapted from Gagné, R.M., personal correspondence)

bring about learning. There is another concept that we must discuss to make this unit complete: the domain of attitude formation. In many instructional situations one of the most desired outcomes of instruction is the formation of particular attitudes by students.

Researchers disagree as to what constitutes the best procedures for teaching attitudes, and therefore it would be inappropriate to imply that instructional design techniques will solve this problem. It is possible, however, to convert attitude goals to a set of specific behavioral outcomes desired of students. That is, if students do in fact learn (or accept) certain attitudes, then they will behave or make decisions in a particular manner.

If an instructional goal were stated in terms of an attitude, as opposed to a specific type of behavior, it should be possible to describe one or more types of behavior that would be representative of that attitude. For example, if the instructional goal were that the student would be an effective citizen, it would be fruitful to analyze this objective into several subordinate behaviorally stated subgoals such as "campaign for a candidate for a school election" or "volunteer for participation in a service organization." Given attitudinal goals, it is usually possible to identify subordinate competencies a student would need in order to display that attitude. In our example, if the student were to assist in a campaign, it would be important to know who the candidates were, what the issues were, and the appropriate techniques for carrying out an election campaign.

While we know that simply having knowledge about a situation does not dictate how a person will use that knowledge, we do know that it is very difficult to behave in certain ways without that knowledge. Therefore, by using hierarchical analysis techniques it is possible to identify the intellectual skills that must be combined with certain other types of reinforcement and motivational properties of the instruction to shape particular kinds of attitudes. In addition to careful analysis of the skills and information required, the instructor needs to plan other activities which are believed to enhance attitude acquisition. These activities include dramatization or modeling showing desired attitude, knowledge of consequences, peer pressure, affiliation, and credibility of source. All these kinds of activities are planned during the instructional strategy which is discussed in chapter 7.

Differentiate Among the Types of Analyses

At the beginning of the instructional analysis, it is sometimes difficult to determine whether your particular analysis will prove to be procedural, hierarchical, or a combination of the two. The analysis should be performed using whatever technique or combination of techniques you find works best in identifying your subskills. Gagné (1977) suggests that you should do (or decide not to do) the procedural analysis first, and then proceed to the hierarchical analysis.

If in the process of applying an instructional analysis procedure you find that it is *impossible* for students to *learn* the elements of one skill without first learning those of a preceding skill, then the relationship of these skills is described as hierarchical. An example of this learning dependence can be seen in a comparison of the objective examples in Figure 3.8 on page 46. A student cannot locate a specified point or object on a map without first learning how to use the legend and the letter and number grid. The student must acquire these subordinate skills before he or she can learn to actually use a map to find a specified object in a specified location.

One way that appears to help differentiate between a hierarchical and a procedural instructional goal is that of determining whether the goal describes the performance of a whole string of subskills or whether it describes only the performance in the terminal (or last) subskill. To look at this difference more closely, you should review the various instructional analyses in this chapter. The procedural analyses appear in Figures 3.1, 3.4, and 3.7. Notice that in all these instructional goals, the goal is not the last behavior performed but rather an umbrella description of all the subskills. The learner does not proceed directly from the last identified subskill into initiating and performing the instructional goal. It has already been accomplished by performing all of the skills listed.

On the other hand, it appears that in hierarchical analyses, the instructional goal describes the last skill that the learner will perform. It seems that the last subskill is sufficient to subsume all the subordinate subskills and that the final subskill to be performed is synonymous with the instructional goal. This can be observed in the hierarchical analyses in this chapter which are included in Figures 3.2, 3.5, and 3.8. In all these examples, all the subskills lead directly into the instructional goal. This structural relationship between the type of analysis and the instructional goal is diagrammed as follows.

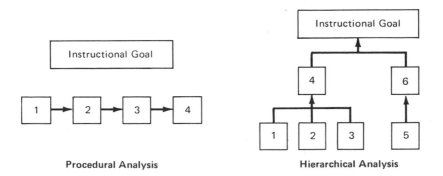

Procedural Analysis   Hierarchical Analysis

Notice the absence of the directional link between any one subskill and the instructional goal in the procedural analysis, and notice the existing link between subskills 4 and 6 and the instructional goal in the hierarchical analysis.

The Instructional Analysis Diagram

When diagrammed, any particular set of subskills required to reach a terminal objective can have a variety of structural appearances. Traditionally, procedural tasks are placed in a straight line to indicate that none is dependent upon or subordinate to another. The following diagram is generally used to represent a procedural analysis. There are no subordinate learning-dependent subskills, so all the skills are diagrammed in one continuous line.

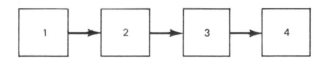

It is also traditional to place learning-dependent subskills above the skills on which they are dependent. In this way, the reader will automatically recognize the implied learning relationship of the subskills. This is illustrated in the following diagram. Notice that subskills 1, 2, and 3 are not dependent upon each other, but that learning objective 4 requires the previous learning of 1, 2, and 3. Objectives 5, 6, and 9 are not interdependent, while 7 and 8 must be learned prior to 9. The ordering of subskills 4, 5, 6, and 9 may reflect a logical order of those skills, a chronological order, or input, process, and output steps in a procedure.

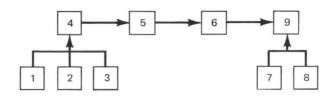

The following diagram illustrates the dependence of subsequent skills upon those preceding them.

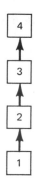

The student must learn subskill 1 before learning to perform subskill 2. Likewise, before subskill 4 can be learned, subskills 1, 2, and 3 must be mastered. Thus, these skills form a hierarchy.

An understanding of these diagramming conventions should help you grasp the implied relationship of subskills in an instructional analysis diagram. The order of instruction for each skill is also implied through such a sequencing of skills.

Why is the instructional analysis process so critical to the design process? It is a process the instructional designer can use to identify those skills which are really needed by the student to achieve the terminal objective, and to help exclude those skills which are unnecessary. This may not appear to be a terribly strong argument for a particular instructional goal which you might select. You might feel that you are so thoroughly familiar with the content and skills required of the student that this type of analysis is superfluous. You may be assured, however, that as you become involved in a variety of instructional design projects there is no way in which you can be a subject-matter expert in all areas. It will be necessary to engage in analytic processes of this type with a variety of content design personnel to identify the critical skills which will result in efficient and effective instruction.

EXAMPLES

Further examples of instructional analysis will be included in this section. Examples of procedural, hierarchical, and combination type analysis for psychomotor skills are included, as well as an analysis for attitudinal objectives.

Procedural Instructional Analysis

Procedural analysis is best performed if you carefully write down each step students need to take and the sequence in which they need to take them to complete the task. You should include everything they must do to complete each step of the procedure, any information or material needed to begin each step, and any information or material they have as a result of completing each step.

Topic: As an example, let us consider analyzing how to teach the use of a copy reduction machine.

Instructional goal: You will reduce a 14-by-18-inch chart to fit onto an 8½-by-11-inch piece of paper, leaving at least 1-inch margins on all sides.

Major Steps to Take
1. Turn machine on.
2. Determine reduction size specifications for this machine.
3. Determine size of paper to be reduced.
4. Determine how much photo reduction is required to fit a 14-by-18-inch page onto an 8½-by-11-inch piece of paper.
5. Turn reduction dial to desired reduction specifications.
6. Check paper supply to make sure there is enough paper of the appropriate size in the machine.
7. Add more paper if needed.
8. Place copy to be reduced face down on copy tray.
9. Set number of copies selection button on 1.
10. Press button to make one copy.
11. Examine copy to determine whether reduction is sufficient.
12. Set number of copies selection button on desired number of copies.
13. Press button to make desired number of copies.
14. Register number of copies made to department.

A diagram of this procedure appears in Figure 3.4 on page 38. For a complete discussion of the analysis of psychomotor skills, see Singer and Dick (1974) as referenced at the end of this chapter.

Hierarchical Instructional Analysis

The instructional analysis below represents a hierarchical arrangement of tasks and subtasks. Students must learn to perform tasks at the lower levels of the chart before they can learn and fully understand tasks at the top of the chart.

Topic: Roman numerals.

Instructional goal: You will be able to form specified Roman numerals with values between 1 and 1000.

The hierarchical analysis appears in Figure 3.5. The structure of this analysis can be considered to explain why it is classified as hierarchical. The purpose of the numbers on the boxes in the instructional analysis is to facilitate the discussion of the order of the skills and to relate the numbers

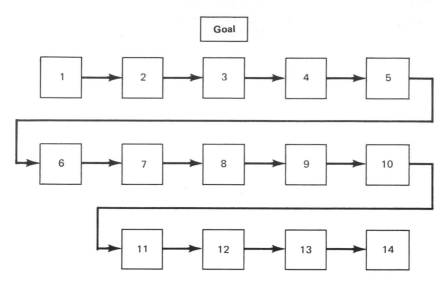

Figure 3.4 Diagram of the Sequence and Flow of a Procedural Analysis on Copy Reduction

to the objectives. Refer to box number 12. Could students learn to equate Roman symbols with Arabic symbols of equal value if they did not know the value of Arabic numbers? Could students add Roman numerals (subskill 14) if they could not yet add Arabic numbers (subskill 7)? Another example of the learning dependent relationship in the hierarchy can easily be seen in subskills 15, 16, and 17. It would be impossible for students to learn to add and subtract numerals within the same number (subskill 17) if they did not already know how to interpret Roman numerals requiring subtraction (subskill 15) and how to interpret Roman numerals requiring addition (subskill 16). The determining fact that makes the subskills within this analysis hierarchical is that students must *learn* to perform subordinate skills before it is possible for them to *learn* to perform skills in a higher position in the hierarchy.

A hierarchical analysis of this type not only illustrates skills, concepts, and information that need to be taught, but it also provides a logical sequence for instruction.

Combination Instructional Analysis

Topic: Opening and maintaining a checking account.

Instructional goal: You will be able to open a checking account, keep a check register of account activities for two months, and balance the account.

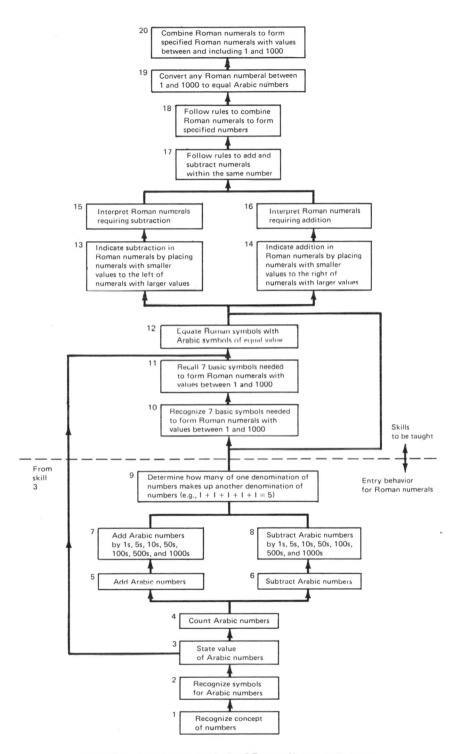

Figure 3.5 Hierarchical Analysis of Roman Numerals Objective

Procedures and skills needed to perform each step:

Procedures

1. Compare costs of checking accounts in your area. (Minimum balance, cost per check, automatic savings, discounts, etc.)
2. Compare locations of banks relative to your home, office, and school.
3. Compare bank-by-mail procedures (deposit by mail, transfers from savings to checking accounts, etc.).
4. Select a bank that would most likely meet your needs.
5. Determine different checking plans and monthly costs of each.
6. Determine discounts for minimum balance.
7. Determine costs for obtaining checks.
8. Determine penalty charges for overdrafts.
9. Determine exact costs of various checking plans.
10. Determine amount of checking activity you plan.
11. Approximate the normal balance range you anticipate.
12. Select the best checking plan for your needs.
13. Determine whether a joint account or private account would best suit your needs.
14. Determine who will be included in the account.
15. Obtain signature cards and obtain all the appropriate signatures and required information.
16. Return the signature cards to the bank.
17. Open an account.

18. Determine how currency and checks are entered on the deposit slip.

19. Determine how to indicate depositing part of a check and having part returned to you as cash.

20. Complete a deposit slip and open a checking account.

    20.1 Add two-place decimal numbers with carrying.

    20.2 Subtract two-place decimal numbers with borrowing.

21. Obtain a check register from the bank and define all the terms on the register.

22. Identify the appropriate places to enter (1) the check number, (2) to whom checks were issued, (3) deposits, (4) withdrawals, (5) service charges, and (6) the current total.

23. Enter the amount of your first deposit in the balance-brought-forward column.

24. Retotal the amount in the balance column each time there is activity in the account.

    24.1 Add two-place decimal numbers with carrying.

    24.2 Subtract two-place decimal numbers with borrowing.

25. Determine the date of any service charges or automatic withdrawals from the account.

26. Subtract the amount of service charges or automatic withdrawals from the balance on the appropriate date.

    26.1 Subtract two-place decimal numbers with borrowing.

27. Add the amount of any deposits or credits to your balance.

    27.1 Add two-place decimal numbers with carrying.

28. Identify checks returned with the bank statement on your check register.

29. Sum the amount of the returned checks, (those which have cleared through the account) and any service charges or automatic withdrawals.

    29.1 Add two-place decimal numbers with carrying.

30. Sum your original balance with any deposits or other credits made to the account.

30.1 Add two-place decimal numbers with carrying.

31. Subtract the amount of debits (cleared checks and charges) from the credits (previous balance and deposits). The remainder is the balance in the checking account on the day the bank prepared the routine statement.

31.1 Subtract two-place decimal numbers with borrowing.

32. Compare your balance for the account with the balance on the statement from the bank.

33. Recheck calculations if your figures do not agree with the bank's.

33.1 Add two-place decimal numbers with carrying.
33.2 Subtract two-place decimal numbers with borrowing.

34. Obtain information from the bank about any activity in the checking account which you cannot justify.

35. Balance your records with the bank's records.

35.1 Add two-place decimal numbers with carrying.
35.2 Subtract two-place decimal numbers with borrowing.

Open and Maintain a Checking Account

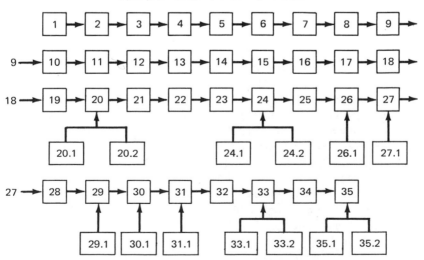

Figure 3.6 Combination Analysis for Bank Book Objective

Let us consider why we classified the previous analysis as a combination of types of learning. (Refer to the diagram in Figure 3.6.) The boxes in the diagram are keyed by number to the steps explained in detail previously. Steps 1 through 19 require the student to follow a procedural analysis where the output of one step becomes the input for the next step in the process. At this point a combination of procedural and hierarchical components exist.

Several steps require addition and/or subtraction skills, and instruction required to teach these mathematical skills is hierarchical. Math skills include adding and subtracting decimal numbers as well as adding and subtracting mixed negative and positive numbers. Though most people who open checking accounts have these skills in addition and subtraction (based on practical experience, bankers often question this hypothesis), if these skills do need to be taught, there would be a hierarchical arrangement in the instructional analysis for them.

PRACTICE AND FEEDBACK

Practice

In the exercises that follow you will be asked to complete an instructional analysis for procedural and hierarchical goals. Work through each example, and then compare your analysis with the example analysis. If your analysis is different, locate the differences, and determine whether you would like to make any revisions in your analysis. You may like your analysis better than the example, but you should be able to explain and justify differences.

Procedural Analysis

Topic: Changing a tire.

Instructional goal: You will change a tire on an automobile, and all work must be considered correct as well as safe.

The diagram below will help you get started.

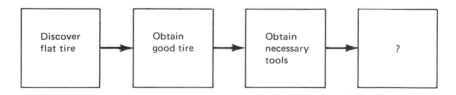

The best way to complete the analysis is to change a tire mentally step by step and note what you must do first, second, third, and so forth. A way to check your procedure is to ask yourself: "What would I need to begin each step (tools, position of car, etc.), and what would I have as a result of completing each step?" This procedure will help you carefully analyze each step and it will help you recall a step or procedure you may have overlooked. Complete your analysis on paper, check to make sure your steps are in the order you desire, and then look at Figure 3.7 and compare your analysis with the example there.

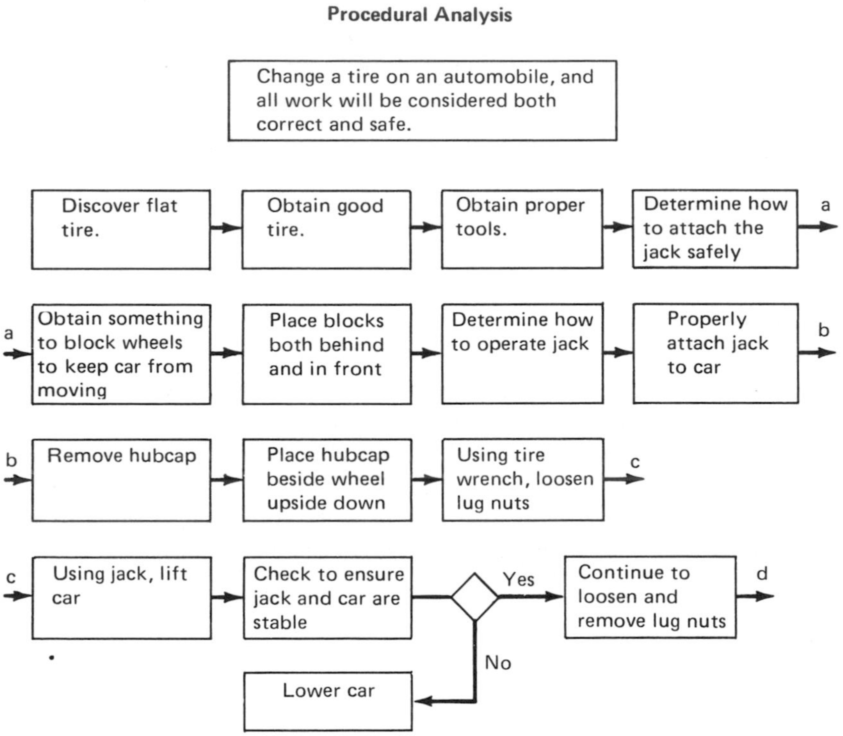

Procedural Analysis

Change a tire on an automobile, and all work will be considered both correct and safe.

| Discover flat tire. | Obtain good tire. | Obtain proper tools. | Determine how to attach the jack safely | a |

| a | Obtain something to block wheels to keep car from moving | Place blocks both behind and in front | Determine how to operate jack | Properly attach jack to car | b |

| b | Remove hubcap | Place hubcap beside wheel upside down | Using tire wrench, loosen lug nuts | c |

| c | Using jack, lift car | Check to ensure jack and car are stable | Yes | Continue to loosen and remove lug nuts | d |

No → Lower car

Figure 3.7 Feedback on Procedural Analysis Task Related to Changing an Automobile Tire

Hierarchical Analysis

In the example shown below, demonstrate your ability to do a hierarchical analysis.

Topic: Reading a city map of your own town.

Instructional goal: You will be able to read a map of (your town) recognizing symbols from the legend, locating points on the map indicated by symbols, calculating distances between given points, and locating specified streets on the map.

The best way to complete this analysis is to start with the instructional goal and ask yourself, "What would the learner have to know in order to be able to perform this objective?" Write down all the information and skills required. Now, given those new subobjectives, ask yourself, "What would a learner have to know or do in order to be able to complete these subtasks?" At each level, compare the interrelatedness of subskills one with another. You may want to rearrange or omit subskills after reconsidering each step.

When you complete your hierarchical analysis, compare your hierarchy with the one in Figure 3.8 on page 46. Analyze and try to explain any differences.

IMPLEMENTATION

The ideas presented in this chapter can be organized into the input, process, and output framework.

Input

The input required to conduct an instructional analysis consists of a clearly stated instructional goal.

Process

1. Rather than deciding which instructional analysis approach should be used to analyze your instructional goal (this decision is usually not made until after the analysis has taken form and you analyze the relationship that exists among subcomponents), you should begin with the instructional goal and ask yourself, "What does the student have to do in order to perform this task?"

2. As you begin to identify subtasks, subskills, and/or supporting information you believe should be included, you will build a collection of substatements. While the appropriate procedure for designers is to work deductively from the instructional goal, some do work inductively from the entry behaviors (which are described in the next chapter). You should use whichever procedure or combination of procedures that works best for you.

3. After you have made a "first pass" through the analysis, you are far from finished! (Write identified subskills on 3-by-5-inch cards so they can be reordered, added, and deleted in subsequent analysis activities.)

4. Again analyze the subskills you have identified. Ask yourself whether they are complete, whether they are in the right order, and whether they are at the desired level of specificity. One way to perform this analysis is to identify exactly the behavior required to perform each subskill.

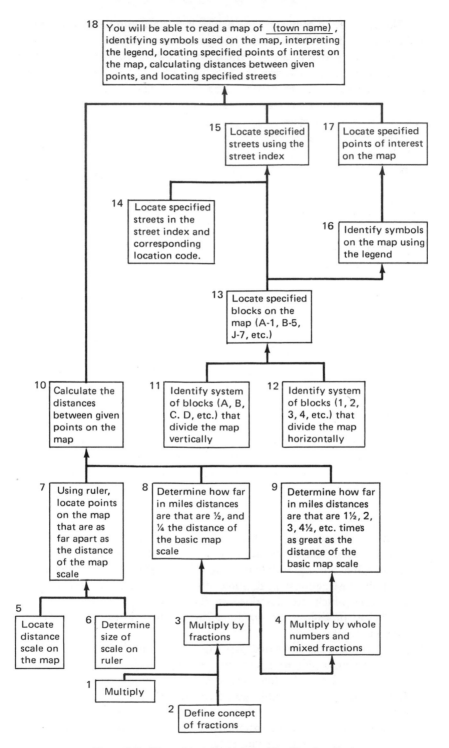

18. You will be able to read a map of __(town name)__, identifying symbols used on the map, interpreting the legend, locating specified points of interest on the map, calculating distances between given points, and locating specified streets

15. Locate specified streets using the street index

17. Locate specified points of interest on the map

14. Locate specified streets in the street index and corresponding location code.

16. Identify symbols on the map using the legend

13. Locate specified blocks on the map (A-1, B-5, J-7, etc.)

10. Calculate the distances between given points on the map

11. Identify system of blocks (A, B, C, D, etc.) that divide the map vertically

12. Identify system of blocks (1, 2, 3, 4, etc.) that divide the map horizontally

7. Using ruler, locate points on the map that are as far apart as the distance of the map scale

8. Determine how far in miles distances are that are ½, and ¼ the distance of the basic map scale

9. Determine how far in miles distances are that are 1½, 2, 3, 4½, etc. times as great as the distance of the basic map scale

5. Locate distance scale on the map

6. Determine size of scale on ruler

3. Multiply by fractions

4. Multiply by whole numbers and mixed fractions

1. Multiply

2. Define concept of fractions

Figure 3.8   Hierarchical Analysis for Map-Reading Goal

5. You may want to verify or discuss your analysis and sequence with another knowledgeable person(s) before finalizing your analysis. This verification step may help identify other important subskills or subskills included unnecessarily, or the fact that you have identified far too much or too little material that is reasonable for the time or money available.

Output

The product you have at this stage is a well-analyzed instructional analysis which includes both the instructional goal and all the subskills and information required for the learner to achieve the goal. Each subskill should be behaviorally stated and the relationship among subskills identified.

REFERENCES

Briggs, L. J. *Handbook of procedures for the design of instruction.* Pittsburgh: American Institute for Research, 1970, 73-92.
  Instructional activities are provided for determining the learning structure of objectives.
Cook, J. M., & Walbesser, H. H. *How to meet accountability with behavioral and learning hierarchies.* College Park, Md.: Bureau of Educational Research and Field Services, College of Education, University of Maryland, 1973, 88-111.
  In these special materials designed for teachers, the authors suggest the use of a "topical" hierarchy before developing an instructional hierarchy.
Davis, R. H., Alexander, L. T., & Yelon, S. L. *Learning system design.* New York: McGraw-Hill, 1974, 129-158.
  The authors' coverage of instructional analysis emphasizes techniques for examining procedural, sequential types of learning tasks.
Gagné, R. M. *Conditions of learning.* (Third edition). New York: Holt, Rinehart, and Winston, 1977.
  While the author specifically describes the analysis of psychomotor procedures, his book is a classic related to many aspects of instructional design.
Gagné, R. M., & Briggs, L. J. *Principles of instructional design.* New York: Holt, Rinehart, and Winston, 1974, 99-119.
  A number of examples of the application of hierarchical analysis to intellectual skills are provided.
Singer, R. N., & Dick, W. *Teaching physical education: A systems approach.* Boston: Houghton-Mifflin, 1974, 142-162.
  The chapter on student evaluation stresses the various domains of learning and provides a variety of assessment techniques for each.

4 Identifying Entry Behaviors and Characteristics

OBJECTIVES

1. *You will be able to describe entry behaviors and distinguish them from general characteristics of students in a target population.*

2. *You will be able to derive entry behaviors when given an instructional analysis and a specific target population.*

BACKGROUND

Have you ever picked up a textbook that you were highly motivated to read, but found you could not get past the first few pages? Or, have you ever enrolled in a course and found that you already knew much of the material that was being taught? These are typical examples of mismatches between instructional materials and the abilities of students using them. In the chapter on instructional analysis we were concerned with identifying the skills that must be taught to a student in order to achieve an instructional goal. In this chapter, we will be looking at the other side of that coin—the skills students must have before they begin instruction. In order to have effective instructional materials or, for that matter, any type of successful instructional experience, there must be a match between students and materials.

Perhaps one of the most costly mismatches between students and materials occurred in the late 1950s and 1960s in the United States when a large number of curriculum projects were funded to update the content of the instructional materials being used in the high schools. These projects revealed that the instructional materials were extremely effective for only the top

25 percent of U. S. high-school students. The huge majority of 75 percent found them too difficult. It is interesting to note that many of the ideas which we are presenting in our instructional design model were researched during this same time period, and that at least some of the new processes were developed in response to the criticisms of curriculum development efforts during that era.

The problem of overestimating or underestimating the ability of learners is still of great concern today and probably will be for a number of years. It is a matter of fact that some instructional designers are far removed either by age or socioeconomic status from the learners whom they hope to serve through their materials. Therefore the designer must make a conscientious effort to identify the critical characteristics of students to design instructional materials appropriately. One example may suffice to make the point. Students in public schools today have watched thousands and thousands of hours of television—some studies indicate that more hours are spent watching television than in the classroom. The results of this are beginning to become evident in testing situations. Students are improving their perceptual skills while their verbal skills have tended to remain unchanged. This certainly has implications for the design of instructional materials.

In this unit we will highlight the critical importance of identifying very specific skills which a student must have before beginning a unit of instruction, of identifying relevant general characteristics of students, and of identifying how these two might interact with the format of instructional materials.

CONCEPTS

This unit will focus on the concepts of entry behaviors and general characteristics of the target population. Let's first consider what is meant by *target population*. This term refers to the group of students for whom instruction is intended. Typically, the target population is described in terms of age, grade level, and sometimes sex. For example, a set of materials might be intended for kindergarten children, fifth-grade reading classes, junior high school boys' football, or college algebra classes. These examples are typical of the descriptions usually available for instructional materials. But, it is important for the instructional designer to go beyond these general descriptions and be much more specific about the entry behaviors and general characteristics of the students for whom the materials are intended. The target population is also sometimes referred to as the *target audience* or *target group*.

Target populations can be described both in terms of general characteristics and specific entry behaviors. The instructor is interested in identifying general characteristics of the entire group of students, which might be important considerations for the design of instruction. For example, the target population may be very young and have a limited attention span; thus the instructional units should be kept quite short. Or, the population may contain many low-ability readers, and thus many visuals should be included in the instruction.

Entry behaviors of the target population are those *specific skills* that a student must be able to demonstrate *prior to* beginning an instructional activity. Entry behaviors should be described at the same level of detail as any task that might be identified through instructional analysis procedures. A statement of an entry behavior should include a verb that describes what students do when they perform this task.

General characteristics of the target population are much more inclusive than entry behaviors. As noted above, mathematics materials are often described as being appropriate for first-grade students or fourth-grade students, and a home economics text might be for girls in the seventh grade. This is a general description of a target population for whom instructional materials should (or might) be appropriate. We use the word *might*, because it is possible that a number of the students who would be included in the target population lack the specific entry behaviors required for beginning an instructional unit. If a mathematics textbook is intended for use in fourth grade, but a majority of a particular fourth-grade class has not yet learned to add two-digit numbers, it is clear that while the students are technically in the fourth grade, they would probably not have the critical entry behaviors to begin using the textbook. Age is not the prerequisite of interest.

How then do instructional designers determine the target population who will use their instructional materials? The target population for any set of materials is decided most often by circumstances which originally resulted in the design of the materials. If the instructional designer is employed on a project to develop career education modules for a county school system, then the initial target population would typically be upper elementary students in county "X." If designers have more ambitious goals for the use of their materials, they may describe the target population as being those students in the upper elementary grades of a particular state or a particular county. Whether the materials will ever reach this target population is often beyond the powers of the individual who designed the instruction.

If the instructional designer is employed on a national curriculum project whose materials will be disseminated by a national publisher, then it would be reasonable to identify a national target population. However, this population might be restricted to college-bound high-school seniors. These examples indicate that the target population is identified in terms of the general characteristics of students for whom the materials are intended.

It is important to identify the major characteristics of the target population so that potential users of instructional materials will have such a description. At this stage it is even more critical to identify these characteristics because of their implications for the instructional development process. It is imperative that instructors consider the characteristics of the target population for whom instruction is being planned.

One of the most important characteristics of a target population is its general intellectual capability. In this regard, the work of Piaget on the psychology of intellectual development is of interest. Piaget has theorized, and research has tended to support, the concept of intellectual stages of growth which are common to all individuals. In recognizing these stages, their characteristics, and the approximate ages at which they occur, the designer possesses critical knowledge about the intellectual capabilities to be expected from a given target population.

Piaget has classified intellectual development into four stages. The first period, labeled the sensorimotor stage, begins with birth and continues to about the age of one and a half years. During this time, a child's intellectual development consists primarily of the coordination of actions and perceptions, and there is little formal language development. The preconceptual and intuitive stage that follows lasts from approximately a year and a half until age seven. During this time period the child can label particular objects but is unable to classify or to determine interrelationships among objects. At approximately the age of seven, the child enters the stage of concrete operations, in which he or she begins to make classifications and establishes relationships. However, these intellectual skills are limited to actual objects or to those which can be easily imagined. At about age twelve the child enters the stage of formal operations. This stage continues to develop for approximately three to four years, during which time children begin to use symbols and manipulate objects in abstract and imaginative ways.

It must be recognized that these age classifications for each stage are not exact, for there is a range of individual differences among children. It does appear, however, that most children's thinking develops through these four stages.

What are the implications for instructors of Piaget's theory and research? Piaget's major interest is in the description of how children think. He has not developed elaborate instructional strategies to teach content to children at each stage. Nevertheless, his findings can lead to inferences about general learner characteristics. For instance, suppose a designer wished to prepare materials for high-school level children—those who are moving from the concrete stage into the formal operations stage. It can be hypothesized that effective instruction should build on the students' prior experience. The designer begins with what is concrete and real to the child at this age, and builds toward more abstract concepts. He or she should make sure that verbal descriptions of phenomena precede other representational forms such as formulas.

Similar types of information about the physical and emotional characteristics of the target population can be used to draw implications about possible interests and skills. This information should be taken into consideration during the instructional development process, and such information is even more critical when the designer is planning for a special subgroup of learners such as the handicapped or the intellectually gifted. Their special characteristics must be considered when formulating any instructional strategy.

Identifying entry behaviors or skills required of students before beginning instruction is a much more specific task. These behaviors should be derived directly from the instructional analysis. If we consider the sample instructional analysis from the previous chapter on estimating points on a linear scale (Figure 3.2), we can identify required entry behaviors. Figure 4.1 shows a modified version of that hierarchical analysis.

Notice in Figure 4.1 that three more skills have been added to the analysis chart, and a dotted line has been drawn across the page. The dotted line indicates that all skills that appear *above* the line will be taught in the instructional materials. All the skills that appear *below* the line will be assumed to be skills already attained by students prior to beginning instruction.

Each of the new skills, which includes the reading of whole numbers and decimal numbers, was derived directly from a superordinate skill that already appeared on the instructional analysis chart. Each was derived by asking the question, "What does the student have to be able to do in order to be given

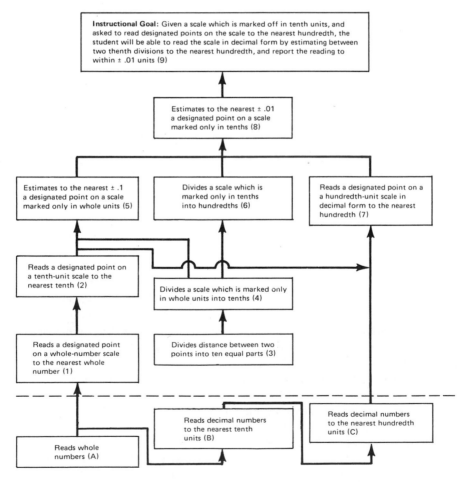

Figure 4.1 Instructional Analysis for Scale-Reading Example

instruction on this skill?" Note that even the entry behaviors identified in Figure 4.1 have a hierarchical relationship to each other.

Instructional designers should identify expected entry behaviors of students by continuing the instructional analysis to the point that skills identified become basic for their target population. The designer must assume that most, if not all, of the students in the target population will have these skills. It is then a matter of simply drawing a dotted line through the instructional analysis chart to separate skills to be included in the instruction from skills students in the target population are assumed to have already learned. This decision is extremely important to the instructional design process.

There are basically two types of errors that can be made when identifying entry behaviors for instructional materials. The first was alluded to earlier when we said that some curriculum materials were designed for only 25 percent of a target population. This situation would be reflected in an instructional analysis chart if the dotted line which separated skills to be taught from skills assumed to be known appeared high on the chart. This suggests that target population students already have the majority of skills described on the chart. When assumed entry behaviors are incorrect, instructional materials lose their effectiveness with a large number of students in the target population. Without adequate preparation in the prerequisite skills, students' efforts are inefficient and the materials are ineffective.

The second error occurs when the dotted line is drawn too low on the instructional analysis. In this situation it is presumed that students have few or none of the skills required to achieve the instructional goal. An error of this type is costly both in terms of developing instructional materials which are not really needed by students and in terms of the time required for students to study objectives they have already mastered.

The description thus far has related entry behaviors to a hierarchical instructional analysis. This same approach can be taken with the procedural and combination analyses. If a procedural analysis has a sequence of already attained skills which must be linked together, the assumption is made explicitly that students already have the individual skills, and the designer's task is simply to show how to link the skills together. The skills would be included in the statement of entry behaviors as well as in the task itself. If a combination approach is used in which subordinate skills and knowledge are identified for major components in procedural analyses, then the identification process can be continued until basic skills are identified.

You should be aware that the examples which we have used have been rather clear-cut in that they either describe general characteristics of a total group of students or specific skills related to specific instructional goals. There are some descriptors of students which may be considered as either specific entry skills for a particular instructional unit or as descriptive of the general target population. Consider the question of students' reading levels. It is apparent that instructional materials typically depend heavily upon the reading ability of students; students must have some minimum level of reading ability to become involved with the materials. Is the specification of reading level a description of a general characteristic of the target population or is it a specific entry behavior which must be possessed by students prior to beginning instruction? Clear arguments could be made on either side of this issue. You may be able to identify other factors which would produce similar problems.

A test you might employ to identify the appropriate category for such an ability is to determine whether you think it would be worthwhile or feasible for an instructor to test a student for that particular skill prior to permitting the student to begin instruction. If the answer to that question is "yes, it would be worth the time to test the student," you have probably identified a specific entry behavior. If, on the other hand, it would seem to be inappropriate to test the skill of the student (such as giving a reading test) before instruction, then the factor which you have identified is probably better classified as a characteristic of the target population for which the unit is intended.

How you go about identifying the specific entry behaviors for your materials will depend upon where you stopped when you conducted your instructional analysis. If you identified only those tasks and skills that you plan to include in the instructional materials, then you will need to take each of the lowest skills in the hierarchy and determine the subordinate skills associated with each. These would be listed on your instructional analysis chart beneath a line which clearly differentiates them from subordinate skills which will be included in the instructional materials.

If your instructional analysis were carried out to the point of identifying basic, low-level skills, then it should be possible for you to simply draw a line through the chart above those skills which you assume a majority of students in the target population already have learned.

It should be noted that the designer is making a set of assumptions at this point about the target population. If time is available, it is possible to interview and test members of the population to determine if the majority have the assumed entry behaviors. If time does not permit this, then the assumption will have to be tested at a later time in the development process.

One last word. When developing instructional materials about topics of general interest which emphasize information objectives, it is sometimes found that there are apparently no required entry skills other than simply the ability to read the materials and use adult reasoning skills to reach the instructional goal. If you find that you have identified such an area, then it is perfectly legitimate to indicate that while the materials are intended for a certain target population, there are no specific entry behaviors required to begin the instruction.

EXAMPLES

Identifying entry behaviors and student characteristics is a very important early step in designing instruction for a specified target population. Consider the procedural instructional analysis on opening and maintaining a checking account in chapter 3. Some possible target populations for that instruction could be:

1. college-bound high-school seniors
2. commercial or work-study high-school freshmen or sophomores
3. any person inquiring about opening an account, either personal or commercial, from a bank
4. sixth-grade students using a simulation of the exercise as a realistic practice in mathematics class

The designer would proceed differently through the instruction for these different groups. There would be differences among the groups in purposes, entry skills, motivation, and perhaps outcomes. The designers would need to provide a more detailed description of the target population before beginning. Target population 3 above, any person, would result in the most general type of instruction, while instruction directed to either college students or work-study groups would differ in vocabulary, problems, practical examples, practice, and amount of feedback.

General characteristics of target populations can be described using general group descriptors such as age, grade, interests, professions, health, motivation, achievement level, abilities, socioeconomic status, or foreign-language status. After these descriptions, reference can be made to specific skills required to enter a particular set of instruction.

Target population 1 above, college-bound high-school seniors, might be further described as having a high reading level, as not requiring math review, as good problem solvers, and as interested in the subject due to its relevance to their new money-management responsibilities.

Target population 2, commercial or work-study students, might be further described as having a limited vocabulary and reading skills, limited math skills, moderate problem-solving skills, and a general disinterest in school related activities.

Target audience 4, sixth-grade students, might further be described as having a limited vocabulary, limited math skills, limited understanding of banking, and good to poor problem-solving techniques.

By carefully defining the general characteristics of the target populations, using general predictors of ability and interests, it will be easier to determine whether you have indeed selected the correct population and to determine what type of approach or vocabulary you will need to use in the tests and in instruction.

Broad general descriptions of target populations such as the example in 3, any person seeking to open a checking account, will make the resulting instruction more general and therefore more applicable to a wider audience, but it might lose its relevance for particular groups. Decisions must be made about whether the effort to design relevant material and the resultant learning are worth the additional effort and cost of designing very specific materials for a limited audience.

Entry Behaviors

Entry behaviors should always be *stated behaviorally* and include *specific skills* the student should be able to perform before entering instruction.

Although the descriptions of general characteristics of target populations will differ, the skills needed to perform the instructional goal will not. If specific skills are required to perform the instructional goal, then they will be required for all persons. The varying factor among the groups would be the skills they possess when they enter the instruction. Their skill level would determine which skills would be considered entry behaviors and which would be included in the instruction. Figure 4.2, the checking account analysis, shows different entry levels for various target populations. Notice the different points at which the various groups enter the instruction. All the skills in the categories below each entry point are assumed entry behaviors for that group.

The actual steps included in the instruction will change not only according to entry skills of the students, but also according to the purpose for the instruction. If the purpose is to have students actually open a checking

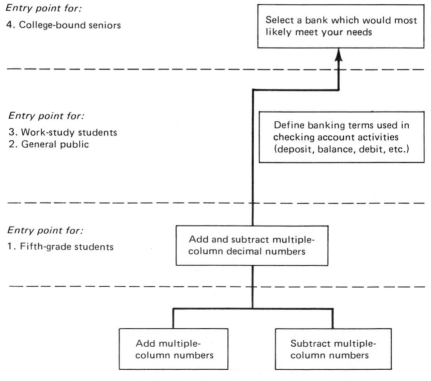

**Figure 4.2 Instructional Analysis for Checking Account Example
Illustrating Varying Entry Points for Varying Target Audiences**

account, then all the steps included in the instructional analysis of opening checking accounts in the previous chapter would be advisable. If the purpose of the instruction is to teach vocabulary and math skills using a realistic exercise, however, then the instructional goal would change and emphasis on opening an account would be reduced to merely putting the exercise in context, while blocks requiring the use and practice of math and language skills would be emphasized.

The same principles apply for hierarchical instructional analyses. Given a complete hierarchical instructional analysis and any particular target population, the designer can predict where in the analysis the students should begin. It could be at the beginning (lower portion) of the analysis or at some intermediate point.

For an illustration of this, consider the instructional analysis in Figure 4.3. The broken line separates subskills the designer predicts will be entry skills and those he or she predicts should be included in instruction.

The target population for instruction depicted in Figure 4.3 is kindergarten children who (1) cannot read, (2) are highly motivated, and (3) have a very short attention span.

A careful description of the target population will help the designer determine the speed of instruction, level of difficulty, instructional time, and occasionally the instructional medium. In the example above, since the majority of the population most likely cannot read, a pamphlet or book would be inappropriate, and another presentation medium should be used.

Another benefit of carefully describing the target population is that the designer can then verify when the target population has been correctly identified. If healthy, normal kindergarten students cannot perform the skills in the analysis after instruction or can already perform all the skills, then the target audience has been incorrectly identified.

There are different solutions to this problem. If the major purpose is to teach the discrimination of shapes and generalize to the environment, then the designer should redefine the target population and select advanced kindergarten/first-grade students if the task was too difficult, or select nursery-school students if the task proved too easy. If the major purpose was to identify instruction for kindergarten students, the designer would need to develop a new instructional goal and begin again.

By placing the dotted line in Figure 4.3 above the skills relating to matching names with illustrations and shapes, the designer assumes that all students in kindergarten have had instruction, either at home or in nursery school, in recognizing the five shapes.

It would be an easy matter to test whether students have the necessary entry behavior skills. The designer could select several children, including those who readily understand and those who tend to need additional examples and practice, and test whether students can match the names of shapes with wooden, plastic, or diagram representations of the shapes. If they can master this block, can they also master other associated blocks? By testing students' performance on specific tasks, the designer can identify those skills

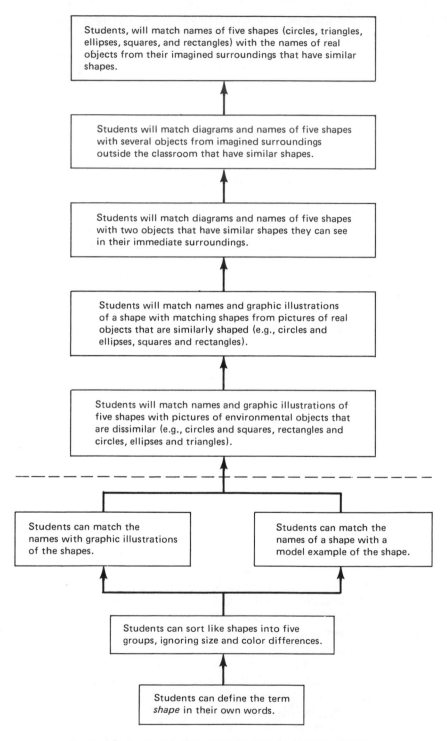

Figure 4.3 Example Instructional Analysis for Matching Shapes

all students, some students, and no students from the target population can perform. This type of testing also helps verify the exact entry behaviors for a given instructional goal. The designer may find members from the target population performing at many different levels in the hierarchy. This is a good argument for designing instruction to cover a large portion of the instructional analysis. Students should enter the instruction at their own levels, since this might prevent boredom for advanced students and confusion for beginning students.

PRACTICE AND FEEDBACK

Practice

I. From the statements below, select those that might refer to general characteristics of the target population (GC) and those that might refer to descriptions of specific entry behaviors (EB).

_EB_ 1. To identify examples of fur-bearing animals
_EB_ 2. To define performance objectives
_GC_ 3. Highly motivated beginning swimmers
_GC_ 4. Frightened nonswimmers
_EB_ 5. To float facedown for thirty seconds
_GC_ 6. Twelfth-grade chemistry students
_GC_ 7. Beginning typing
_EB_ 8. To type at least thirty words per minute
_GC_ 9. Undergraduate business majors
_GC_ 10. High-school sophomores
_EB_ 11. To park a car between markers within ten inches of the curb
_EB_ 12. To write terminal objectives for instruction

You may check your responses with those in the Feedback section.

II. For the instructional goal below, identify a logical target population for the instruction and identify what you would expect to be entry behaviors for that population. Base your judgments of entry behaviors both on the goal and on your expectations for the target population.

Instructional goal: To identify nouns and verbs in a paragraph

Target population: remedial
7th grade language arts
students

start here *to identify characteristics of*
concepts – noun a verb

Entry behaviors: ✓ *to define nouns, to define verbs*
to identify nouns and verbs in sentences)

Check your answers with those presented in the Feedback section.

Feedback

I. 1. EB   2. EB   3. GC   4. GC   5. EB   6. GC   7. GC
    8. EB   9. GC   10. GC   11. EB   12. EB

II. *Instructional goal:* To identify nouns and verbs in a paragraph.

Target population: There could be several responses here. A few might include:

1. Adults learning to read
2. Foreign-speaking students learning English
3. Advanced primary-school students with large word-recognition vocabularies
4. Slow-reading eight-year-old students with limited word-recognition vocabularies

Can you see how instructional approaches and vocabularies used in instruction would need to differ to be appropriate for these four different populations?

Entry behaviors: The entry behaviors would differ according to the target population. Advanced primary-school children would be expected to already know the concept and definition of both a noun and a verb. Instruction would probably begin with teaching "noun" and "verb" as names of components of a sentence as illustrated in Figure 4.4.

    The same objective with slow-reading eight-year-olds would require different entry behavior skills, as illustrated in Figure 4.5.

    These students have little previous knowledge of language structure upon which to build new skills. They must start at the beginning, and entry skills should include all those skills required to teach the terminal objective which will not be included in the instruction. If students cannot perform skills identified as entry behaviors, then those skills should be moved and be included in the instructions. Look at your own entry behavior statements, and answer the following questions.

1. Are they behaviorally stated?
2. Can you logically expect all (or nearly all) members of the target population to possess these skills?
3. How can you check to ensure your judgments about students' entry performance are correct? *pre – test*

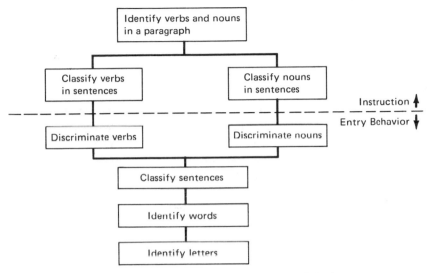

Figure 4.4   Example of Instruction and Entry Behaviors
for Advanced Primary-School Children

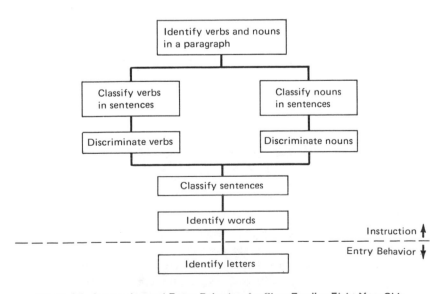

Figure 4.5   Instruction and Entry Behaviors for Slow-Reading Eight-Year-Olds

IMPLEMENTATION

The ideas presented in this chapter can be organized into an input, process, and output model.

Input

Input at this stage consists of the instructional goal and, usually, all the subskills required to meet that goal. In addition, you may already have a rough idea of the target audience for which the materials are being designed. By rough idea, the description you have may be beginning engineering students, beginning telephone operators, experienced ambulance drivers, kindergarten children, or advanced algebra students. Even this preliminary idea about the target audience will provide you with the information necessary to identify the entry behaviors and characteristics of the students.

Process

1. The designer may begin by identifying the general characteristics of the target population. Examples of general characteristics might include age, attention span, interests, sex, grade level, previous experience, vocabulary or reading level, general motivation for learning, and so forth.
2. Secondly, the designer should identify the entry behaviors which target students bring to the instruction. These are specific skills which are identified from the instructional analysis. These skills do not need to be included in the instructional materials because the target audience already possesses them. Examples of such behavior are: can add two-digit numbers with borrowing, can capitalize proper names in a paragraph, or can load 35mm film into a camera.

Output

The output from this process includes a description of the target population's general characteristics and entry behaviors. The description of general characteristics is valuable in identifying the appropriate instructional strategy (pace, amount of instruction, motivation, etc.) for a particular group of students. The description of specific entry behaviors of the target population identifies where in the instructional analysis the instruction should begin. Often the designer discovers that target groups possess a wide range of entry behaviors, and that is an important consideration for where to begin instruction as well.

REFERENCES

Beard, R. M. *An outline of Piaget's developmental psychology*. New York: Basic Books, Inc., 1969.

    This brief book provides a complete description of Piaget's major theories and supporting research as well as the implications of his theories for teachers.

Davis, R. H., Alexander, L. T., & Yelon, S. L. *Learning systems design*. New York: McGraw-Hill, 1975, 93-98 and 184-191.

    The authors describe entry behaviors and characteristics of students and relate them to the task-analysis process.

DeCecco, J. P. *The psychology of learning and instruction: educational psychology*. Englewood Cliffs, N.J.: Prentice-Hall, Inc., 1968, 54-82.

    This is perhaps the most complete description available of the concepts of entry behaviors and characteristics and how they relate to the design of instruction.

5 Writing Performance Objectives

OBJECTIVES

1. *You will be able to identify and describe the components of a properly written performance objective.*

2. *You will be able to write performance objectives for skills which have been identified in an instructional analysis. These objectives should include the conditions of the performance, the performance, and the criteria.*

BACKGROUND

Perhaps the best-known component of the instructional design model is the writing of performance objectives, or, as they are more commonly called, behavioral objectives. Since publication of his book on objectives in 1962, Robert Mager has influenced the total educational community through his emphasis on the need for clear, precise statements of what students should be able to do when they complete their instruction. The term *behavioral objective* became familiar to many educators in the 1960s.

During that time, many workshops were set up for public-school teachers throughout the country. Thousands of teachers have been trained to write behavioral objectives "in order to become accountable for their instruction." However, at least two difficulties have emerged with this approach to instruction. These difficulties arose when the process of defining objectives was not included as an integral component of a total instructional design model.

Without such a model it was difficult for instructors to determine how to derive objectives. Therefore, although instructors could master the mechanics of writing an objective, there was no indication as to what was to serve as the stimulus for writing the objective. As a result, many instructional designers reverted to the tables of content of textbooks to identify topics for which they would write behavioral objectives.

The second and perhaps more critical concern was what to do with the objectives after they were written. Most instructors were simply told that objectives should be incorporated into their instruction, and that they would be better teachers because they now had them for their instruction. In reality, thousands and thousands of objectives were written and then placed in desk drawers never to have their first ounce of impact on the instructional process.

A number of researchers have asked whether it makes a difference if objectives are used or not. In almost all the research studies this question has been asked in the context of an operational instructional setting. In a typical experiment, one group of students receives a sequence of instruction which is preceded by statements of what they should be able to do when they complete the instruction. A control group receives the same instructional materials, but without the statements of the instructional objectives. The results of this type of research have been ambiguous. Some studies have shown significant differences in learning for those students who receive objectives; other studies have shown no differences.

In the instructional design model used in this text, objectives are a key component. It would be impossible to remove this step without significantly influencing the instruction which results from using the model.

Objectives serve as the basis for developing testing instruments used to gauge the effectiveness of instruction. The objectives guide the designer in selecting content and developing the instructional strategy. Therefore, objectives are critical to the design of instruction, whether they are presented to students during instruction or not. Objections to the use of behavioral objectives have been raised. For example, instructors can point to seemingly trivial objectives that appear in some instructional materials. Often, however, these objectives are not based on a carefully conducted instructional analysis illustrating the relationship of each new behavior to one previously acquired. Similarly, many educators acknowledge that writing objectives in some areas, such as humanities, is more difficult than in others. Instructors in these areas, however, do evaluate student performance. The use of objectives requires instructors in these disciplines (a) to specify the behaviors they will teach, (b) to determine the strategy for instruction, and (c) to establish criteria for evaluating student performance when instruction ends.

Statements of what students should be able to do when they complete a given set of instructional materials are useful not only to designers but also to students, instructors, curriculum supervisors, and administrators. If objectives for a unit or course are made available to students, they have clearcut guidelines for what is to be learned and tested during the course. Few students are likely to be lost for long periods of time, and many more are likely to master the instruction when they know what they are supposed to be learning.

While some instructors may see objectives as detrimental to free-flowing classroom discussion, they really serve as a check on the relevance of discussion. Objectives can increase the accuracy of communication among instructors who must coordinate their instruction. Statements describing what students should be able to do when they complete their instruction provide a clear description of what students will be "covering," thus helping to prevent instructional gaps or duplication. Objectives can also indicate to parents and administrators what students are being taught. General course goals, which are often used for this purpose, may sound interesting and challenging, but seldom indicate what it is that students will know or be able to do when a course is completed.

CONCEPTS

The most important concept associated with this chapter is that of a performance objective. We will define a performance objective as a detailed description of what students will be able to do when they complete a unit of instruction. First, it should be pointed out that there are three terms which are often used synonymously when describing student performance. Mager first used the term *behavioral objective* to emphasize it is a statement that describes what the student will be able to do. Some educators have strongly objected to this orientation. Other, perhaps more acceptable, terms have been substituted for "behavioral." Therefore you will see in the literature such terms as *performance objective* or *instructional objective*. When you see these you can assume that they are synonymous with *behavioral objectives*. You should not be misled to think that an instructional objective describes what an instructor will be doing. It describes the kind of behavior which the instructor will be attempting to produce in the learner.

We have said previously that the instructional goal describes what students will be able to do when they complete a set of instructional materials. Similarly, we said that the skills that can be derived through an instructional analysis of the instructional goal are called *subordinate skills*. The objectives that pave the way to the achievement of the terminal objective are referred to as subordinate or enabling objectives. These latter two terms, *subordinate* and *enabling*, are also used synonymously. Likewise, when you convert the instructional goal to an objective, it is referred to as the *terminal objective*. The terminal objective describes exactly what the student will be able to do when he or she completes a unit of instruction.

Though the paragraphs above may seem to you to be filled with jargon or educational gibberish, these terms will become meaningful to you as you use the instructional design model. In the description which follows on the development of objectives, it is important to know that these terms, which you will see in a variety of educational contexts, are essentially synonymous.

Now, on with the task of writing performance objectives. The first question: where do they come from? The answer: they are derived from the instructional analysis. At least one or more objectives can be written for each of the skills identified in the instructional analysis. This includes the writing of objectives for the skills identified as specific entry behaviors. The skills identified in the instructional analysis provide the key when you start to develop the performance objectives.

The generally accepted model for an objective is a statement that includes three major components. The first component describes the skill or behavior identified in the instructional analysis. The objective must describe what it is the student will be able to do.

The second component of an objective describes the conditions which will prevail while the students carry out the task. Will they be given a paper and pencil test? Will they be allowed to use a dictionary? Will their time be limited? Will they be given a paragraph to analyze? These are all statements of the conditions under which the students will work.

The third component of the objective describes the criteria that will be used to evaluate the performance of the student on the objective. The criterion is often stated in the limits, or range, of answers or responses that will be acceptable. The criterion answers the student's question, "Does my answer have to be *exactly* correct?" The criterion indicates the tolerance limits for the response. The criterion may also be expressed in terms of a qualitative judgment such as the inclusion of certain factors in a definition or a physical performance which is judged to be acceptable by an expert.

The following statement contains all three components of an objective: "Given two points on a line and asked to divide the distance between the points into ten equal parts, the students will divide the distance into ten equal parts by drawing nine equal lines between the two points. They will do this within a tolerance of 10 percent." In other words, the behavior the students will exhibit is: "students divide the distance into ten equal parts by drawing nine equal lines between the two points." The conditions that will prevail when they are asked to do this are: "given two points on a line and asked to divide the distance between the two points into ten equal parts." The criterion is explicit: "they will do this within a tolerance of 10 percent."

Note that the objective leaves unanswered the question of how many times the students must demonstrate they can divide a line into ten equal parts. The question of "how many times" or "how many items correct" and similar statements are questions of *mastery*. The designer must determine how many times the students must demonstrate a behavior in order to be sure that they have mastered it. This decision is usually made when test items or assessment is developed. The important point is that the criterion in the objective describes what behavior will be acceptable or the limits within which a behavior must fall.

A large number of objectives will not be reviewed at this point. Examples and practice are provided in later chapters. Other texts can be used as references in this area. It is perhaps more important here to discuss several issues related to the writing of objectives.

It has been stated that objectives are derived directly from the instructional analysis. Thus they must express precisely the type of behavior already identified in the analysis. If the subskill in the instructional analysis includes, as it should, a clearly identifiable behavior, then the task of writing an objective becomes simply adding criteria for behavioral assessment and describing the conditions under which the behavior must be performed. For example, if the subskill is "divides a scale into tenths," then a suitable objective might be stated thus: "Given a scale divided into whole units, the student will be able to divide one unit into tenths. The number of subunits must be ten, and the size of all units must be approximately the same."

Sometimes, however, the designer may find that subskill statements are too vague to write a matching objective. Therefore, the designer should carefully consider the verbs that may be used to describe behavior. Most intellectual skills can be described by such verbs as *discriminate, identify, classify, demonstrate,* or *generate.* These verbs, as described by Gagné and Briggs (1974), refer to such specific activities as grouping similar objects, distinguishing one thing from another, or solving problems. Note that the list does not include such verbs as "know" or "understand."

The instructor must review each objective and ask, "Could I observe a student doing this?" It is impossible to observe a student "knowing" or "understanding." Often these verbs are associated with *information* which the instructor wants the student to learn. To make it clear to students that they are supposed to learn certain skills, it is preferable to state in the objective exactly how students are to demonstrate that they have learned the skills. For example, the student might be required to state that New York and California are approximately three thousand miles apart. If students are able to state (or write) this fact, it may be inferred that they know it.

Usually objectives that relate to physical activity are easily expressed in terms of a behavior (e.g., running, jumping, or driving). In this case, it is more difficult to state the criteria for judging the adequacy of the performance. These criteria sometimes include a frequency count or a time limit, a checklist of activities to be completed for acceptable performance, or a description of the body's appearance as the skill is performed.

When objectives involve attitudes, the student is usually expected to choose a particular alternative or sets of alternatives or to complete an attitude questionnaire. Or, it may involve the student making a choice from among a variety of activities.

While writing the objectives, the designer must be aware that these statements will be used to develop the tests for the instruction. Therefore, the designer might again check objectives by asking, "Could I design a test that indicates whether a student can successfully do what has been described in the objective?" If it is difficult to imagine how this could be done in the existing facilities and environment, then the objective should be reconsidered.

One problem that sometimes occurs is that although an objective may not convey any real information, it may meet the criteria for being an objective. For example, consider the following objective: "Given a multiple-choice test, the student will complete the test and achieve a score of at least nine out of ten correct." While this may be a slightly exaggerated example, it can be referred to as the universal objective in the sense that it meets all the criteria for being an objective and is applicable to almost any cognitive-learning situation. It says nothing, however, in terms of the behavior that is to be taught and evaluated. You should always make sure that your objectives are not universal objectives.

Another problem that can arise in certain types of instructional settings is reference to the use of expert judgment or instructor judgment as the criterion for judging student performance. It is wise to begin with a determination to avoid listing this as the criterion for an objective. It is not helpful to you or to the students. It only says that someone else will judge their performance. In situations in which a judge must be used, try to consider what types of things you would look for if you were the expert who was judging the student's performance. Develop a checklist of the types of behaviors and include these in the statement of the objective to ensure a clear understanding of the criteria.

Gagné and Briggs (1974) have recognized the two problems described above and have suggested that an objective should describe not only the actual behavior to be observed when the student is performing an objective but also should describe the intent of that behavior, a distinction also made by Mager (1975). For example, students might demonstrate their ability to identify Latin words by circling such words in a mixed list of English and Latin words. This statement of an objective not only describes what the students will be doing, namely, "circling a response," but it also describes the capability that will be demonstrated, namely, "identifying." In other words, the intent of the objective is not to have the students demonstrate their ability to draw circles, but rather, to demonstrate their ability to identify examples of Latin words.

Gagné and Briggs also suggest that the criterion for acceptable performance not be stated in the objective. They reason that if you say that the student will have to answer nine out of ten problems correctly, you have in fact predetermined the format of the evaluation. There must be, in this example, at least ten problems on the test for the objective. They suggest that it would be preferable to indicate the mastery level which the student must achieve in the assessment instrument itself. For example, no mastery level would be mentioned in an objective, but the instructions at the top of the test would indicate to the students that they must correctly answer nine of the ten items to get credit for achieving this objective. The Gagné and Briggs approach has the major advantage of avoiding empty statements about student performance, and it puts the criterion for acceptable performance in the context of the assessment situation.

The instructional designer should choose one or a combination of the two approaches to stating objectives. The intent of both approaches is to communicate what it is students will be able to do when they have completed the instruction.

Objectives should be written for each of the skills identified in the instructional analysis, including the instructional goal. You should clearly indicate the relationship between the skill and the objective. You may find that sometimes it will require two or three objectives to describe adequately the types of behavior which are represented by a skill in the instructional analysis. The need for four or more objectives suggests that the task itself is too large and should be reanalyzed into subordinate skills in order to provide a more fine-grained analysis of what it is that you are attempting to teach.

Another suggestion which may be of help is that you should not be reluctant to use two or even three sentences to adequately describe your objective. There is no requirement to limit objectives to one sentence. Also, you should avoid using the phrase "after completing this instruction . . . " as part of the conditions under which a student will perform a skill as described in an objective. It is assumed that the student will study the materials prior to performing the skill.

One final word. Don't allow yourself to become deeply involved in the semantics of objective writing. Many debates have been held over the exact word that must be used in order to make an objective "correct." The point is that objectives have been found to be useful as statements of instructional intent. They should convey to the designer or subject-matter specialist in the field what it is that the student will be able to do. However, objectives have no meaning in and of themselves. They are only one component in the total instructional design process and only as they contribute to that process do they take on meaning. Therefore, the best advice at this point is to write them in a meaningful way and then move on to the next step in the instructional design model.

EXAMPLES

Subskills from the instructional analysis on identifying shapes are listed in the left column; on the right are matching performance objectives which include:

1. a description of the behavior the student is expected to perform
2. the conditions under which the performance will be carried out
3. the criteria for acceptance of performance as sufficient to pass the objective

Subskill Statement from Instructional Analysis	*Matching Performance Objective*
A. Students will match the diagrams and names of the five shapes with the shapes of several objects from imagined surroundings outside the classroom.	A. Given a diagram and the names of a circle, an ellipse, a square, a rectangle, and a triangle, the students can verbally name objects that they cannot see in the classroom (home, playground, store, etc.), which match the shapes of the diagrams.

B. Students will match the diagrams and names of five shapes with two objects that have similar shapes, which they can see in their immediate surroundings.

C. Students will match names and graphic illustrations of five shapes with pictures of real objects which are similarly shaped.

D. Students will match the names and graphic illustrations of five shapes with pictures of real objects which have the same shape from among pictures of real objects which have dissimilar shapes (e.g., square from a triangle and circle, rectangle from a circle and an ellipse).

B. Given a diagram and the names of a circle, an ellipse, a square, a rectangle, and a triangle, the student can verbally name and point to objects that they can see in the classroom which have similar shapes.

C. Given the names and a diagram of a circle, an ellipse, a square, a rectangle, and a triangle, the student can point to pictures of objects with the exact shapes from among several pictures of real objects which are similarly shaped.

D. Given the names and a diagram of a circle, an ellipse, a square, a rectangle, and a triangle, the student can point to pictures of real objects which have the same shape from among pictures of objects which have dissimilar shapes.

In the examples above, the *conditions* in each objective are:

Objective A: Given diagrams and the names of the shapes, objects cannot be seen in classroom.

Objective B: Given diagrams and the names of the shapes, objects can be seen in classroom.

Objective C: Given diagrams and the names of the shapes, selects from among given pictures.

Objective D: Given diagrams and the names of the shapes, matches from among given pictures.

The *performance* in each objective is:

Objective A: Verbally name objects which have similar shapes

Objective B: Verbally name and point to objects which have similar shapes

Objective C: Point to pictures which have similar shapes

Objective D: Point to pictures which have similar shapes

The criterion for acceptably passing **A** through **D** is the same, namely, the student must correctly identify similarly shaped objects. An additional criterion in objective **A** is that the objects must be from outside the classroom. In objective **B** the objects can be seen in the classroom. In objective **C** the shapes must be selected from among pictures of real objects. In objective **D** the shapes must be matched with pictures of similar objects.

The performance required in the objective should match the performance suggested by the parallel subskill in the instructional analysis. If students are required to recognize a picture from among like pictures, the objective should read: "Given several similar pictures, select an example of . . . " If it is necessary for students to define some terms, then the behavioral objective should read: "In your own words, define the following terms . . . "

The idea of matching the required performance with the test item is often ignored because of the time involved or the difficulty of testing and evaluating some performance objectives. Any deviation from the performance required casts doubt upon the student's ability to perform the actual task.

Below is an example of a common mismatch between an item in the instructional analysis and the parallel performance objective.

Instructional Analysis
Compare the prices charged for a motor tune-up at five local garages and, itemizing exact work, parts serviced, parts replaced, and convenience, determine the "best buy" for the price charged.

Performance Objective
Describe how to determine the "best buy" in automobile motor tune-ups including work, parts serviced, parts replaced, and convenience.

The intention of the skill description in the instructional analysis is for the student *to perform* a cost analysis on a specific automobile maintenance task. The objective, however, requires the students *to describe* what they would do to perform the cost analysis. The teacher can determine from this objective whether students can describe the correct procedure to use to gather pertinent costs, but cannot determine whether they can actually gather the information and select the best buy. A correct objective might read: "Given the yellow pages of a phone book, call and request cost estimates for motor tune-ups from five local garages. Compare the costs of labor, parts serviced, parts replaced, and the convenience (i.e., hours, distance, etc.) at each garage. Select the best buy for the prices charged and justify your decision."

We have said that objectives are written for tasks that have been identified in your instructional analysis. This includes writing an objective for your instructional goal, which becomes the terminal objective for your instruction. Listed below are some possible instructional goals and the terminal objective for each.

Goal: The student will be able to punctuate sentences.

Objective: Given a paragraph which includes both description and dialogue, the student will be able to insert all the appropriate punctuation marks, including commas, periods, question marks, exclamation points and colons.

Goal: The student will make choices that reflect a rejection of racial stereotypes.
Objective: Given a list of statements about racial groups, the student will reject as false all those statement that reflect racial stereotyping.

Goal: The student will be able to throw a baseball accurately.
Objective: Given a standard baseball, the student will throw it to another student standing ninety feet away. The throws should be accurate enough to be caught in the air by the receiver while remaining in a specific target area.

Goal: The student will be able to describe the causes of the wars in which the United States was involved.
Objective: In an essay, the student will identify the major causes of three wars involving the United States. The student will analyze the causes discussed and describe the differences and similarities among the causes identified.

PRACTICE AND FEEDBACK

Practice

I. Below are several statements of performance objectives. Some are acceptable as they are written; others need to be revised. Read each objective and determine whether:

a. It is acceptable the way it is written.
b. The performance required is stated unclearly.
c. The conditions required are omitted.
d. The criteria required are omitted.

Place the letter of the appropriate response(s) from above in the space provided by each objective below. Some items have more than one problem.

_____*a*__ 1. Given several black-and-white photographs, the student will select all those that have a mat finish.
_*c*_ _*d*_ 2. The student will develop four black-and-white photographs of animals.
_____*a*__ 3. Using an IBM electric typewriter, the student will type at least thirty words per minute from typed copy with no more than three errors per typed page.
_____*a*__ 4. Given a line with two points, you will divide the distance between the two points into ten equal parts.
_____*a*__ 5. In your own words, write the correct definition (in keeping with that in the text) of four of the following five terms: plutonium, radioactive, fallout, reactor, and fission.

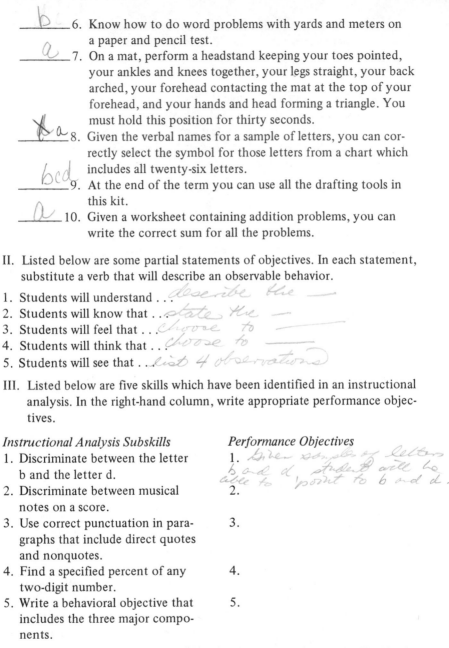

_____b____ 6. Know how to do word problems with yards and meters on a paper and pencil test.

_____a____ 7. On a mat, perform a headstand keeping your toes pointed, your ankles and knees together, your legs straight, your back arched, your forehead contacting the mat at the top of your forehead, and your hands and head forming a triangle. You must hold this position for thirty seconds.

___X a___ 8. Given the verbal names for a sample of letters, you can correctly select the symbol for those letters from a chart which includes all twenty-six letters.

___bcd___ 9. At the end of the term you can use all the drafting tools in this kit.

_____a____ 10. Given a worksheet containing addition problems, you can write the correct sum for all the problems.

II. Listed below are some partial statements of objectives. In each statement, substitute a verb that will describe an observable behavior.

1. Students will understand . . . *describe the* _____
2. Students will know that . . . *state the* _____
3. Students will feel that . . . *choose to* _____
4. Students will think that . . . *choose to* _____
5. Students will see that . . . *list 4 observations*

III. Listed below are five skills which have been identified in an instructional analysis. In the right-hand column, write appropriate performance objectives.

Instructional Analysis Subskills

1. Discriminate between the letter b and the letter d.

2. Discriminate between musical notes on a score.

3. Use correct punctuation in paragraphs that include direct quotes and nonquotes.

4. Find a specified percent of any two-digit number.

5. Write a behavioral objective that includes the three major components.

Performance Objectives

1. *Given samples of letters b and d, students will be able to point to b and d.*

2.

3.

4.

5.

Compare your behavioral objectives with the examples in the Feedback section.

Feedback

I. 1. a 2. c, d 3. a 4. a 5. a 6. b 7. a 8. a
    9. b, c, d 10. a

II. All of the verbs in the statements refer to internal states of the students—how they will feel or think. Possible alternatives would be:

1. Students will list the characteristics of . . .
2. Students will measure the distance on a map with the use of the legend.
3. Students will state orally that . . .
4. Students will express their feelings by choosing to . . .
5. Students will analyze a given set of data and . . .

III. The five objectives you have prepared will no doubt be different from the ones below, because the conditions and criteria which can be applied to these subskills are numerous. The five activities below, however, are all correct examples of behavioral objectives that match the specific subtasks, and you can use them as examples.

1. Given pictures of the symbols for the letter b and the letter d, the student will correctly identify verbally the b and the d.

   or

   Verbally given the name of the letter b or the letter d, the student will point to the matching symbol on charts illustrating the two letters.
2. Given a musical score, students will graphically record each different type of note that appears and write the corresponding name of the note.
3. Given a paragraph of printed text containing direct quotes and non-quotes, the student will correctly punctuate the paragraph using quotation marks, commas, and periods or question marks.
4. Given several problems requiring the student to find a specified percent of a given two-digit number, the student will correctly solve the problems using paper and pencil.
5. Given paper, pencil, and subskills from an instructional analysis, the student will write behavioral objectives which include the conditions of the behavior, the behavior expected, and the acceptable performance criteria.

IMPLEMENTATION

The concepts presented in this chapter can be organized into the input, process, and output model.

Input

The products available as inputs for this phase include the instructional goal, instructional analysis, entry behaviors, and the general characteristics of the target population.

Process

1. Begin with the instructional analysis and write one performance objective for the instructional goal. This is the terminal objective. Then write an

objective for each subskill that is above the entry behaviors line in the instructional analysis. It is not necessary to write performance objectives for entry behaviors if instruction related to those skills is not included as part of the materials and no tests for entry behaviors will be developed.

2. Make sure that for each performance objective you have included (a) the conditions under which the performance will occur, (b) the exact performance that is expected, and (c) the criteria by which the performance will be judged.

3. Check the objectives the way they are written to ensure that (a) the behavior stated in the subskill is parallel to the matching subskill, and (b) the objective as it is stated (conditions, performance, and level of performance) is compatible with the capabilities of the target audience and the constraints of the intended learning environment (classroom, airfield, auditorium, learning center, etc.).

Output

The product of this component consists of the terminal objective and a complete list of performance objectives for the instructional materials. The objectives include the conditions of performance, the required performance, and the criteria for judging performance successful.

REFERENCES

Gagné, R. M., & Briggs, L. J. *Principles of instructional design*. New York: Holt, Rinehart, and Winston, 1974, 75-97.
    The authors describe a five-component behavioral objective, and relate objectives to the various domains of learning.
Kibler, R. J., Cegala, D. J., Barker, L. L., & Miles, D. T. *Objectives for instruction and evaluation*. Boston: Allyn and Bacon, 1974, 29-64.
    Kibler et al. propose a five-component model for behavioral objectives. Attention is given to common difficulties which arise when writing objectives.
Mager, R. F. *Preparing instructional objectives*. Palo Alto, Calif.: Fearon Publishers, 1975.
    This is the original text by Mager on objectives. Mager's humor is well served by the branching programmed-instruction format.

6 Developing Criterion-Referenced Tests

OBJECTIVES

1. *You will be able to identify the characteristics of a criterion-referenced test.*

2. *You will be able to describe the characteristics of an entry behaviors test, a pretest, embedded tests, and a posttest.*

3. *Given a variety of objectives, you will be able to write appropriate criterion-referenced test items which reflect the behavior required of students as stated in the objective.*

BACKGROUND

We have been testing the general and specific abilities of students for many, many years. We have used general ability tests such as the Stanford-Binet as well as tests designed for specific courses. You are perhaps most familiar with instructor-made tests which are used to obtain data to assign grades to students. Quite often these tests are written after instruction has been provided to students, and are made more or less difficult depending upon the ability of the students in the class or the perception of the instructor of how well certain topics were taught. The format of this type of test is sometimes determined by the interests and ability of the instructor rather than by the nature of the content that has been taught.

There are also full-time professional test writers who sample from a large domain of content to select those items for a test which will result in a wide range of scores. In order to develop this type of test, writers must throw out items that are answered either correctly or incorrectly by nearly all students. Although this process tends to increase the reliability of the test, its effect on the validity of the test may be questioned.

During the last ten years, classroom testing has taken a very different turn. Much of this change can be attributed to the impact of Mager's writings about behavioral objectives. As more and more emphasis has been placed on statements of explicit behaviors which students must demonstrate, it has been increasingly obvious that a fair and equitable evaluation system is one that measures those specific behaviors. That is, after students have been told what they have to do to be successful on a learning unit, they should be tested accordingly.

Tests which are designed to measure an explicit set of objectives are called criterion-referenced tests. This type of testing is important to (a) test and evaluate students' progress, and (b) to provide information about the effectiveness of the materials to the instructor. The results of criterion-referenced tests indicate to the instructor exactly how well students were able to achieve each instructional objective. Thus, criterion-referenced testing is a critical feature of almost every instructional design model.

You may wonder why test development appears at this point in the instructional design model rather than after instruction has been developed. The major reason is that test items which are constructed should correspond on a one-to-one basis with the objectives which have just been developed. The performance required in the objective must match the performance required in the test item. Likewise, the nature of the test items which are given to students serves as a key to the development of an instructional strategy.

CONCEPTS

The major concept in this chapter is criterion-referenced testing. A criterion-referenced test is composed of items that directly measure the behaviors described in a given set of behavioral objectives. The term *criterion* is used because test items serve as a benchmark to determine the adequacy of a student's performance in meeting the objectives; that is, success on these items determines whether a student has achieved the objectives of the instructional unit. However, more and more often the term *objective-referenced test* is being used rather than *criterion-referenced test*. The purpose is to be more explicit in indicating the relationship between test items and behavioral objectives. Test items are referenced directly to the performance required by objectives for the instructional materials. Therefore, you may consider these two terms to be essentially synonymous.

There are often two ways the term *criterion* is used when referring to criterion-referenced test items. The first refers to the relationship between the performance objective and the test items. If students manage to *perform adequately* the *behavior* stated in the *objective*, then they have reached criterion or mastery on that objective, as *mastery* on the objective was the *criterion* for moving ahead.

The second use of the word "criterion" relates to the specification of the *adequacy of performance* required to be described as mastery. Examples of this second type of criterion include such benchmarks as "the student will answer all the items correctly," "the student will add all punctuation omitted," and "the student will make a cut with 5-degree accuracy." This type of criterion specification may be established for one test item written for one behavioral objective, several test items written for one objective, or several test items written for many objectives. Clarity in specifying objectives and criteria for adequate performance is necessary as a guide to adequate test construction. Based on a particular behavioral objective and established criteria, a posttest may require only one test item or it may require several.

Therefore, in order to determine whether a test item is truly criterion referenced, the instructor should determine both whether the *performance* required in a test item(s) *matches or is parallel to behavior* stated in the behavioral objective, and second, whether criteria have been established to specify *how well* a student must perform the skill in order to master the objective.

Four Types of Criterion-Referenced Tests

There are basically four types of tests which the instructor may utilize in a module. The first is an entry-behaviors test. This is a criterion-referenced test designed to measure skills which the instructor has identified as being critical to beginning the instructional materials. The second type of test is a pretest. A pretest is criterion referenced to objectives which the designer intends to teach in the module. If you consider a hierarchical instructional analysis, an entry behaviors test measures all the skills that appear below the "line" while a pretest measures all the skills that appear above the "line."

The third and most common test used by the instructor is the posttest. This criterion-referenced test is parallel to and sometimes identical to the pretest. Like the pretest, it measures objectives taught in the instructional program.

The fourth type of test is an embedded test. This is not necessarily a single test, but rather represents clusters of criterion-referenced test items which are interspersed throughout the module. Sometimes embedded tests are ignored by instructors and excluded from instruction. However, they serve two important functions. The first is the testing of students immediately after instruction and prior to the posttest, which provides valuable data for the formative evaluation of the instruction. The second purpose is associated with the eventual implementation of the instruction. It may be of value to an instructor to have embedded tests to check the progress of students, and, if needed, provide remedial activities prior to a more formal posttest.

Designing a Test

How does one go about designing and developing a criterion-referenced test? The designer writes one or more test items for each of the entry behaviors and behavioral objectives which has been identified. The important factor is that there are questions on the test that correspond directly to each entry behavior and each performance objective. Questions related to skills excluded from the instructional analysis are also excluded from an objective or criterion-referenced test.

Objectives in the cognitive or intellectual domain generally require paper and pencil assessment items or items which call for a specific product or performance. Generally, it is relatively easy to determine achievement of a cognitive objective; either students "know" the appropriate response or they do not. Assessment in the affective or attitude domain is more difficult. Affective objectives are generally concerned with the student's attitudes or preferences. As there is no way to directly measure students' attitudes (e.g., whether they enjoy baseball), items for affective objectives generally require that either the students state their preferences or that the instructor observes the students' behavior. For example, if students voluntarily engaged in baseball games on three different occasions, the instructor may infer that they enjoy baseball. From these stated preferences or observed behaviors, inferences about attitudes and preferences can be made.

Items for objectives in the psychomotor domain are most like items in the cognitive domain—they require demonstration of a specific performance. While an objective in the cognitive domain might require students to demonstrate their ability to make oral presentations that meet prespecified criteria, an objective in the psychomotor domain might require them to demonstrate their ability to properly execute a chip shot in golf, again according to prespecified criteria. Similarly, items for objectives of a social nature are like items in the affective domain: there is no direct way to determine whether a student is a "good citizen." As with affective objectives, the assessment of social objectives relies primarily on observation of student behavior and, to a lesser degree, on students' self-reports.

Writing Test Items

It goes without saying that regardless of the type of learning that is involved in the objective, appropriate test-item writing techniques should be applied to the development of criterion-referenced tests. There are several things the instructor should remember while writing criterion-referenced test items. First, the items constructed should match the behavior and the conditions specified in the objective. The items should also provide students with the opportunity to meet the criteria necessary to demonstrate mastery of an objective.

To match the response required in a test item to the behavior specified in the objective, the instructor should consider the learning task or verb prescribed in the objective. Objectives that ask the student to state or define, perform with guidance, or perform independently will all require a different set of questions and responses.

It is critical that test items measure the exact behavior described in the objective. For example, if an objective states that a student will be able to match descriptions of certain concepts with certain labels, then the test items must include descriptions of concepts and a set of labels which the student will be asked to match.

Let's look at an example. Given a scale which is marked off in tenths and asked to read designated points on the scale in tenths, the student will read the designated points in decimal form in units of tenths. The corresponding test item for that objective is shown below.

Report your answer to both questions below in tenths of units.
What is the reading at A? _____
What is the reading at B? _____

You can see in this example that the objective requires the student *to identify exact points* on a scale which is divided into units of one tenth. The test item provides the student with such a scale and two letters that lie at exact points on the scale. The student must indicate the value of each point in tenths' units.

You will encounter more illustrations similar to this in the examples and practice sections. It is important to note carefully the behavior described by the *verb* of the objective. If the verb is to match, to list, to select, or to describe, then you must provide a test that allows a student to match, to list, to select, or to describe. The objective will determine the nature of the item.

The test item must take into account the conditions under which a skill is to be performed. An open-book examination differs greatly from an examination from which reference material is forbidden. The expected conditions of performance included in the performance objective serve as a guide to the test-item writer. The conditions specify whether the student is to respond from memory, use references, or have certain equipment available.

Sometimes the classroom fails to provide the environment or contain the equipment necessary to reproduce exact performance conditions. Instructors must sometimes be creative in their attempts to provide conditions as close to reality as possible. The more realistic the testing conditions can be made, the more reliable the students' responses will be. For example, if the behavior is to be performed in front of an audience, then an audience should be present for the exam. The behavioral objective also includes the *criteria* used to judge mastery of a skill. There is no rule which states that performance criteria should or should not be written into a test item. Sometimes it is necessary for students to know performance criteria and sometimes it is not. Students usually assume that in order to receive credit for a question, they must answer it correctly.

A major question has developed concerning the proper number of items needed for an objective. How many items do students need to answer correctly to be judged successful on a particular objective? If students answer one item correctly, can you assume they have achieved the objective? Or, if they miss a single item, are you sure they have not mastered the concept? Perhaps if you gave the students more items per objective and they answered them all correctly or missed them all, you would have more confidence in your assessment. There are some practical suggestions that may help you determine how many test items an objective will require. If the item or test requires a response format that will enable the student to guess the answer correctly, then you may want to include several parallel test items for the same objective. If the likelihood of guessing the correct answer is slim, however, then you may decide that one or two items are sufficient to describe the student's ability to perform the skill.

In deciding on the number of items to include, you must also consider the likelihood of simple errors being made in response to the item. Examples of this can be found in arithmetic tests. If a student is asked to add fifteen and fifteen and gets twenty for an answer, it is impossible for the instructor to know for sure whether the student does not know how to carry a number to the next column or whether the student simply forgot to add the one to the next column in this problem. If two or three items were included, however, and the student's answers all indicated a failure to carry forward, then the instructor can be sure the student does not know this process. The instructor should always include enough items to be assured that students actually can perform the prescribed skill. A sufficient number of items should eliminate the possibility of students' accidentally stumbling over the correct answer or missing the correct answer because of a minor calculation error.

As you can see, there is no correct answer for the number of items required. What little research has been done in this area generally indicates that the more narrowly stated an objective is, the fewer the items required to correctly measure students' performance. A more broadly stated objective, on the other hand, will require many more items if it is to be adequately tested.

Another important question to consider is, "What type of test item will best assess students' performance?" There are many different test item formats. Several common ones are true/false, completion, fill-in-the-blank, matching, multiple-choice, and definitions.

The behavior specified in the objective provides clues to the type of test items that can be used. In the following chart, the left column lists the type of behavior prescribed in the behavioral objective. Across the top are the types of test items that can be used to evaluate student performance for each type of behavior.

Type of Behavior from Objective	Types of Test Items						
	Essay	Fill-in-the-blank	Completion	Multiple Choice	Matching	True/False	Free Response (building, design, etc.; not paper and pencil)
State	X	X	X				
Identify	X	X	X	X			
Discuss	X		X				
Define	X	X	X				
Select				X	X	X	
Discriminate				X	X	X	
Solve	X	X	X	X		X	X
Develop	X		X				X
Locate	X	X	X	X	X	X	X
Construct	X	X	X				X
Generate	X		X				X

Certain types of behavior can be tested in different ways. Although it is possible to use several different methods to test performance, some test items can assess specified behavior better than others. For example, if it is important for students to remember a fact, asking them to *state* that fact is better than requesting reactions to true/false or multiple-choice questions. Using the objective as a guide, select the type of test item which gives students the best opportunity to demonstrate the performance specified in the objective. In constructing multiple-choice test items, for example, it is often hard to think of adequate distractor items that are not tricky. Another disadvantage of this type of format is that students can use some cue inside the item to guess the correct answer accurately.

There are other factors to consider when selecting the test-item format to use. Each type of test item seems to have its benefits and its weaknesses. To select the best type of item from among those considered adequate, consider such factors as the responding time required by students, the scoring time required to grade and analyze answers, the testing environment, and the probability of guessing the correct answer.

The time required for students to complete a test is important for you to consider. If a behavioral objective requires students to define terms, and limited testing time is available, the instructor may want to construct test items that require students to fill in key words in the definition, rather than the type that requests a complete statement of the definition.

Certain item formats would be inappropriate even when they speed up the testing process. It would be inappropriate to use a true/false question to determine whether a student knows the correct definition of a term. Given such a choice, the student does not define, but rather discriminates between the definition presented in the test item and the one learned during instruction. In addition to being an inappropriate response format for the behavior specified in the objective, the true/false question provides students with a 50–50 chance of guessing the correct response.

Test items can be altered from the "best possible" response format to save testing time and scoring time, but the alternate type of question should still provide students with the opportunity to actually demonstrate the behavior prescribed in the objective. This is often difficult and challenges the creativity of the instructor.

Another important factor in item selection is the time required to analyze and grade students' responses. Current grading practices encourage the use of computer-scored response forms. The facility of grading provided by these forms often encourages the use of multiple-choice or true/false response formats. These two types of formats permit correct guessing more than any other type of response; however, time limitations and pupil-to-teacher ratios sometimes make their use mandatory. Whenever time permits, construct test items to minimize guessing (e.g., fill-in-the-blank, state the definition, explain the phrase, locate the position, match the following list, describe the features, construct the object, etc.). Response formats of this type increase both assessment time and scoring time, but they provide more reliable estimates of the student's ability to perform tasks specified by objectives.

The testing environment is also an important factor in test-item selection. What equipment, facilities, and "givens" are available for the test situation? Can students actually perform a skill specified in an objective? If not, can realistic simulations, either paper and pencil or others, be constructed? If simulations are not possible, will questions like, "list the steps you would take to . . . " be appropriate or adequate for your situation? The further removed the behavior in the test item is from the behavior specified in the objective, the less accurate is the prediction that students either can or cannot perform the behavior specified. Sometimes the exact performance is impossible and performance will have to be assessed in other, less desirable, ways.

The probability of guessing the correct answer is another factor that should be considered when writing test items. Some response methods enable pupils to guess the correct answer more so than others. True/false questions provide students with a 50–50 chance of guessing the right answer, while multiple-choice questions with three, four, or more responses also give them the opportunity to guess the right answer, though the odds of doing so are not as high. By giving extra thought to the responses being requested, instructors can sometimes reduce the likelihood that students will guess correctly. It is more difficult to guess the correct answer in a long line of ten or more matching items than it is to select the correct answer from among three or four. It is also more difficult to guess the correct answer to a fill-in-the-blank question than it is to select the correct term from among two to four choices.

Once you have decided on the best test-item format, the next step involves the actual writing of "good" test items. You will have to consider such things as vocabulary, the "setting" of the item, compound questions within an item, and the trickiness of items.

The vocabulary used in the directions for completing a question and in the question itself should be appropriate for the intended students. Test items should not be written at the vocabulary level of the instructor unless that level is the same as that expected for target learners. Students should not miss questions because of unfamiliar terms. If the definition of certain terms is a prerequisite for performing the skill, then such definitions should have been included in the instruction. The omission of necessary terms and definitions is a common error made by many instructors.

The "setting" of the item is another important consideration. Items can be made unnecessarily difficult by placing the desired performance in an unfamiliar setting. When this is done, the instructor is not only testing the desired behavior, but is also testing additional, unrelated behaviors as well. Though this is a common practice, it is an inappropriate item-writing technique. The more unfamiliar the examples, question types, response formats, and test-administration procedures, the more difficult completion of the test becomes. An example of this "staged" difficulty would be to make up verbal arithmetic problems using contrived, unfamiliar situations. The setting of the problem, whether at the beach, at the store, or at school, should be familiar to the target group. In another example, students could be required to write a paragraph about an unfamiliar topic when the real object of the test item would be to discover whether they can write a paragraph that includes a topic sentence, supporting descriptive sentences, and a summary sentence. Students could demonstrate this skill better using a familiar topic rather than an unfamiliar one. If the item is made unnecessarily difficult, it may hamper accurate assessment of the behavior in question.

Compound questions usually create unnecessary difficulty in test items. Each question can have one or more responses, but a question that permits only one response should not have multiple parts. Compound test items occasionally occur in true/false questions, as instructors seek to increase the difficulty of selection. Being tested is the students' ability to identify each section of the question, to determine whether the sections are equally true, equally false, or partially true. This type of question requires students to figure out exactly what is being asked. The true/false format does not allow them to explain or qualify their responses, and therefore creates justified frustration.

Items written to "trick" students often result in the testing of behaviors other than the one specified in the objective. Instructors would be well advised to spend their creative talents constructing good simulation items rather than inventing tricky questions. If the object is to determine how well students can perform a skill, then a series of questions ranging from very easy to extremely difficult would provide a better indication of students' performance levels than one or two tricky questions (e.g., double negatives, misleading information, compound questions, incomplete information, etc.). If instructors wish to challenge or evaluate advanced students, they could best use their time in constructing test items at a higher difficulty level.

Constructing Tests

Test items are clustered together to form the pretest and posttest. At this time there are two major factors to consider: the order that items will appear on the test and the directions that explain to students what they are to do on the test.

There are no hard and fast rules that guide the order of item placement on a test. There *are* suggestions that can guide placement, but final decisions are usually based on the specific testing situation and the performance to be tested. Some suggestions for item placement are to scramble the order of items so that you do not naturally lead students through a step-by-step procedure with the flow of content in the items. When possible, scramble test items—avoid placing them in the order of natural occurrence or in the order students practiced them during class exercises.

Cluster items so that like types of questions are together. Matching items should all be together; fill-in-the-blank items should be together; essay-type questions should be together; and so forth. Within each type of question, the content of the questions can vary across the content included in the objectives. Each time the expected response mode of students changes, they have to change their thought and response patterns. Unnecessary switching back and forth across types of test items can cause a test to be unnecessarily difficult. Your real purpose is to test performance related to content and not the test sophistication of students.

Tests should always include clear, concise directions for completing the test. Beginning a test usually causes anxious feelings among students who will be judged and placed in instruction according to their performance on the test. There should be no doubt in their minds about what they are to do to perform correctly on the test. There are usually introductory directions to an entire test and subsection directions when the type of test item changes.

The nature of the directions changes according to the testing situation, but the following kinds of information are sometimes found in test directions: a test title that suggests the content to be covered rather than simply pretest or "Test I"; a brief statement of the objectives or performance to be demonstrated; the amount of credit which will be given for a partially correct answer; whether students should guess if they are unsure of the answer; whether words must be spelled correctly to receive full credit; whether students should identify themselves as individuals or as members of a group; whether there is a time limit, word limit, or space limit for responses; and whether they need any special things to respond to the test such as number 2 pencils, mark sense answersheets, a special text, or special equipment such as calculators or maps.

It is difficult to write clear and concise test directions. What is clear to you may be confusing to others. Write and review directions carefully to ensure that students have all the information they need to respond correctly to the test.

Evaluating Tests and Test Items

Test directions and test items should undergo formative evaluation before they are actually used to assess student performance. A test item may seem perfectly clear to the person who wrote it but thoroughly confusing to the individual required to respond to it. Many things can go wrong with a test. The instructor should ensure that (a) test directions are clear, simple and easy to follow; (b) that each test item is clear and conveys to students the intended information or stimulus; (c) that conditions under which responses are made are realistic; (d) that the response methods are clear to students; and (e) that appropriate space, time, and equipment are available for students to respond appropriately.

After writing a test, the instructor should administer it to a student or individual (not one from the actual target group) who will read and explain aloud what is meant by both the directions and questions, and actually respond to each question in the intended response format. In constructing a test, the instructor can unknowingly make errors, and this preliminary evaluation of the test can save many anxious moments for students, wasted time for students and teachers, or even invalid test results. Incorrectly numbered items will result in scrambled answers on response sheets. The same applies to unclear directions, confusing examples or questions, and vocabulary which is too advanced for the students being tested. A preliminary evaluation of the test with at least one person, and preferably several persons, will help pinpoint weaknesses in the test or individual test items that can be corrected prior to exam time.

Even after an exam is actually given, the instructor should assess the results. Test items that are missed by most of the students should be analyzed. Instead of measuring the performance of the student, such questions might point to some inadequacy in the test item, the directions for completing the test item, or the instruction. Items that are suspect should be analyzed and possibly revised before the test is administered again.

A practical testing problem exists for instructors who test several different groups of students on the same objectives at the same time. To guarantee the integrity of students' answers, instructors in these situations may need to construct several different versions of a posttest. Thus, in addition to the pretest and the embedded test, as many as five or six versions of a posttest may be required.

In this situation, the instructor may want to construct several different test items, or a pool of items, for each performance objective. When this is done, the instructor will need to ensure that all items constructed for one objective are parallel and at the same level of difficulty. By setting a question in an unfamiliar situation or using more difficult terminology, the difficulty of items can be increased. This can cause the item to assess behavior other than that intended. When many different items are used, the instructor should confirm that items are parallel by asking colleagues to judge whether the multiple items are parallel in assessing performance and at the same level of difficulty.

When constructing test items—and tests in general—the instructor should keep in mind that tests measure the adequacy of (a) the test itself, (b) the response form, (c) the instructional materials, (d) the instructional environment and situation, and (e) the achievement of students.

All the suggestions included in this discussion should be helpful in the development of test items for criterion-referenced tests. If you are an inexperienced test writer, you may wish to consult additional references on test item construction. Several references on test-item writing techniques are included at the end of this chapter.

Criterion-Referenced Tests and Norm-Referenced Tests

There are at least three basic differences between norm-referenced tests and criterion-referenced tests. First is the way each type of test is developed. Second is the standard used to judge students' performances on the tests. And third is the purpose for which each type of test is constructed.

Test development. As stated previously, criterion-referenced tests include only test items that are based on specified behavioral objectives. Each item requires students to demonstrate the performance stated in an objective. Standards for acceptable performance on the test are based upon criteria stated in the objectives.

Norm-referenced tests are constructed differently. It is usually unnecessary for the exact performance desired to be described in behavioral terms prior to item or test construction. Test items are not necessarily based on instruction students receive or on skills or behaviors that are identified as relevant for student learning. Items that are developed from a given domain for norm-referenced tests are administered to a variety of students from the target population. Those items that cause the greatest spread or range in students' responses are selected for inclusion on a norm-referenced test. The range of scores is usually expected to resemble a normal or bell-shaped curve, hence the name "norm-referenced."

Assessment of student performance. A second difference between criterion-referenced tests and norm-referenced tests is the manner in which student performance is judged and interpreted. In criterion-referenced testing, the performance standard, or criterion, is established in the behavioral objective. Each individual student's performance on test items is measured against the established standard of performance. Students either master objectives or they do not. Their performance is interpreted in terms of the number of the required objectives they have mastered. It is possible for all students in a group to master all the objectives assessed or for all students to fail all objectives tested. The distribution of students' scores is not expected to resemble a normal curve.

Scores on norm-referenced tests are not reported in terms of the number of specified objectives an individual completes, but rather in terms of the number of questions the student answers compared to other students completing the test. Each student's performance is relative to the performance of all other students in the group. Standard scores such as percentile ranks, stanines, and grade equivalents will allow the performance of each student to be compared with the performance of others, regardless of the nature of the performance being evaluated. Student performance is sometimes reported as, "The student performed better than 80 percent of the group." Normative scores reflect relative performance.

Testing purposes. Whether it is appropriate to administer a criterion-referenced test or a norm-referenced test depends upon the instructor's purpose. If instructors need to classify a person, diagnose learning, or prescribe instruction, then it is important for them to construct or select criterion-referenced tests to assess performance. The performance of each individual will indicate skills that have been mastered and those that have not. This performance-based assessment is especially appropriate for training or job-placement purposes.

If, on the other hand, the purpose of testing is to select a few outstanding individuals, then norm-referenced tests that cover a wide range of skills which are not especially objective related can be used to spread out student performance and isolate outstanding individuals from the remainder of the group.

Today in education, criterion-referenced tests are designed to assess student performance on specified objectives. It is becoming common practice to use these same criterion-referenced tests not only to assess the progress of individuals, but also to compare the relative performance of students on a set of behavioral objectives. There are many reasons for doing this. Sometimes the comparative results are used to determine which students work faster, to determine which go beyond minimum criteria or standards, to identify the placement of the group on any of the skills in a continuum, or to select outstanding, average, or poor performers for special programs.

Although criterion-referenced tests are now being used for normative comparisons within or among groups, and although the performance of a group at any one time may resemble a normal curve on a set of objectives, the method in which the items for a criterion-referenced test are constructed and selected differs from that used to construct what is traditionally called a norm-referenced test.

Test Reliability

When constructing tests that will be used again and again, the instructor should take the time to determine the reliability of the test. Reliability refers to whether the test and each item within a test consistently measures the behavior for which it is intended. For example, if you have four questions that you believe assess the same skill, and a student can perform the skill, you would expect the student to answer at least three of the four correctly. If the student was unable to perform the skill, you would expect the student to miss consistently questions based on that skill. Test items should be reviewed and revised if they are consistently missed by students who know the skill the items supposedly tap. Test items that are correctly answered by pupils who do not possess the intended skills are also suspect and should be revised. These items, or other questions on the test, no doubt provide cues that enable students to answer correctly without following the intended thought process.

Certain statistical procedures will allow you to obtain a numerical index of the reliability of a test. Most elementary statistics books provide formulas which will show you how to obtain a reliability index for a test. If you have computer-scoring services available, reliability indexes are usually provided as part of the data on each group of responses. By checking the reliability index of your test, you can determine whether test items need revision. It should be noted, however, that most reliability indexes were designed for use with norm-referenced tests. Their direct application to criterion-referenced tests is not advised.

We mentioned previously that there are four types of criterion-referenced tests: entry behaviors tests, pretests, posttests, and embedded tests. How do you decide which of these to use? If you have identified specific entry behaviors, then it is in your best interest to measure these prior to having students begin instruction so you know whether they have the entry behaviors which you identified as important. If you have no explicit entry behaviors for a particular set of instructions, then, of course, you will have no test.

Typically, designers like to have a pretest that covers the content they are going to teach in order to obtain data on students' prior knowledge of that content. These data can also be used to measure gains in knowledge students make during instruction. Therefore, it is generally true that a pretest is of value to the designer. If you are certain, however, that few or none of the students in your target population will have prior knowledge on the topic you have selected, then it is a waste of your time and theirs to pretest entry performance. It simply becomes a frustrating experience for both you and the students if pretest scores are nearly all zeroes.

On the other hand, we can say unequivocally that you will need a post-test that measures students' achievement of objectives in the module. There is almost no exception to this recommendation.

As you design the instructional strategy for your unit, you may find it is valuable to have a number of criterion-referenced test items which are parallel to the behavioral objectives. These can be inserted into the instruction for students to use as practice. These embedded items help students to understand the level of criterion performance which is expected of them and to

90   *Developing Criterion-Referenced Tests*

determine if they have sufficient understanding and skills to take the posttest successfully.

EXAMPLES

Test items should be parallel to the behavioral objectives they intend to measure. The performance required in the test item should match the performance indicated in the objective. Below are several behavioral objectives and matching test items designed to measure skills defined by the objectives.

Objective 1
Given pictures of the symbols for the letters b and d, the student will correctly identify the b and the d.

Four test items could be used to measure students' ability to perform this objective. The performance required of the students is a key to writing the items. They are to see examples of letters, *recognize* the b and d, and state the names of the b and d. It is unnecessary for students to be able to print the letters when they hear them, but rather to *state the names* when they see them. The following test items illustrate correct measures for this objective.

Test Items
    1. Hold up a card containing the letter b and say, "What is the name of this letter?" Students can respond orally.

    2. Hold up a card containing the letter d and say, "What is the name of this letter?" Students can respond orally.

    3. Hold up a card containing both the letter b and the letter d and say, "Point to the letter b." Students can respond by pointing to the letter b.

4. Hold up a card containing both the letter b and the letter d and say, "Point to the letter d." Students can respond by pointing to the letter d.

Objective 2

Given pictures of musical notes, the student will write and spell the name of each note correctly.

The behavior required in this objective is to write and spell the names of musical notes correctly. Therefore, the test item will be paper and pencil and the students will write the names of notes they see. Criteria for scoring include the correct spelling of names. By stating this in the objective, it cues the student to attend to spelling when learning names. The two items below are appropriate test items for this objective.

Test Items
Write the name of each note pictured below in the corresponding blank. Names must be spelled correctly for credit.

Objective 3

Given a paragraph of printed text containing direct quotes and non-direct quotes, the student will correctly punctuate the paragraph using quotes, commas, periods, and question marks.

This objective requires multiple behaviors, so the test must provide adequate opportunities for students to perform the skills. The item would be written since the student is required to actually punctuate. Caution should be used here to ensure that other cues like capital letters remain intact. Otherwise the test may require behavior not stated in the objective. The capital letters serve as cues to the punctuation task requested.

Test Item
Punctuate the paragraph below by inserting (") quotation marks, (,) commas, (.) periods, and (?) question marks where needed in the paragraph.

> The sky looked overcast when Josh looked up and said I believe it might rain We can really use some rain around here How long has it been since we have had a good shower He looked back at his book but was unable to read He rose from his chair went to the window and watching the dark clouds form he said to himself I sure hope this one doesn't pass us by.

To test this objective adequately it is necessary to provide opportunities for students to perform the required behaviors.

Objective 4
Given five problems requiring the student to find a specified percent for a given two-digit number, the student will correctly solve four of the problems using only pencil and paper.

To test this objective, the test developer must consider both the behavior required (find a specified percent for a given two-digit number) and the criteria of performance required. The student must be presented with more than one test item to test this objective adequately, since simple errors in mathematics are common and do not always reflect whether a student understands how to solve the problem.

Test Item
In the problems below determine the correct answer and write it in the blank beside the number. Show your work.

        _____ 1. What is 40 percent of 50?
        _____ 2. What is 3 percent of 10?
                3. What is 30 percent of 90?
        _____ 4. What is 200 percent of 60?
        _____ 5. What is 43 percent of 45?

Objective 5
Given several subskills from an instructional analysis, the student will write behavioral objectives for all the subskills which include (a) the conditions under which behavior will be demonstrated, (b) the behavior expected, and (c) acceptable performance criteria.

This objective has multiple requirements including the testing conditions, the criteria for performance, and the performance. The test item must provide the student with the guidance and opportunity to perform the skills required by the objective. The following test item exemplifies these requirements.

Test Item
For the instructional analysis below, write one behavioral objective for each

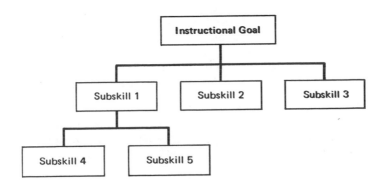

of the five subskills that includes (a) the conditions under which the behavior will be demonstrated, (b) the expected behavior, and (c) the acceptable criteria.

Subskill 1: _____

Subskill 2: _____

Subskill 3: _____

Subskill 4: _____

Subskill 5: _____

Objective 6
Students will correctly write the definitions of *flora* and *fauna* in their own words which do not deviate in meaning from the definitions given in the text.

This objective sets the text definition of the terms as the standard by which students' responses will be scored. This information cues the students for study purposes and guards against their believing that their original renditions of the term definitions will be acceptable. The two items below provide the student with the word cue and the opportunity to make their written response. Since "write" was specified in the objective, then these items meet the behavior required. For practice and feedback during the unit, however, students may be asked to define the terms orally. It should be kept in mind, however, that oral responses and written responses are not equal in a student's ability to respond.

a. flora _____

b. fauna _____

Objective 7
Given a sick child, parents will never knowingly send the sick child to school.

This objective differs from the previous ones in that it requires the assessment of a person's beliefs and motives. Observations of behavior can be used to infer that the parent believes a certain thing. The test item below would be one way to collect behavioral evidence concerning parents' motives.

Test Item (performance measure)
Tally and keep a record of children who arrive at school ill. Using the recorded tally, determine whether sending ill children to school appears to be unintentional or intentional.

Objective 8
Given the company incentive plan, trained sales personnel will spend at least forty hours each week developing leads and pursuing sales contracts.

Again, this objective will require the direct observation of behavior for final analysis. The item below provides a sample of behavior from which behavior patterns can be inferred.

Test Item
Observe the sales personnel for a seven-day period, and record the amount of time they spend each day (morning, afternoon, evening) on sales activities.

Another, but less valid, procedure would be to require sales personnel to self-report the number of hours spent and the pattern of hours spent on the activities in question. This procedure is less reliable, since they may, for any number of reasons, distort the time-analysis chart they prepare.

Objective 9
Given a small flower garden plot, students will prepare the soil, select plants appropriate to the soil and climate, plant, and maintain healthy plants in a garden for three months.

The test for this objective will be complex. It will require longitudinal observations of a quantative/qualitative nature.

Test Item
Observe the garden plot. Are the plants appropriate for the soil and climate? Are the plants healthy, and do they show signs of appropriate maintenance such as fertilizing, spraying, and weeding?

Objective 10
Given an adjustable mitre box, a backsaw, and appropriate wood stock, the student will make specified mitre cuts accurate within $\pm 1°$.

In order to test this objective, the student will actually have to make woodcuts and have them judged according to the $\pm 1°$ criteria.

Test Item
Using an adjustable mitre box, a backsaw, and 1-by-3-inch wood stock, make mitre cuts of $30°$, $45°$, and $60°$. After completing cuts, check the accuracy of your own work with a protractor. Any cuts varying more than $\pm 1°$ must be redone before satisfactory completion of this task.

PRACTICE AND FEEDBACK

Practice

I. Below are some statements about criterion-referenced test items. Mark the item T if you believe it is a correct statement and F if you believe it is an incorrect statement.

_T_ 1. A criterion-referenced test is composed of items that measure behavior.

_T_ 2. A criterion-referenced test is the same as an objective-referenced test.

_F_ 3. Test items in criterion-referenced tests need not measure the exact type of behavior which is described in a behavioral objective.

_F_ 4. Test items for criterion-referenced tests are developed directly from subtasks identified in the instructional analysis.

_T_ 5. Embedded tests are used mainly to give students practice and feedback on their performance during instruction.

_F_ 6. It is always a good idea to construct a test of entry behaviors.

_T_ 7. Entry behavior test items are developed to measure skills students should possess before entering instruction.

_T_ 8. Pretests are used prior to instruction to indicate a student's prior knowledge about what is to be taught.

_F_ 9. Pretest items are developed from behaviorally stated objectives in the entry behavior section of an instructional analysis.

_T_ 10. Criterion-referenced test items are written directly from behavioral objectives, which in turn are written directly from the subskills in an instructional analysis.

II. Below are seven behavioral objectives written from various instruction analyses. For each behavioral objective, write matching test items which will measure a student's ability on the objective using the stated criteria.

Objective 1
Given a chart containing the letters of the alphabet, the student will say the name of all the letters when they are randomly selected.

Test Item

Objective 2
Given a work sheet of subtraction problems, the student will correctly subtract a two-digit number from a three-digit number with borrowing.

Test Item

Objective 3
Given pencil and paper the student can correctly convert measures in yards to comparable meters.

Test Item

Objective 4
The student can write the formula for converting yards to meters.

Test Item

Objective 5
The student can drain oil from an automobile engine and replace it with the proper amount of new oil as measured by the oil gauge.

Test Item

Objective 6
Given a standard model color television, service manual, and appropriate tools, the student will correctly remove and replace UHF and VHF tuners within forty-five minutes.

Test Item

Objective 7
Given a laboratory situation in which the use of acids is required, the student will choose to practice appropriate safety procedures.

Test Item

Compare your test questions with those in the Feedback section. Your questions may not directly match the ones given, but the important issues are whether you have enough questions to enable the student to meet the criteria established in the objective and whether the performance you require in your questions matches the performance specified in the objective.

III. Using the instructional analysis diagram that follows, indicate by box number the behavioral objectives that should be used to develop test items for:
   1. An entry behaviors test _____ 1, 2, 3, 4 _____
   2. A pretest _____ 5, 6, 7, 8, 9, 10, 11, 12, 13, 14 _____
   3. An embedded test _____ some _____
   4. A posttest _____ some _____

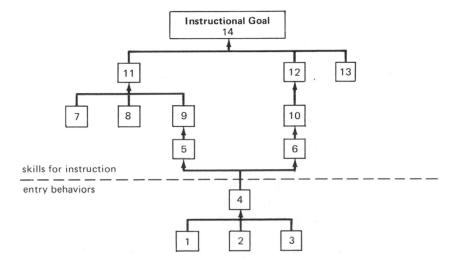

Feedback

I. 1. T   2. T   3. F   4. F   5. T   6. F   7. T   8. T   9. F
10. T

II. *Objective 1*
The teacher would use a chart showing all twenty-six letters and say, "Look at this chart. When I point to a letter, you say the name of the letter. For instance, if I point to this letter, you would say 'A.' Now I'll point to letters and you say the names." The teacher should point to all twenty-six letters and note any letters the student does not recognize, for the student must recognize and name all twenty-six letters to pass the criteria stated in the objective.

Objective 2
Because it is often easy to make a simple calculation error, more than one problem should be included. Those problems included should represent different examples of typical problems the student would encounter.

a) 402	b) 396	c) 404	d) 200	e) 152
-21	-28	-20	-47	-67

In this case, borrowing is required in some problems during the first operation, in others, during the second. In some problems zero is subtracted from a number, whereas in others the students are required to subtract a number from zero. Note that there are three-digit numbers on the top row, two-digit numbers on the bottom row, and borrowing is required in each problem.

Objective 3
There must be enough questions to test students' performance on this objective so that the instructor is sure that the student knows or does not know how to perform this skill.

a. 5 yards = _____ meters
b. 7.5 yards = _____ meters
c. 15 yards = _____ meters

Objective 4
Only one question should be needed to test this objective. The student must answer it correctly to receive credit.

a. In the space below, write the formula for converting yards to meters.

Objective 5
Actual performance on an automobile is required for this test. Any special conditions placed on this item such as time, oil weight selected, neatness, and so on would have to be included as part of the behavioral objective. In this particular objective, no conditions were specified except that a proper amount of oil, as measured by the gauge, should be replaced.

a. Drain the oil from an automobile engine into a disposable container and replace the oil in the engine with the proper amount of new oil as measured by the oil gauge.

Objective 6
Actual performance is again required to test this objective.

a. Using a standard model color television, the service manual, and appropriate tools, remove and replace the UHF and VHF tuners. You have forty-five minutes to complete the work.

Objective 7
You will need to observe students' performance while experimenting with acids in the laboratory. Note whether the students practice safety procedures all the time. A test or quiz on students' knowledge of safety procedures would be insufficient to test this objective. Systematic observation of actual performance is required.

III. Generally speaking, behavioral objectives which should have test items included on:
  1. an entry behaviors test are 1, 2, 3, and 4
  2. a pretest are 5 through 14
  3. an embedded test (or tests) are 5 through 14
  4. a posttest are 5 through 14

IMPLEMENTATION

Consider the ideas presented in this chapter in terms of the input, process, and output structure.

Input

The input for this component is the performance objectives which are based on the instructional analysis.

Process

The process required to develop test items which are appropriate for each behavioral objective is:
  1. Determine whether you will use a pretest, embedded test, and/or posttest.
  2. Determine how many test items are required to assess performance at the criteria levels stated in the objective.
  3. Study the exact performance specified in the objective and the conditions under which the performance should be made.

4. Write multiple, parallel test items to measure each performance objective. Judge the items yourself to determine whether for one objective (a) they are of equal difficulty, (b) they are parallel to each other, and (c) they are all directly related to the behavior and conditions stated in the objective. You may find that you have an objective that is so specific that it need be tested with only one test item. If this is the case, then the item on the pretest, embedded test, and posttest will be exactly the same.
5. Designate each test item for either the pretest, embedded test, or posttest.

Output

The output for this component is test items that measure performance for each behavioral objective, and have been divided into a pretest, embedded test, and/or posttest.

DESIGN EVALUATION

It is important at this stage in the design of instruction to evaluate the design you have created. The materials you have at this stage make up the framework for many hours of future development and conceptualization. By determining whether flaws exist in your design and correcting errors that are found to exist, many hours of less-than-satisfying developmental work may be saved.

Exactly what is to be evaluated? The materials that should be evaluated are (a) the instructional goal, (b) the instructional analysis, (c) the performance objectives, (d) the criterion-referenced test items, and (e) the adequate selection and description of the target population.

Who should evaluate your design? There are several options here, and the nature of your materials and time you have available for the evaluation will be major factors in selecting the evaluators. Some persons you might want to consider are:

1. Colleagues who are considered *content experts* or *instructional designers* who can validate (a) the need for such instruction, (b) the importance of the behavior stated in the instructional goal, (c) the accurateness of subskills that were identified in the instructional analysis, (d) the accurateness of the sequencing of subskills in the instructional analysis, (e) the relationship among subskills identified in the instructional analysis, (f) the parallelism between subskills in the instructional analysis and behavioral objectives, (g) the clarity of performance desired and criteria established for the behavioral objectives, (h) the parallelism between behavioral objectives and test items, and (i) the equality of multiple test items constructed to measure performance on the same objective.

2. *Peers* could be asked to evaluate whether (a) there is a need for instruction identified, (b) it is an area in which their students often experience learning difficulties, (c) such instruction would be feasible in their classroom (equipment, space, etc.), (d) any subskills have been omitted from the instructional analysis, and (e) there is any deviation from the required parallelism among the instructional goal, instructional analysis, behavioral objectives, and test items.

3. *Target students* could react to whether (a) they would find learning the material interesting, (b) they perceive a need for the behavior identified in the instructional goal, and (c) they experience any difficulty understanding vocabulary and required procedures when explained. Given time, the designer may also choose to administer a sample pretest to determine how target students can perform on the tasks without previous instruction. This may provide an early sign of whether the appropriate target students have been selected. If they can already perform most of the skills or if they are totally baffled, they may be the wrong group.

How can you best organize and present your materials so that you can evaluate them? One criterion is that each component builds upon the product from the previous one and, therefore, the materials should be presented in a way that enables comparisons among the various components of your design. The designer should, at a glance, be able to see if the components are parallel and adequate. One way to achieve this is to organize the materials such that related components are together. Consider the structure in Table 6.1. Each segment of the table contains all three elements. The first line is distinguished

Table 6.1
Structure of the Design Evaluation Chart

Instructional Goal	Behavioral Objective	Test Item(s)
Subskill 1	Performance Objective 1	Test item (a)* Test item (b) Test item (c)
Subskill 2	Performance Objective 2	Test item (a) Test item (b) Test item (c)
Subskill 3	Performance Objective 3	Test item (a) Test item (b) Test item (c)
. . .		
Terminal Objective	Performance Objective	Test item (a) Test item (b) Test item (c)

*(a) Test item(s) selected for pretest
 (b) Test item(s) selected for posttest
 (c) Test item(s) selected for embedded test

in that it contains the instructional goal, the terminal objective, and the test item(s) for the terminal objective. The evaluator(s) can, at a glance, determine whether the three elements are parallel and also determine the adequacy of test items to enable students to demonstrate whether they have mastered the objective.

Table 6.2 contains an example of the type of material that would be included in each section of Table 6.1. Note that there is only one test item for subskill and behavioral objective 1. That item would appear on any test given, whether pretest, posttest, or embedded test, because there is only one way to answer that question correctly. However, objective number 2 provides the opportunity for many questions and answers.

Table 6.2
Example of a Design Evaluation Chart

Subskills	Behavioral Objectives	Test Item(s)	
1. Write the formula for converting yards to meters	1. The student can *write* the formula for converting yards to meters with *100 percent accuracy*	1. In the space provided below, write the formula used to convert yards to meters. It must be exactly correct to receive credit	(a) * (b) (c)
2. Convert measures in yards to comparable meters in two out of three problems	2. Given pencil and paper, the student *can convert* measures in yards to comparable meters in *two out of three problems*	2. 5 yds. = _?_ meters 7.5 yds. = _?_ meters 15 yds. = _?_ meters ----- 4 yds. = _?_ meters 65 yds. = _?_ meters 19 yds. = _?_ meters ----- 3 yds. = _?_ meters 8.25 yds. = _?_ meters 12 yds. = _?_ meters	(a) (b) (c)

*(a) pretest questions
 (b) posttest questions
 (c) embedded test questions

Check the performance required in all three components in Table 6.2 to ensure it is parallel. In addition, check the criteria stated in the objective to determine whether the number of test items or the nature of a test enables students to perform to criteria. Are there enough items to construct a pretest, posttest, and an embedded test? Are items which are earmarked for the various tests equal in difficulty? It is inappropriate to construct a difficult "zinger" for the final when performance at that level has not been taught.

The sequence of subskills presentation on your chart is important. If you place them in the order you believe they should be taught, then you will be able to receive additional feedback from your evaluator(s) concerning the logic you have used for sequencing skills and presenting instruction. This additional feedback may save steps in rewriting or reorganizing your materials at a later point.

One additional way to show content experts and other evaluators the relationship among subskills which you have identified is to prepare a numbered instructional analysis chart. All items should be keyed to the number of the subskills in the analysis. This diagram can be used with your design evaluation table to present a clearer representation of your content analysis and design. Figure 6.1 contains three examples of such diagrams.

After you have received feedback concerning the adequacy of your design and made appropriate revisions in your framework, you will have the input required to begin work on the next component of the model, namely developing an instructional strategy. Having a good, carefully analyzed design at this point will facilitate your work in future activities.

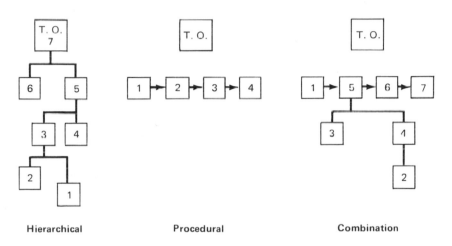

| Hierarchical | Procedural | Combination |

Figure 6.1 Diagram of Relationship and Sequence of Subskills

REFERENCES

Gagné, R. M., & Briggs, L. J. *Principles of instructional design.* New York: Holt, Rinehart, and Winston, Inc., 1974, 150-182.

    The chapter on assessing student performance includes not only the development of objective-referenced assignments, but also the concept of "mastery" and norm-referenced measures which are not covered in this book.

Kibler, R. J., Cegala, D. J., Barker, L. L., & Miles, D. T. *Objectives for instruction and evaluation.* Boston: Allyn and Bacon, 1974, 114-142.

    Kibler et al. include a discussion of norm versus criterion-referenced assessment and the use of mastery learning strategies.

Millman, J. Criterion-referenced measurement. In Popham, W. J. (Ed.) *Evaluation in education: current applications.* Berkeley, Calif.: McCutchan Publishing, 1974, 309-398.

The discussion of the criterion-referenced and domain-referenced testing is extensive and includes some of the quantitative, as well as qualitative, issues associated with them.

Payne, D. A. *The assessment of learning: cognitive and affective*. Lexington, Mass.: D. C. Heath and Co., 1974.

This is an excellent text which relates various types of test items to the varieties of instructional objectives. It emphasizes techniques for writing effective test items.

Singer, R. N., & Dick, W. *Teaching physical education: a systems approach*. Boston: Houghton-Mifflin Co., 1974, 142-162.

This chapter on student evaluation stresses the various domains of learning and provides a variety of assessment techniques for each.

7 Developing an Instructional Strategy

OBJECTIVES

1. *You will be able to identify and describe the major components of an instructional strategy.*

2. *You will be able to develop an instructional strategy for a set of objectives for a particular group of learners.*

BACKGROUND

If you have a textbook nearby, pick it up and look it over. In what ways is the book structured to facilitate learning by the student? The typical text, particularly for adults, usually has an introduction, a body of information, references, and an index. Sometimes test items have been prepared and appear at the end of the chapters or in a teacher's manual. In essence a textbook serves primarily as a source of information. The instructional strategy that will be employed to bring learners into a state of full knowledge must be generated by the reader or an instructor. Usually, an instructor must do nearly everything to bring about learning: define the objectives, write the lesson plan and tests, motivate the students, present information, and administer and score tests.

In a well-designed instructional module, the module itself must contain many of the strategies or procedures that a teacher might normally use with a group of students. Therefore, it is necessary to develop an instructional strategy that employs, to the degree possible, that knowledge which we have about facilitating the learning process.

Educational psychologists have conducted much research over the past fifty years to determine appropriate relationships between particular types of stimuli and responses by learners. They have also studied the use of reinforcement, punishment, behavior modification, and other teacher behaviors. If you have read any of this research you may feel that it often seems esoteric and greatly removed from any type of real-life learning situations. Psychologists have been successful, however, in identifying several major factors in the learning process which, when present, almost always will facilitate mastery of the instructional materials. These three areas are those dealing with motivation, prerequisite and subordinate skills, and practice and feedback.

This unit relies heavily on the work of various educational psychologists and especially on that of Robert Gagné and Leslie Briggs. In this chapter, procedures will be described that can be used to design an idealized instructional strategy with regard to a particular set of instructional objectives. In the next chapter you will be shown how this instructional strategy applies directly to the development of an instructional module, the selection of instructional materials, and the development of classroom procedures.

CONCEPTS

An instructional strategy describes the general components of a set of instructional materials and the procedures that will be used with those materials to elicit particular learning outcomes from students. You should carefully note that an instructional strategy is more than a simple description of the content which will be presented to the learner. For example, it would be insufficient to say that in order to have students learn how to add two-digit numbers that you would first teach them single-digit numbers without carrying and then single-digit numbers with carrying and then present the main concept of adding two-digit numbers. This is certainly a part of an instructional strategy and refers to the sequence of presentation of information, but this says nothing about what you will do before you present that information, what students will do with that information, or how it will be tested.

There are five major components in an instructional strategy:

1. Preinstructional activities
2. Information presentation
3. Student participation
4. Testing
5. Follow through

We will look at each of these components in some detail, because the instructional designer must plan an approach to each of these steps after obtaining a set of objectives, a description of assumed entry behaviors, and the criterion-referenced test(s).

Preinstructional Activity

Prior to beginning the formal instructional activities, there are a number of activities that you should consider. The first of these is the motivation level of the learners who will use your instructional module. You might assume that students will be assigned this module or that you will be dealing with highly motivated adults and therefore assume that no effort is required on your part to establish a high motivation level. You may be right; but, you may wish to use some type of special techniques such as an attractive color scheme, a cartoon, a human-interest story, or some other approach to gain the attention of the learners and "hook" them into your module. In order to do this properly, it takes a great deal of knowledge about the learners and what will in fact hook them and what will turn them off.

Part of the motivational process may include showing students what they will be able to do when they have completed the module. For certain learners it may be sufficient to state the objectives in the same form that you have them in your instructional design. For others, you may wish to reword the objectives into lay terms so that students will better understand what the module is about. There may be situations in which the terminal objective is so remote from the students' present level of understanding that it would be distracting and discouraging to be told about it. In this rare case, you might consider the wisdom of describing that type of objective.

Another source of motivation may be to remind the learners about knowledge that they have already acquired which will relate directly to what they are about to learn. This can serve not only to inform the learners that this is appropriate material for them but also serve as a bridge into the instructional materials.

Information Presentation

One of the questions you will need to answer is: What sequence should I follow in presenting information to the student? The most useful tool in determining the answer to this question is your instructional analysis. If you have done a hierarchical analysis, then you would begin with the lower-level skills, that is, those just above the line that separates the entry behaviors from those skills which are to be taught, and then progress up through the hierarchy. At no point would you present information on a particular skill prior to having done so for all related subordinate skills.

The instructional sequence for a task which is a procedure would, of course, logically be sequenced from the left, or beginning point, and proceed to the right, or terminal objective. If there are subordinate capabilities for any of the major steps in the procedure, they would be taught prior to going on to the next major component. As an aside, some psychologists argue that with a learning task, which is essentially a linear string of tasks, it is more efficient to begin with the final task and to work backwards. For beginning design efforts, however, an orderly progression from the first step to the final step is the recommended approach.

The next question in your instructional strategy deals with the size of "chunk" of material you will provide in your module. At one extreme of the continuum is the linear programmed-instruction approach, which tends to break all the information down into very small units and requires constant responding by the student. At the other extreme of the continuum is the conventional textbook in which a chapter is usually the unit of information. You may decide that in your module, you will present your information on an objective-by-objective basis with intervening activities or you may wish to present the information on all objectives prior to any kind of student activity.

Three factors you should take into consideration when determining the size of "chunk" are the age level of your learners, the type of learning taking place, and whether the activity can be varied, thereby increasing attention time to the task. For younger children it is almost always advisable to keep the module and the chunks within it relatively small. More mature learners will be able to handle larger chunks of information. Regardless of the age of the learner, when information presented is varied with performance and feedback activities, the learners do not seem to tire of the activity as quickly.

The next step is to determine exactly what information, concepts, rules, and principles need to be presented to the student. This is the basic explanation of what the unit is "all about." The primary error in this step is to present too much information, especially if much of it is unrelated to the objective. It is important not only to define any new concepts but to explain their interrelationships with other concepts. You will also need to determine the types and number of examples you will provide with each of the concepts in your module. Many research studies have investigated how we learn concepts and how we use examples and nonexamples to accomplish that task. We know that learning is facilitated by the use of examples and nonexamples, components which should be included in your instructional strategy.

Student Participation

One of the most powerful effects in the whole learning process is that of practice with feedback. You can enhance the learning process greatly by providing the student with activities which are directly relevant to the objectives. Students should be provided an opportunity to practice what you want them to be able to do. Not only should they be able to practice, but they should be provided some type of feedback or information about their performance. Feedback is sometimes referred to as "knowledge of results." That is, students are told whether their answer is right or wrong, or are shown a copy of the right answer from which they must infer whether their answer is correct. Feedback may be provided also in the form of a reinforcement. Reinforcement for adult learners is typically in terms of statements like "great, you are correct." Young children often respond to forms of reinforcement such as an approving look from the instructor or even the opportunity to do some other activity.

Testing

Part of your instructional strategy will involve the testing or evaluation of the learner. The student participation activities discussed above are a part of that testing procedure in the sense that students are assessing for themselves their level of competence as they go through the module. You may wish to insert embedded test items, which usually resemble practice and feedback items, *but* have no feedback. These items are used to determine if the student can perform the desired behavior at this point in the instruction. These data will be valuable for formative evaluation, and these items may be retained in the final form of the instruction as progress checks that an instructor may wish to use. You should also determine as part of your instructional strategy how the data from the pretest and posttest will be used with regard to student performance. For example, if you teach a topic in which some of the students have prior knowledge of the content, you could use that information to branch or direct students directly to those parts of the module which they have yet to master. This would save them time by not repeating material which they already knew.

You will also be required to make decisions about the module with regard to differing levels of performance on the posttest for the module. Recommendations should be made to the teacher and student as to what should be done as a result of particular outcomes. For example, if students do not reach some predetermined level of performance such as 80 percent on the posttest, what should they do? Will they simply be branched back to repeat certain parts of the module or will other materials be made available to them? If students do reach the predetermined level of mastery, should they continue with the next module or will there be other enrichment activities available to them? This leads into the final component of the instructional strategy.

Follow-Through Activities

As a part of your module, you will want to have materials, or at least recommendations, about what students should do as a result of a particular level of performance on the posttest. Will you have separate remediation materials available for them? If so, what type of strategy will be involved with them? Will you have certain enrichment materials or proposed instructional activities which students who are successful with the module might participate in while other students are reaching mastery? These decisions have implications not only for helping with the learning process, but also for the directions necessary to implement your instruction in the classroom.

Instructional Strategy Components

A summary of all the components of a complete instructional strategy follows.

A. Preinstructional activity
    1. Motivation   2. Objectives   3. Prerequisite knowledge
B. Information presentation
    1. Sequence   2. Size of instructional unit
    3. Content presentation   4. Examples
C. Student participation
    1. Practice   2. Feedback
D. Follow-through activities
    1. Remediation   2. Enrichment
E. Testing
    1. Entry behaviors   2. Pretest   3. Embedded test   4. Posttest

Developing an Instructional Strategy

It would be inappropriate to go directly from a list of behavioral objectives to developing a set of instructional materials without first planning and writing out your instructional strategy. The instructional strategy is an actual product which can be used (a) as a prescription to develop instructional materials, (b) as a set of criteria to evaluate existing materials, (c) as a set of criteria and a prescription to revise existing materials, or (d) as a framework from which class lecture notes, interactive group exercises, or homework assignments can be planned. Regardless of the availability of existing instructional materials, the instructor should develop an instructional strategy for identified behavioral objectives before selecting, adapting, or developing instruction.

What is needed to develop an instructional strategy? The instructor should begin with an evaluated instructional design which includes (a) a statement of the subskills, (b) a statement of behavioral objectives, (c) test items, and (d) a diagram of the relationship and sequence of subskills.

Having completed all these steps, you are ready to develop your instructional strategy. At this point you should realize that you have already completed some of the work needed to develop an instructional strategy. You have already (a) identified objectives, (b) identified prerequisite knowledge (through your analysis of the relationship among subskills in the instructional analysis), (c) identified the sequence for presenting instruction (when you completed your design evaluation table and your analysis diagram), (d) identified the content required (when you analyzed the knowledge and skills during the instructional analysis), and (e) identified appropriate test items for each objective. All this information, already included in your design evaluation table and chart, can act as input for the development of the instructional strategy.

Even though we recommend that instructional events occur in the order presented in the previous section (preinstructional activities, presentation of information, student participation, testing, and follow through), we do not recommend that you try to develop your instructional strategy in this order. The developmental sequence differs from the suggested order in which students encounter instructional events during a lesson.

Following are three major steps we recommend for the development of the instructional strategy.

1. Refer to the behavioral objectives included in your instructional design table and estimate how much time will be required for students to learn each objective in the chart. In this rough time estimate, be sure to include for each objective the amount of time required for introduction, presentation, review, practice, and summary. Remember, this is just a rough estimate and you may have to adjust these approximations later.
2. Cluster all the subskills together into lessons or into the number of objectives that can be learned during one instructional period.
3. List the objectives for one instructional period in a table. Then, for each objective, analyze the instructional events that should occur during that period or lesson. Repeat this analysis procedure for each separate lesson or cluster of objectives. You will have to construct a separate strategy table for each lesson containing objectives and instructional strategies. Use the instructional strategy table as a guide for developing, selecting, and adapting instructional materials.

To develop the instructional strategy according to these three steps, you will need an instructional design table such as the one illustrated in Table 7.1. First, study the objectives in the instructional design table. Then assign to each objective the amount of time, in hours and minutes, you believe will be required to learn the skills. Remember to include for each objective the amount of time required for the following: introduction, presentation, review, practice, and summary.

Once you have estimated the amount of time required for each objective, you are ready to assign objectives to lessons or class periods. Obviously, the amount of time available for a lesson depends on the length of a class period, be it thirty minutes or two hours. The number of objectives included in each class period depends upon the estimated amount of learning time for each. Your lesson analysis might look like the one included in Table 7.1.

Table 7.1
Estimated Time Required for Each Objective in the Instructional Analysis and the Lesson Assignments for Objectives Based upon Estimated Time Requirements

Objective	Estimated Time Required	Lesson Time = 30 minutes
1	15 minutes	1
2	15 minutes	
3	15 minutes	2
4	10 minutes	
5	1 hour	3, 4
6	30 minutes	5
7	15 minutes	6
8	15 minutes	

In Table 7.1, the left column lists the objectives. The center column indicates the estimated learning time for each objective, while the column on the right notes the number of the lesson assignment. In this example, instruction is planned for thirty-minute instructional periods. (Remember that introductory, practice, and clean-up time is included in the rough estimate for each objective.) Only the first two objectives will fit into the first thirty-minute lesson. The second lesson will deal with objectives 3 and 4. Because objective 5 has an estimated learning time of one hour, it is assigned to both lessons three and four. The eight objectives illustrated in Table 7.1 will require an estimated six separate lessons.

The instructional strategy for lesson one can be developed using a format similar to the one illustrated in Table 7.2. Remember, you have already determined the sequence of instruction and size of instructional unit. Thus, they are not included in this table.

By filling in the boxes beneath each objective and beside each lesson event, you can use Table 7.2 to develop an instructional strategy. The instructional strategies you plan for each lesson can guide your development, selection, evaluation, and revision activities when you begin to develop your instruction.

EXAMPLES

The following example describes a terminal objective, the instructional analysis for that terminal objective, and the target population. For the purpose of this discussion, the behavioral objectives and test items have been omitted. These components would normally be completed before the instructional strategy is considered; in this example, however, only the framework of the terminal objective, target population, and instructional analysis will be used to illustrate the implications of these basic components for the instructional strategy.

Terminal objective: The student will be able to form specified Roman numerals with values between 1 and 1000.

Target population: Sixth-grade students between the ages of eleven and twelve. Students are below average, average, and above average in math achievement, having a variety of entry skill levels.

Instructional analysis: The instructional analysis appears in Figure 7.1.

The first step to take in analyzing the instructional strategy is to analyze the sequence of objectives and the estimated learning time required for the skills specified in each objective. The objectives and learning time estimates are based on the sample instructional analysis that appears in Figure 7.1.

Table 7.3 includes a rough analysis of the time required for pupils to learn the specified skills. Of course, the time required to learn a set of specified

Table 7.2
An Instructional Strategy Format for Two Objectives

Instructional Activity		Objectives		
Preinstructional Activity	Motivation			
	Objectives			
	Prerequisite Skills			
Presenting Information	Content Presentation			
	Examples			
Student Participation and Embedded Tests	Practice			
	Feedback			
Follow-Through Activities	Remediation			
	Enrichment			

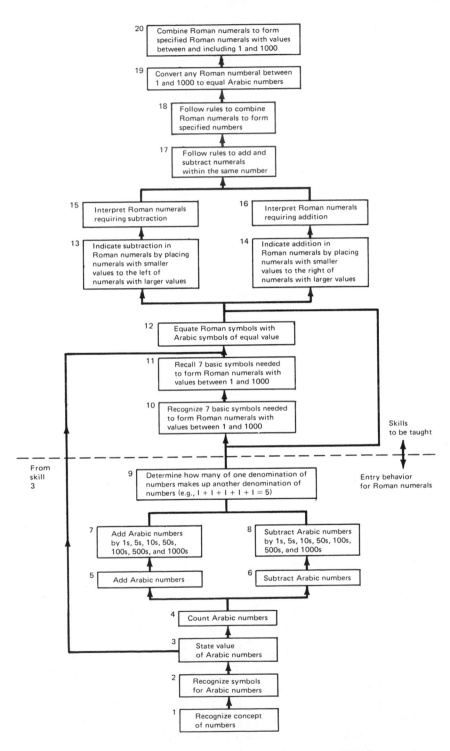

Figure 7.1 Hierarchical Analysis of Roman Numerals Objective

skills will vary according to the characteristics of the target students. The analysis here is simply an example of how it would be done if the instructor had prior knowledge of the time needed for each task. When estimating student learning time, consider such things as attention span, behavior, work habits, facilities, and personnel. All these factors will affect the learning time necessary for each of the skills in the analysis.

Table 7.3
Estimated Time and Objective Clustering
for the Roman Numeral Objectives in Figure 7.1

Objective	Estimated Time Required (in minutes)	Lesson
1. Introduction/overview/pretest	30	1
2. 10	15 ⎫	2
3. 11	15 ⎭	
4. 12	15	3
5. 14	15 ⎫	4
6. 16	15 ⎭	
7. 13	15 ⎫	5
8. 15	15 ⎭	
9. 17	15 ⎫	6
10. 18	15 ⎭	
11. 19	15 ⎫	7
12. 20	15 ⎭	
13. Summary, Posttest	15	8

Upon studying the analysis and lesson assignment in the example in Table 7.3, you will discover that lessons 1, 2, 4, 5, 6, and 7 require 30 minutes, while the time required for lessons 3 and 8 is only 15 minutes. This was done because the instructor thought that related objectives (13 and 15, 14 and 16) should be learned in the same lesson. This means that lesson 3 deals only with objective 12. There are several different ways the instructor can plan for the extra fifteen minutes available in lesson 3. Review, practice, or embedded tests covering materials from objectives 10, 11, and 12 might be planned. Enrichment or remedial exercises for members of the group needing additional instruction might be provided. It would probably be wiser to allow a whole lesson for objective 12. This would be preferable to clustering objectives 12 and 13 together into one unit and leaving objective 15 until the next lesson.

In summary, time required to learn a skill is only one factor to consider when clustering objectives into lessons. The instructor must also consider the relationship and interdependence of the objectives in the analysis. Whenever possible, related objectives should be placed together in the same lesson. Avoid unnecessary interruptions of the learning sequence.

At this point, the instructor is ready to design the instructional strategy for the unit of instruction and for each lesson within the unit. Table 7.4 and Table 7.5 contain sample instructional strategies for objectives 10, 11, 12, and 13 from the analysis in Figure 7.1.

Table 7.4
An Instructional Strategy for the Roman Numeral Analysis (Figure 7.1)

Instructional Activity		Objectives	
		10 (Lesson Two)	11 (Lesson Two)
Preinstructional Activity	Motivation	1. Why should they learn these symbols? 2. What can they do with them?	Same as Objective 10.
	Objectives	Recognize symbols used to count in Roman numerals from 1 to 100.	Recall from memory the seven Roman numerals.
	Prerequisite Skills	1. Subskills 1-9. 2. Perhaps a few sample questions to provide review and recall of the most important skills.	1. Mastery of subskill 10.
Presenting Information	Content Presentation	1. Roman numerals different from Arabic numerals. 2. Roman numerals are letters instead of numbers. 3. There are seven Roman numerals to be learned. 4. The numerals are I, V, X, L, C, D, and M.	1. Represent the seven numerals. 2. Present any mnemonics or hints for memorizing the numerals (order, spell word, letters in phrase, etc.).
	Examples	1. Roman = L, C, D, etc.; and Arabic = 1, 2, 3 . . . 2. LCD = letters like in the alphabet. 3. Show numerals in several different uses (outlines, headings, counting).	Provide examples of hints for remembering numerals.
Student Participation and Embedded Tests	Practice	Write practice examples that go from easy to more difficult that allow students to recognize numerals from other things. Exercises like: Pick out all the Roman numerals: 1. (I, *, C); 2. (I, V, X, 4, 3, V, 10); 3. (A, B, C, D, E, F, G). Give students several opportunities to select the correct numeral.	Provide exercises enabling students to write numerals, say numerals, and repeat the writing and saying several times.
	Feedback	Provide students with your reactions to their selections whether correct or incorrect. You may need to analyze incorrect patterns of selecting and add additional information for them to use in selection.	Provide feedback enabling students to check to see which ones they forget each time they repeat the list.
Follow-Through Activities	Remediation	1. Remind students of prerequisite skills again. 2. Repeat content presentation. 3. Repeat criteria for selecting them. 4. Provide more practice and feedback, selecting from very dissimilar to very similar symbols.	1. See list of numerals. 2. Review that there is a total of seven. 3. Review any mnemonics used. 4. Repeated practice recalling total list.
	Enrichment	Provide students with the opportunity to recall from memory some of the numerals, rather than to select from a list or group.	Practice guessing how much each of the seven numerals is worth in value.

Table 7.5
An Instructional Strategy for the Roman Numeral Analysis (Figure 7.1)

Instructional Activity		Objectives	
		12 (Lesson 3)	14 (Lesson 4)
Preinstructional Activity	Motivation	If you learn to equate the values of numerals and numbers, you can use the numerals to count.	The 7 numerals can be put together to form all the numbers between 1 and 1000. It only takes 7 numerals.
	Objectives	Equate Roman numerals with Arabic numerals of the same value.	Put basic numerals together and add the independent values to form other numbers.
	Prerequisite Skills	Provide summary or review questions to help students recall skills in subskills 10 and 11.	Provide review exercises for recalling the value of each numeral (subskill 13).
Presenting Information	Content Presentation	1. Each Roman numeral has an equal Arabic number. 2. By equating the numerals and numbers you can count using numerals. 3. I = 1; V = 5; X = 10; L = 50; C = 100; D = 500; M = 1000.	1. By placing numerals side by side you can form other numerals. 2. The values *add* together almost like Arabic numbers. 3. To add numerals together, place the numerals side by side starting on the left with the largest and working to the right to the smallest.
	Examples	*Show* students examples of Roman numerals and corresponding numbers.	1. Form other numerals: L + V 2. Values add together: 50 + 5 = 55 3. Go from left to right, from largest to smallest (C, L, X, V, I).
Student Participation and Embedded Tests	Practice	1. Provide exercises for students to recall the Roman numeral when given the corresponding number (i.e., 10 = _?_ ; 100 = _?_ ; etc.). 2. Provide exercises for students to recall the Arabic number when given the Roman numeral. (e.g., X = _?_ ; C = _?_ ; etc.)	1. Develop exercises from simple to complex, changing Roman numerals to numbers (e.g., II = _?_ ; MDXXIII = _?_). 2. Develop exercises from simple to complex, changing numbers to numerals (e.g., 3 = _?_ ; 1523 = _?_).
	Feedback	Provide responses to students' practice exercises. Branch students to remedial or enrichment exercises based on their responses.	Provide responses to students' practice exercises. Branch students to remedial or enrichment exercises based upon their responses.
Follow-Through Activities	Remediation	1. Each Roman numeral has an equal Arabic numeral. 2. You can learn the numbers that match the numerals. 3. I = 1; V = 5; X = 10; L = 50; C = 100; D = 500; M = 1000.	1. Roman numerals can be combined to make other numbers. 2. They are added together like numbers. Provide examples like: I+I+I=III=1+1+1=3; V+I=VI=5+1=6.
	Enrichment	Provide exercises for students to put numerals together and see if they can make new numbers. Relate the Roman numeral system to the hand (five-finger) gestures.	1. Do you know how to subtract using Roman numerals? 2. If you place more numerals on the *right* to add, where might you place them to subtract? 3. Can you make Roman numerals using your hand? 4. What system of counting would be used if humans had six fingers on each hand?

Before you begin to analyze the content of Tables 7.4 and 7.5, notice that the original introductory and motivational ideas for the whole unit on Roman numerals are not included. Only embedded test items used for practice and feedback are included in these tables. The motivational and introductory material was left out because the motivational ideas for the whole unit on Roman numerals do not fit into the instructional activities table for one lesson. The comprehensive pretest and posttest for the unit do not really fit into the instructional strategy framework for specified objectives for one lesson. Keeping in mind that these are missing, look at the instructional strategies in Tables 7.4 and 7.5. Notice that, under preinstructional materials, all the motivational information appears at the beginning of the session. Notice also that, because both objectives 10 and 11 are taught during the same session, it is unnecessary to provide review and practice on subskill 10 before moving on to instruction for subskill 11. This is different in Table 7.5. Because subskill 13 is taught in the next lesson, review and practice of subskills 10 and 11 precede instruction on subskill 12. Likewise, because subskill 14 is taught in a subsequent lesson, review and practice on subskills 10, 11, and 12 precede instruction for subskill 14.

For content presentation activities, note each rule or important fact in the strategy and include an example of each. Examples should range from simple to difficult, with simple examples presented first. Students should not have to learn the content of your example along with the idea or process you are trying to teach through the example. Example content should be kept simple.

Practice and feedback items should be similar to your embedded test items in the instructional analysis chart. Check to ensure that you have included a range of items. In the instructional strategy examples, you should include samples of the types of items to be included in the lesson.

You can include examples of remediation and enrichment instruction. Remediation activities might be based on a repetition of the content presentation steps (especially rules), examples, and practice exercises. Sometimes this involves repeating the same materials. At other times, you will want to use easier or different examples, along with easier practice exercises. If students have difficulty learning materials, you may want to retest prerequisite skills. Remedial instruction can include embedded test items covering either prerequisite or lesson objectives.

Enrichment activities usually involve students in more difficult practice exercises, in playing competitive games using the new skills, or in trying to solve problems from the next objective. Repetition during these activities will enhance students' retention of the material learned.

At this point you may be asking "In the instructional strategy charts in Tables 7.4 and 7.5, what happened to lesson one, to the motivational material for the unit, and to the pretest and posttest?" These were omitted from the charts because they are inappropriate for the instructional strategy table.

Lesson one was omitted because overall unit motivational activities were unrelated to any of the instructional objectives in the diagram in Figure 7.1.

It is usually wise to defer planning motivational activities for the whole unit until after you have a clear idea of what material and activities students will complete during the unit. After finishing the instructional strategy for all the lessons, you should be familiar enough with the unit to have developed very good motivational ideas. These activities are then planned for lesson one. Following are some motivational possibilities for the unit on Roman numerals.

1. Discuss Roman civilization and the time period in which it flourished. Who were the Romans? What was their alphabet like? What was their language? What was their system of numbers like?
2. Show pictures of costumes, and locations of cities on a map.
3. Discuss and show examples of ways Roman numerals are used today in America.
4. Indicate that, using Roman numerals, students need only learn 7 new symbols to count from 1 to 1000.
5. Compare 10 symbols in American system of numbering (Arabic) with 7 symbols in Roman numerals needed to form any number between 1 and 1000.
6. Show some examples of Roman numerals either printed or cut out of cardboard, plastic, or wood.

Neither the pretest nor the posttest are a part of an instructional strategy for an objective. Instead, they cover all the objectives in the unit. The pretest can be included along with motivational activities in the first thirty-minute lesson of the unit. The posttest can be scheduled, along with other summary activities, at the end of the unit.

PRACTICE AND FEEDBACK

Practice

For these practice exercises, refer again to the instructional goal and instructional analysis on Roman numerals in Figure 7.1. This time, assume your target population is low-achieving eighth-grade math students. Your target population may require different instructional strategies for the same objectives.

Referring to the subskills listed in Figure 7.1, complete the following table by:

1. Determining the attention span and optimum length of one lesson for this group.
2. Arranging the order or sequence of subskills for presentation to low-achieving eighth graders.
3. Estimating the time required for students to learn each subskill.
4. Clustering subskills into lessons based upon (a) the amount of time available for one lesson, (b) the number of subskills fitting into one lesson, and (c) the relationship among the content of subskills (i.e., related or dependent skills, natural breaking places, etc.).

Table 7.6 can be used to plan the sequence, time, and lesson assignment for each instructional objective in Table 7.1. Remember that you may want to include prerequisite skills as well, since the target population was described as low-achieving math students.

Check your analyses of sequence, time required, and lesson assignment with the analysis in Table 7.8 in the Feedback section. Remember, there is no one right answer. The analysis in the Feedback section should simply be used for comparison.

Table 7.6
Sequence of Objectives, Time Estimates, and Lesson Assignments
for the Objectives in Table 7.1

	Sequence of Objectives (1 - 20)	Time Required	Lesson Assignment
1			
2			
3			
4			
5			
6			
7			
8			
9			
10			
11			
12			
13			
14			
15			
16			
17			
18			
19			
20			
21			
22			

5. Table 7.7 contains an instructional strategy form. Included in the table are two subskills taken from the Roman numeral analysis in Figure 7.1. The subskills are numbers 13 and 14, covering the subtraction procedures required to read Roman numerals. Complete this sample instructional analysis and then compare your ideas with those included in Table 7.8 in the Feedback section. Again, there is not just one answer for each of these boxes. The right answers are the ones that provide the most efficient, enjoyable instruction.

Table 7.7
A Practice Instructional Strategy for Subskills 13 and 15

		Objectives	
Instructional Activity		13	15
Preinstructional Activity	Motivation		
	Objectives	Indicate subtraction in Roman numerals by placing numerals with smaller values to the left of numerals with larger values.	Interpret Roman numerals requiring subtraction.
	Prerequisite Skills		
Presenting Information	Content Presentation		
	Examples		
Student Participation and Embedded Tests	Practice		
	Feedback		
Follow-Through Activities	Remediation		
	Enrichment		

Feedback

1. The length of each lesson is set at thirty minutes. If you discover during field tests that thirty minutes is too long a period, then adjust the length of the lesson to accommodate the target group.
2., 3., and 4. See the sample sequence, time estimates, and lesson assignments in Table 7.8.
5. Table 7.9 contains the sample instructional analysis for subskills 13 and 15.

Table 7.8
Sample Strategy for Roman Numeral Instructional Analysis

Sequence of Objectives		Time Required	Lesson Assignment
Order	Objective	Minutes	
1	Introduction, Pretest	30	1
2	10	15 ⎫	
3	11	15 ⎬	2
4	3	5 ⎫	
5	4	5 ⎬	3
6	12	20 ⎭	
7	5	5 ⎫	
8	7	10 ⎬	4
9	9	10 ⎭	
10	14	15 ⎫	
11	16	15 ⎬	5
12	6	5 ⎫	
13	8	10 ⎬	6
14	13	15 ⎭	
15	15	15 ⎫	
16	17	15 ⎬	7
17	18	15 ⎫	
18	19	15 ⎬	8
19	20	15	9
20	Summary, Posttest	30	10

IMPLEMENTATION

Consider the work you do on developing an instructional strategy for your materials design in terms of the input, process, and output model.

Input

At this point you have a design for your instructional materials which has been evaluated and revised as needed. It includes the instructional goal, a description of the general characteristics of your target group, the instructional analysis (nature, sequence, and relationship of required subskills), the performance objectives, and criterion-referenced tests to be used as pretests, embedded tests, and posttests.

Table 7.9
Feedback on Instructional Strategy for Subskills 13 and 15

Instructional Activity		Objectives	
		13	15
Preinstructional Activity	Motivation	You can actually subtract using Roman numerals.	Same.
	Objectives	Indicate subtraction in Roman numerals by placing numerals with smaller values to the left of numerals with larger values.	Interpret Roman numerals requiring subtraction.
	Prerequisite Skills	Subskills 6, 8, 9, 10, 11, 12. Review and practice of 8 and 12.	No review necessary if taught in same lesson as 13. If not, review and practice subskills 8, 12, and 13.
Presenting Information	Content Presentation	1. Individual numerals can be put together. 2. You have to subtract the values of the numerals to read the total value of the combined numeral. 3. You put the largest value numeral to the far right and place smaller valued numerals to the left if you want them subtracted.	1. Numerals can be subtracted from right to left to read the value of the numeral. 2. Subtract from largest to smallest, or from right to left.

	Examples	1. IV IX XL
		    ↑Largest ↑Largest ↑Largest
		 2. I←V I←X X←L
		    1←5 1←10 10←50
			IV = the largest value (5) minus the smallest value (1) = 4. Say $5-1=4$. IV = 4. IX = the largest value (10) minus the smallest value (1) = 9. Say $10-1=9$. IX = 9.

Student Participation and Embedded Tests	Practice	Practice exercises should include examples from simple to difficult (e.g., from the following list, put together numerals that require subtraction in order to read the value).	Practice examples should include all seven numerals in order from simplest examples to most complex examples.
	Feedback	Feedback should show correct combinations and provide reasons why any wrong ones are incorrect.	Feedback should show all correct combinations for students to compare answers (e.g., IV = 4 = [4 = V − I]) to not only illustrate correct answer, but also to illustrate process.
Follow-Through Activities	Remediation	1. Numerals can be put together to indicate subtraction. 2. Order goes right to left from highest value to lowest value. 3. E.g.: 4 = IV = I ← V 9 = IX = I ← X 4 = 1 ← 5 9 = 1 ← 10	1. Numerals should be subtracted from right to left (←), larger numeral to smaller numeral (I ← V). Provide easier practice exercises: IV, IX, XL, and so on.
	Enrichment	Use subtraction notation to show the same value as shown in addition notation (e.g., XVIIII = XIX).	1. Have students practice interpreting numbers that have several numbers to subtract. (_?_ = IIVX) 2. Have students try adding and subtracting in the same numeral. (_?_ = XIV)

Process

In order to develop an instructional strategy, all of the components you have are necessary inputs. You will need to:

1. Consider the general characteristics of your target students to identify the level of vocabulary, types of examples, and activities which would be appropriate for your group.
2. Consider your instructional analysis and use either a best-guess procedure or an entry-skills test to determine where to set the starting point for your instructional analysis. If you find that your students lack the required entry skills, then you may need to either select a different target group or designate a different entry point in the analysis.
3. Identify the amount of time allowable for each instructional meeting (thirty minutes, one hour, etc.).
4. Determine the best sequence for presenting instruction on objectives in the instructional analysis.
5. Estimate the time required for students to learn skills specified in each objective.
6. Assign objectives to lessons on the basis of time required for objectives and the relationship among objectives.
7. Prepare an instructional strategy chart for each lesson, including the preinstructional, presentation, practice and feedback, and follow-through activities. This instructional strategy chart can be used to guide (a) materials development, (b) materials selection, (c) materials evaluation, and (d) materials revision. It is a key product and will be used throughout the remaining steps in the instructional design process.

Output

At this point you should have (a) an estimate of the time that will be required for students to use your materials, (b) a time-segmented division of your materials for lesson construction, (c) instructional strategies charts for all the objectives in your instructional analysis diagram, (d) an outline of unit motivational activities from this chapter, and (e) pretests and posttests from previous developmental activities.

REFERENCES

Briggs, L. J. *Handbook of procedures for the design of instruction*. Pittsburgh: American Institutes for Research, 1970.
    Briggs provides an in-depth approach for designing an instructional strategy based upon the type of learning which is involved.

Gagné, R. M., & Briggs, L. J. *Principles of instructional design.* New York: Holt, Rinehart, and Winston, Inc., 1974.

    The chapter on the events of instruction in this book will provide additional background on the major concepts which have been included.

Gagné, R. M. *Essentials of learning for instruction.* Hinsdale, Ill.: Dryden Press, 1974.

    This book includes another description of the events of instruction as they would be incorporated into an instructional strategy.

Note: The *Journal of Educational Psychology* includes a variety of research articles about the effectiveness of various instructional strategies which might be incorporated in individualized materials.

8 Developing Instructional Materials

OBJECTIVES

1. *Given an instructional strategy, you will be able to describe the procedures for developing instructional materials.*

2. *You will be able to develop instructional materials based on a given instructional strategy.*

BACKGROUND

In a typical classroom instructional setting the instructor does many of the things which we described as being components of an instructional strategy. The instructor is often the motivator, the information presenter, the leader of practice activities, and the tester. The instructor makes decisions which effect the whole group as well as individual students. Instructors are usually locked into a strategy and must move the whole class forward or retain the whole class at a particular point until they feel that sufficient understanding has developed within the group.

The hallmark of individualized instruction is that many of the instructional events which are typically carried out by the instructor with a group of students are now presented to the individual student through the instructional materials. As we have said elsewhere, this does not mean that the instructor is removed from the instructional setting. The instructor's role is even more important than that in lock/step instruction. The instructor is still a motivator, as well as a counselor, an evaluator, and a decision maker.

We recommend that if you are developing your first instructional materials package, that it be totally self-instructional. That is, the materials should permit the student to develop the criterion behaviors without any required intervention from an instructor or fellow student. Once having performed this feat as a designer you can very easily move back to the point of using peer discussions or instructor evaluations. Motivation and decision making should be built into the instructional materials. If you were to start your development with the instructor "built in" to the instructional process, it would be very easy to begin to use the teacher as a crutch in order to deliver the instruction.

In essence, you are considering a new form of instructional delivery system. Answers are being sought to the question of how we can meet students where they are and provide them with instruction which is efficient and effective in developing new behaviors.

CONCEPTS

There are four major components in any well-designed instructional materials package. Each component is defined in the following discussion.

Instructional manual. An instructional manual contains the directions to the student on how to use all the resources included in the module. The manual contains the master strategy for students; it tells them what to do first, second, third, and so on. This is a minimal definition of the instructional manual. It may also include some of the instructional materials, examples of test items, statements of objectives, and practice tests.

The manual includes as a minimum the directions to the student on how to use the other components of the package. At most, it may incorporate all of the other parts of the package. In this case, the manual and the instructional materials package become clearer as we describe the other components.

Instructional materials. The instructional materials contain the information, either written or mediated, which a student will use to achieve the objectives. This includes not only those materials for the major objectives, but also any remedial or enrichment materials. Instructional materials refer to any pre-existing materials which are being incorporated as well as those materials which will have to be specifically written for the objectives.

Tests. All instructional materials should be accompanied by tests. These may include an entry behaviors test, and/or a pretest, a posttest and embedded test items. You may decide that you do not wish to have the tests as a separate component in the materials, but prefer to have them appear as part of one of the other components. You may, for example, wish to have the entry behaviors test, pretest, and posttest printed in the instructor's guide so they are not available to the students. You may wish to put the embedded test items directly into the instructional materials at the point at which they complete instruction on a particular topic. The package will be incomplete, however, unless you have included at least a posttest and those other tests which are necessary for using the instructional package.

Instructor's manual. There should be a general description available for the instructor which provides an overview of the materials package and how it might be incorporated into an overall learning sequence for students. It might also include the tests as well as other information which you judge would be important to the instructor.

Development Activities

Now that we have described the four major components of individualized instructional packages, you are ready to develop the package itself. Perhaps the best place to begin is with the development of the instructional materials component. You should refer directly to your instructional strategy to determine the types of materials you will need.

The first step, which is often overlooked in instructional design efforts, is to determine if there are already *existing materials* which fit your objectives. In some situations you will find an abundance of materials available, many either superficial or greatly detailed, which are not really directed to the target population in which you are interested. On the other hand, occasionally it is possible to identify materials which will serve at least part of your needs. When you consider the cost of developing a videotape, or a slide/tape presentation, it is clearly worth the effort to spend several hours examining existing materials to determine if they meet your needs.

If no appropriate materials exist, you are in the materials writing business, and you must make an additional decision with regard to your instructional strategy. What type of medium will you use to develop the materials? There are five important variables to consider.

Media Selection

The first factor is the *type of learning* involved in your objectives. If, for example, you are teaching a psychomotor activity of some type, it is important to use pictorial or moving visuals in order to demonstrate criterion performance to students. If you are teaching students to make auditory discriminations, then you should include some type of audio medium as a part of your instruction. If the task is one of shaping fine discriminations among concepts, then perhaps you should use a medium that can supply feedback to students on their performance.

A second important factor in media selection is the projected *availability of various media* in the environment in which the instructional package will be used. If the materials will be used in a learning resource center of a public school, community college, or university, then a whole array of media devices would probably be available to the learner and thus to you as the instructor.

However, if the package is designed for home study or use in a community center where this equipment is not likely to be available, then you must either develop a means of making that equipment available or limit yourself to paper and pencil types of instructional materials. A related concern is the ability of the teacher and the student to manage the media which you incorporate in the instructional package. If you use a videotape, a slide tape, an audio tape, and a programmed instruction text in combination, the variety of media could create logistical problems. This is a practical consideration you must not overlook.

The third factor in media selection is the *ability of the designer* to produce materials in a particular media format or the availability of persons with this expertise. For example, you may find that computer-assisted instruction would be an ideal medium for a particular instructional objective, but because you do not already have the skills to develop instruction using computers or the time to learn them, or because there is no staff available to do it, another choice must be made. On the other hand, if such resources are available or you have these skills, then certainly they should be used.

The fourth factor is the *flexibility, durability, and convenience* of the materials within a specified medium. If the materials are designed so they require equipment found only in a learning center, is there a learning center available? Is it open during hours when students can participate in independent study? Are the materials in a form that students can handle for themselves without destroying either the materials or equipment required for materials? Should the materials be portable and, if so, how portable can they be with the media you have chosen?

The fifth factor is the *cost effectiveness* of one medium compared to others over the long run. Some materials may be initially cheaper to produce in one medium than another, but these costs may be equalized when one considers savings in other areas such as lecturers, evaluators, and feedback personnel. It might be cheaper to videotape a lecture for students to view again and again as needed. This frees the lecturer or specialist to work with students in a discussion/problem-solving atmosphere.

All the factors discussed here present both theoretical and practical criteria which must be met. Therefore, which media you select is an extremely important decision in the instructional-package development process.

The Instructor's Role in Instructional Development and Delivery

The instructor may become involved in the use of three different types of instructional materials. The differences between the three types lie in the role the instructor plays in developing the instruction and in the actual delivery of instruction to target students. Table 8.1 includes the instructor's role in the design and the delivery process.

Table 8.1

The Role of the Instructor in the Design and Delivery of Instruction

The Instructor's Role in Designing Materials	The Mode of Delivering Instruction for Each Instructional Event				
	Preinstructional Activities	Presenting Information	Student Participation	Follow-Through Activities	Pretest/ Posttest and Unit Motivation
I **Instructor designs individualized instructional materials**	Materials	Materials	Materials	Materials	Instructor/ materials
II **Instructor selects and adapts existing materials to suit the instructional strategy**	Materials and/or Instructor	Materials and/or Instructor	Materials and/or Instructor	Materials and/or Instructor	Instructor/ materials
III **Instructor delivers instruction to suit the instructional strategy**	Instructor	Instructor	Instructor	Instructor	Instructor/ materials

When instructors design and develop individualized materials, or materials that can be delivered independent of an instructor, their role in instructional delivery is passive. In this case, their task during instruction is to monitor and guide the progress of students through the materials. Students can progress at their own speed through the instruction, with the instructor providing additional help for students who seem to need it.

Except for the pretests and posttests, all instructional events are included within the materials. In some materials, even these tests are included and submitted to teachers only when students complete them.

In the second case, when instructors select and adapt materials to suit their instructional strategy, it is probable that the instructor will have an increased role in delivering instruction. Some available materials may be instructor independent, but when they are not, the instructor must provide any instruction specified in the strategy, but not found in the materials.

When an instructor uses a variety of instructional resources, he or she plays a greater role in materials management. By providing a student guide for available materials, instructors may be able to increase the independence of the materials and free themselves to provide additional guidance and consultation for students who need it.

The third type of instruction illustrated in Table 8.1 heavily depends on the instructor. The instructor delivers all the instruction, according to the instructional strategy that has been developed. This commonly occurs in public school or in other settings in which there is a small budget for materials or in which the content to be taught changes rapidly.

The instructor uses the instructional strategy as a guide in producing outlines for lecture notes and directions for group exercises and activities. Most often, the pretest and posttest are the only materials that are typed and duplicated for student use.

This type of instruction has both advantages and disadvantages. A major advantage is that the instructor can constantly update and improve instruction as changes occur in the content. But, instructors spend the majority of time lecturing and delivering information to a group, leaving little time to help individual pupils with problems. Progress through a lesson is difficult because when the teacher stops to answer a question for one student, the progress of the entire group is halted.

The intended delivery mode for instruction is a very important consideration in the development of materials based on the planned instructional strategy. If instruction is intended to be teacher-independent, then the materials developed will have to include all the instructional events from the strategy. The instructor is not expected to play a role in delivering instruction.

If the instructor plans to combine available materials, then instructional delivery will combine materials and instructor. The instructor may not be required to develop any new materials in this mode, but may be required to deliver some of the needed instruction. The amount of original materials developed for this type of instruction will depend upon available time, budget, and secretarial support.

If instructors plan to deliver all the instruction with materials such as lecture notes, an overhead projector, and a chalk board, then they may need to develop little besides lecture outlines, practice worksheets, and formal tests.

Your decision about the intended development and delivery mode should be made prior to materials development. These decisions will affect developmental activities, budget, and staff.

The Instructional Manual, Tests, and Instructor Guide

In conjunction with the development of the instructional package, you will also design the manual which students will use to guide them in the use of the package. You will find it helpful to provide an introductory statement which explains the purpose of individualized instruction and the procedures which the student will follow as he or she goes through the package. You may want to describe the various types of materials the student will be using and include any preinstructional activities in the manual. As indicated earlier, you may wish to include all the printed materials, and perhaps the test, in the manual to make the instructional package convenient for the user.

As you begin to develop your package, you should have already completed the tests which will be included. It is now a matter of determining how the tests will be used and how they will be presented within the package, and it is particularly important to determine how the pretest is to be used. Will students be branched to a particular place in the materials on the basis of their score on the pretest, or will all students start at the beginning regardless of their pretest scores? You will also need to decide how you will integrate practice and feedback items into the instructional materials.

The final task you will undertake if you plan to share the materials you have developed with other instructors is to develop the instructor's guide. If others ask to use your materials to teach, you may wish to develop a guide which includes (in addition to an overview of the set of materials) a list of specific objectives, copies of all the tests (and answers), and suggested procedures for using the package. You may wish to include a general description of the target students for whom the package is intended and specific statements or tests for entry behaviors.

Factors that Affect Materials Development

Instructors must consider many factors in making decisions about how to develop and provide instruction. Some of these include the instructional environment; the degree to which instruction depends on an instructor; the availability of materials; the amount of instruction required; the grouping patterns of students; the size and characteristics of the target group; and available personnel, facilities, and equipment.

The instructional environment. The instructional strategy can be used to guide the development of materials regardless of where instruction is to occur. Some instructors will plan instructional materials to be used in a learning center setting which is independent of instructor explanation or guidance. Others might need to plan instruction for a combination learning center-classroom environment; still others might plan instruction for a classroom setting only. Regardless of where instruction takes place, the instructional strategy is used as a guide to motivational activities, information presentation, student participation and testing, and follow-through activities.

The degree of instructor dependency. Instructional materials will reflect many different degrees of instructor dependency. Some materials are totally instructor-independent, with all components of the instructional strategy and learner guidance included within the materials. In other cases, the instructor and the materials share instructional duties: Both the materials and the instructor provide motivational activities. Students may read a text and see film presentations in addition to hearing an instructor's introductions, lectures, and summaries. Students may complete practice exercises included in the materials and check their own answers in addition to participating in small group activities and classroom simulations directed by the instructor or an assigned monitor.

Frequently, instructional materials are unavailable for a topic and instructors are required to provide verbal motivation, lectures, practice activities, and feedback and follow-through instruction, whether remedial or advanced. The most frequent combinations of instructor-dependent instruction are as follows: Instructor-dependent guidance through a unit lesson, instructor-dependent motivation, textbook-lecture presentation, textbook/workbook-classroom practice, instructor-dependent assessment, and instructor-planned follow through.

Availability of existing materials. The instructional strategy is a necessary guide for (a) original instructional material to be developed, (b) existing material to be adapted, (c) existing material to be adopted in its current form, or (d) a combination of original and selected materials.

The planned strategy can be used to develop original instruction which will ensure that, during instruction, all the events necessary for efficient learning are included.

The strategy can be used to identify existing instructional materials. It can be used to sequence, cluster, and schedule identified materials when they need to be ordered, borrowed, or altered.

The instructional strategy can also be used to determine whether existing materials are adequate as they are or whether they need to be adapted prior to use. Materials can be evaluated to determine whether (a) adequate motivational materials exist; (b) the appropriate content is included; (c) the sequence is correct; (d) all the required information is available; (e) practice exercises exist; (f) adequate feedback is included; (g) appropriate tests are available; (h) adequate follow-up directions are included for remediation, advanced work, or general progress; and (i) adequate learner guidance is provided to move students from one event or activity to the next.

The instructional strategy should be used to evaluate each selected reference. It may be possible to combine references to improve the materials. When materials lack one or more of the necessary instructional activities, such as motivation, prerequisite skills, and so on, they can be adapted so that the missing components are made available for use by students.

Existing instructional materials will frequently lack a systematic guide students can use to progress through the materials. In the situation in which such a guide is missing, the instructor must develop one.

The amount of instruction. The instructional strategy can be used as a framework for entire units of instruction or a daily lesson plan. The instructional events described in the instructional strategy should occur on several different levels. Students need to be informed of long-range goals and be motivated to work toward those goals. It may be necessary to inform them and motivate them for unit goals, for lesson goals, or even for the achievement of one objective. "Why should I?" is a common question being asked by students today, and it applies to the category of motivation and informing the learner.

Presentation efforts will be guided by the amount of instruction that is required. The amount of repetition, review, and summarization necessary for one objective is not usually great, but it increases as the amount of instruction increases to one whole unit or several interrelated units.

Review, repetition, and summary activities are also important considerations when developing practice and feedback activities. While these activities may be simple for one objective, students should have the opportunity to relate the current skills to others learned in previous lessons.

Testing is usually done on an objective level, lesson level, and unit level. The manner in which this is done depends upon the nature of the content and skills being learned, and such testing can range from informal observation to formal examinations.

Follow-through activities are also related to the amount of instruction to be completed. Activities may include review, summary, and generalization both at the lesson level and the unit level.

Individualized or group instruction. Though we have based this discussion of planning materials on the individual learner, obviously classes and groups are made up of a number of individuals. We have assumed in this discussion (and text) that instruction will usually take place in a group or in a classroom. Whether instruction will be read by one or by one hundred, the pace, sequence, and information can be, and often is, the same. Whether a film is viewed or a lecture is heard by one or by a class group of thirty-five, the strategy used to create the film or the lecture remains the same, and the nature of the instructional materials provided remains the same.

The difference in the size of the group participating in an instructional lesson will probably affect the method of presentation and the nature of practice and feedback activities. For years instructors have practiced asking a question, having the whole group ponder the answer, and then calling on one individual to answer. By waiting to name the student who is to answer the question, the instructor allows all the students in the group to practice the process required to answer the question, hear the answer given by a chosen individual, and have the opportunity to compare their answers with response or feedback from the instructor.

When there is insufficient time or opportunity for the instructor to work individually with students on an activity, more mature students working in groups can provide each other with individualized feedback for practice activities. If students are provided with the necessary criteria for evaluating their own work and the work of their peers, valuable individualized practice and feedback can be gained through small-group interaction. Additional learning also takes place when students evaluate the work of peers. Students then have the opportunity to see additional examples of the material and the way in which problems were perceived and addressed by others.

There is one major problem with individualized pacing of instruction in group-mode instruction: The instructor must be able to plan and manage instruction so that all students, regardless of their rate of progress, are busy, challenged, and actively learning the skills they individually need. When adequate materials are unavailable for truly independent pacing of students, the instructor must modify individual progress rates to comply with some kind of subgroup or class progress rate. For example, to achieve specific skills, all students in a group may be required to view a film on a certain date at a specified time. The students will be required to view the film whether they have the prerequisite skills to obtain maximum benefit from viewing the film or not. In these instances, the instructor must try to introduce the film and to summarize the film so that as many students in the group as possible can benefit.

Clustering students into similar groups based on prerequisite skills and learning rates often provides the benefits of individualized pacing of instruction for the majority of students. It enables the instructor to plan additional practice activities for subgroups who need more practice and to provide enrichment activities for the advanced group which will benefit from additional, more difficult examples and activities.

Instructional activities developed or selected which are related to motivation, presentation, and embedded test components are usually the same whether they are planned for one or for a number of students. These activities usually involve viewing, listening, reading, and answering questions. The size of the group instructed affects instruction mainly at the practice and feedback stages. When several students are available, interactive types of practice, discussion, and feedback activities can be planned.

If you are designing instruction for an unknown instructional setting, the best procedure is to design all materials for an individualized, instructor-independent setting. It is far easier for others to modify instruction to include additional group practice and feedback than to provide instructor-dependent motivation, presentation activities, follow-through activities, and pretests and posttests.

Size and characteristics of the target group. The instructional strategy should indicate whether instruction will be presented to one student or to a whole group. In a learning center, instructor-independent materials can be provided for one student or for a hundred. Instructor-dependent instruction is traditionally reserved for class-size groups because of cost-effectiveness (e.g., the instructor's salary and the number of students taught). For example, if certain motivational activities, based on the instructional strategy prescription, are desired, final decisions about whether they will be included may depend upon the number of students to receive instruction and the number of times the instruction will be repeated for other groups. If a large number of students is to receive instruction, the decision may be made to develop elaborate instructor-independent materials. If students are to receive instruction on a particular topic once a year, instructors may be left to contrive and provide instructor-dependent motivational activities on their own. This is not an uncommon situation today. The size of the group to be taught and the frequency of instruction are both important in determining how to implement the events prescribed in the instructional strategy.

The characteristics of the target group also affect the instructional strategy and thus the nature of instructional materials. Whether students can read, see, or hear will affect the nature of the strategy and their instruction. The students' attention span, their social maturity, and their expected behavior and responsibility patterns will also affect the way in which the prescriptions in the instructional strategy are implemented.

Personnel, facilities, and equipment. The instructional strategy for materials development cannot be implemented until available personnel, facilities, and equipment are carefully considered. If a certain event is to take place as prescribed in the strategy, the system to support the event must be available. Otherwise, the instructional strategy will have to be modified. If needed instructors are unavailable, then several or all instructional events in the strategy need to be made instructor-independent. If learning centers are unavailable, materials designed for these centers cannot be developed. If audiovisual equipment is lacking, it will also affect the manner in which the materials are developed.

EXAMPLES

The development examples included here are based on the instructional strategy in Table 7.5 in Chapter 7. Instructional materials are presented for Objective 12—equate Roman numerals with Arabic numbers of the same value. We have assumed that these materials are planned to be included in a self-instructional workbook or text for sixth-grade students.

I. Preinstructional Activities

A. Motivation

Text	Illustration/Cue
You can learn to read Roman numerals if you learn the value of each numeral. It is easy if you just compare the Roman numerals with numbers you already know.	

In this example the motivational information suggests *how* students can learn to interpret Roman numerals and that interpreting numerals is *easy* if students compare numerals with numbers they already know.

The illustration serves as additional motivational material. It shows a sixth-grade boy actually equating numerals and numbers. In addition, he is being admired by a peer for doing so. The use of color in illustrations can be motivational, but it is costly. The funds available for final products will allow the instructor to determine whether the use of color can be planned.

B. Objectives

Text	Illustration/Cue
During this lesson you will learn the values of all seven Roman numerals and be able to associate them with regular numbers. When you see a number, you should be able to say the name of the matching Roman numeral. You should also be able to say the name of the matching number when you see a Roman numeral. Practice until you don't make any mistakes matching numerals and numbers.	Objective

The script for the objective includes the skill the students are going to learn and how well they need to learn it. The illustration accompanying this example is simply a cue informing students of the location of objectives in the lesson. Any symbol or form that they can consistently associate with the location of objectives would suffice. Some ideas might include bold lettering, a box around the objective statement, or script lettering.

C. Prerequisite Skills

Text	Illustration/Cue
It is important to remember the seven letters that are used as Roman numerals. What are they? ? ? ? ? ? ? ?	Remember? ? VIXCDM
The seven letters used for Roman numerals are: I, V, X, L, C, D, M	

By requiring students to recall the names of the letters, you are providing them with a review of previously learned material. This exercise will help them remember the material for a greater length of time. In addition, the student recalls material that is an important component of this lesson. At this point students know the letters used for Roman numerals. In addition they already know Arabic numbers and corresponding values. Now the instructional task is to help them associate the numeral with the appropriate number and value.

II. Presenting Information

A. Content Presentation and Examples

Text	Example
Each of the seven Roman numerals has a corresponding number.	I = 1 V = 5
The value of the Roman numeral is the same as the value of the corresponding number.	5 = V 11111 = IIIII 1111 = IIII
Just as you can count using numbers, you can count using Roman numerals.	I + I + I + I = 4 1 + 1 + 1 + 1 = 4
	V + V + V + V = 20 5 + 5 + 5 + 5 = 20
The values of each of the seven Roman numerals are: *Roman* *Equal Number* I = 1 V = 5 X = 10 L = 50 C = 100 D = 500 M = 1000	

The script presents the information and a corresponding visual example together. The way you would visually arrange the information and corresponding example or the amount of information you would include on one page would be determined at the time you actually produce each page of text. At this point, you know exactly what information to present and how to present and explain it through examples. Pagination, layout, and illustrations can be determined at the time you are actually ready to produce the material.

III. Student Participation

Practice	Feedback
1. Match the following Roman numerals and numbers. Check your answers on page _____ .	

Roman	Arabic	Practice		Feedback
I	500	1. I = _____		1. I = __1__
V	10	2. V = _____		2. V = __5__
X	1	3. X = _____		3. X = __10__
L	50	4. L = _____		4. L = __50__
C	1000	5. C = _____		5. C = __100__
D	5	6. D = _____		6. D = __500__
M	100	7. M = _____		7. M = __1000__

In this exercise, students are given all the Roman numerals and all the numbers, and since students are just beginning, the Roman numerals appear in ascending order. As practice exercises become more difficult these cues are removed. In the next example, the order of the numerals is changed and students can no longer use order as a cue. Also, students will have to exercise more caution selecting their answers, because more than the exact number of answer choices are included.

Practice			Feedback
2. Match the Roman numerals and numbers. Check your answers on page _____ .			
Roman	Number	Value	
X	1	100	X = __10__
D	2	200	D = __500__
M	5	500	M = __1000__
V	16	1000	V = __5__
C	15	10	C = __100__
I	20	25	I = __1__
L	50		L = __50__
	70		

In the next practice exercise, students are asked to remember the values. This is more difficult than selecting the correct value from a list of choices.

Notice that the numerals have again been arranged in correct order, thus providing still another cue.

Practice	Feedback
3. Fill in the blanks with the correct number. Check your answers on page _____ . I = _____ C = _____ V = _____ D = _____ X = _____ M = _____ L = _____	I = _1_ C = _100_ V = _5_ D = _500_ X = _10_ M = _1000_ L = _50_

The recall problem is reversed in the next exercise, and students are requested to recall the appropriate Roman numeral for each number given.

Practice	Feedback
4. Fill in the blanks with the correct Roman numeral. Check your answers on page _____ . 1 = _____ 100 = _____ 5 = _____ 500 = _____ 10 = _____ 1000 = _____ 50 = _____	1 = I 100 = C 5 = V 500 = D 10 = X 1000 = M 50 = L

Again, the numbers in the exercise are placed in numerical order to facilitate recall.

IV. Embedded Test Items

In the following exercise, students are asked to practice recalling both numerals and numbers. Distractor values have been added, and the numbers are not in numerical order.

Practice	
Fill in the blanks with either the correct Roman numeral or the correct number. If there is no matching number or numeral for a question, leave it blank. _____ . 1. I = _____ 6. N = _____ 2. 5 = _____ 7. C = _____ 3. D = _____ 8. 50 = _____ 4. T = _____ 9. B = _____ 5. 10 = _____ 10. 1000 = _____	

This exercise allows students to demonstrate their ability to convert both from Roman numerals to Arabic numbers and from Arabic numbers to Roman numerals.

V. Follow-Through Activities

A. Remediation

Students who were unable to answer all the items in practice exercise or embedded test items should participate in more practice exercises. In addition to practice, they may need further explanations for matching numerals with numbers.

Text	Illustration/Cue
Each Roman numeral stands for a certain number and a certain number of things. The I stands for 1 and for 1 dot. The V stands for 5 and for 5 dots. The X stands for 10 and for 10 dots. The L stands for 50 and 50 dots.	I = 1 = • V = 5 = ••••• X = 10 = •••••••••• L = 50 = •••••••••• •••••••••• •••••••••• •••••••••• ••••••••••

By illustrating the numeral, the corresponding number, and the corresponding value, you may increase the student's understanding of corresponding numbers and values.

For remediation purposes, information may be presented and practiced in smaller portions. Practice exercises could require students to match a smaller number of numerals at one time. In one exercise, they may be asked to equate only numerals I through L. Then information could be presented on numerals C through M and practice exercises on equating only numerals C through M could follow.

After successfully matching smaller groups of numerals they could be asked to recall all seven numerals and their corresponding numbers.

At this point, students can go through the regular practice exercises for additional repetition if it is still needed.

B. Enrichment

Students are often challenged when they are asked to guess the next step in the lesson. Sometimes they can and sometimes they cannot successfully guess the next step. Their ability to guess successfully usually depends upon the difficulty of the next objective. It is highly possible that they can combine the seven basic numerals to form other numerals, because they already know how to do it with Arabic numbers. Therefore, in this lesson a challenging enrichment exercise would be one that asks students to combine numerals to form specified numbers. Remember to specify only numbers that require adding from left to right, because that is the next lesson. You should avoid the issue of subtracting numerals and moving right to left until after the instruction on addition is complete.

Text	Illustration/Cue
If you were a Roman and needed more than seven numbers, how would you make the extra numerals?	
Do you think the Romans had only seven numbers even though they had only seven numerals?	

Text	Illustration/Cue
1. Try to make the following numbers using only the seven numerals you have learned. Check your answers on page _____. 2 = _____ 30 = _____ 3 = _____ 52 = _____ 6 = _____ 110 = _____ 11 = _____ 505 = _____ 15 = _____ 1050 = _____ 22 = _____ 1053 = _____	2 = II 30 = XXX 3 = III 52 = LII 6 = VI 110 = CX 11 = XI 505 = DV 15 = XV 1050 = ML 22 = XXII 1053 = MLIII If you did not get these correct, don't worry. We are going to learn to do this in lesson 4.
2. What do you think the numbers are for these numerals? Check your answers on page _____. XX = _____ XVII = _____ XII = _____ LXVI = _____ LXI = _____ CLXXV = _____	XX = 20 XVII = 17 XII = 12 LXVI = 66 LXI = 61 CLXXV = 175 If you did not get these correct, don't worry. We are going to learn to do this in lesson 4.

These materials for preinstructional activities, presenting information, practice and feedback, and follow-through activities are ready for review, revision, and then actual development.

When making up pages in a workbook or text, you should always keep in mind the general learning characteristics of the target group and the format of the instruction. The same information looks very different when it is arranged on a page. A large border and blank space on a page makes a lesson look easier than a page crowded with materials. In designing each page, try to create an attractive, simple design. Financial considerations are often very important, but the effectiveness of your instructional materials is also important. Your final product may turn out to be a compromise between cost and attractive page design.

PRACTICE AND FEEDBACK

Practice

Use the instructional strategy for Objective 14 in Table 7.5, chapter 7, to design materials for a sixth-grade text or workbook. Compare your designs with those in the Feedback section. It is important to remember that there are many ways to design these materials. The examples in the Feedback section reflect only one of these ways.

Objective 14 from Table 7.5: The student will learn to put several numerals together to form numerals with different values. They will be able to read the value of the new numeral.

I. Preinstructional Activities

A. *Motivation*

Text	Illustration/Cue

B. *Objectives*

Text	Illustration/Cue

C. *Prerequisite Skills*

Text	Illustration/Cue

II. Presenting Information

Text	Examples

III. Student Participation

Practice	Feedback

IV. Follow-Through Activities

A. Remediation

Text	Examples

B. Enrichment

Text	Examples

V. Other Developmental Considerations

1. List below the four major components of an instructional package.
   a. _____
   b. _____
   c. _____
   d. _____

2. In question 1, which of the components are intended primarily for the instructor and which are intended primarily for the students?
   Instructor: _____
   Students: _____

3. What types of information would you be likely to include in an instructional manual intended for students?
   a. _____
   b. _____
   c. _____
   d. _____
   e. _____

4. What types of information would you be likely to include in the instructional materials?
   a. _____
   b. _____
   c. _____
   d. _____

5. What types of materials would you be likely to include in an instructor's guide?
   a. _____
   b. _____
   c. _____
   d. _____

6. What factors are of major importance in deciding the most efficient media for your lesson?
   a. _____
   b. _____
   c. _____
   d. _____
   e. _____

7. Discuss the order in which you believe you will develop the following materials: (a) instructional manual, (b) instructional materials, (c) tests, and (d) instructor's guide.

   There is no set answer to this question, but with your developmental project in mind, it is time to give the developmental procedure some thought. This will enable you to collect pertinent information at the proper time.

Feedback

I. Preinstructional Activity

A. Motivation

Text	Illustration/Cue
It is possible to combine numbers to make any number between 2 and 1000	III IV I
When you learn to combine Roman numerals to form new numbers, you can actually add the numerals together.	$I + I + I = III = 3$

B. Objective

Text	Illustration/Cue
During this lesson you are going to learn to put several numerals together to form new numerals. You will also learn to put the seven basic Roman numerals together and read the total value of the new numeral. You will be expected to give the number value of any Roman numeral given.	8 = VIII 13 = XIII XXI = 21 LXV = 65

C. Prerequisite Skills

Text	Illustration/Cue
You must know the value of each of the seven Roman numerals before you can put them together to form new numerals. Each new numeral depends on the value of all the numerals inside it.	I = 1 V = 5 X = 10 L = 50 C = 100 D = 500 M = 1000

1. What are the values of these numerals? Check your answers on page _____.
X = _____ L = _____ M = _____
C = _____ I = _____ V = _____
D = _____
	1. X = 10 I = 1
	   C = 100 M = 1000
	   D = 500 V = 5
	   L = 50

2. What are the numerals for each of these values? Check your answers on page
 	
_____.
5 = _____   50 = _____
100 = _____   1 = _____
1000 = _____   500 = _____
10 = _____
	2. 5 = V 50 = L
	   100 = C 1 = I
	   1000 = M 500 = D
	   10 = X

II. Presenting Information

Text	Examples
You can make new numerals from the seven basic numerals by placing them side by side.	III VI XV
You can't place numerals side by side in just any order. To add them together, you have to write the one with the largest value first, the second largest value second, and a smallest value last.	largest smallest ↓ ↓ X ⟶ V ⟶ I ↑ next largest
Look at these numerals: XCILV In order to place them together and add them to make a new numeral, you have to place the largest first. You need to place the second largest numeral second.	X, C, I, L, V (1st) (2nd) C L CL
Place the next smaller numerals beside the L.	CL<u>X</u>
How do the rest of the numerals fit together so that they will add to make the new number?	CLX<u>VI</u>

Text	Examples
We have learned that to add numerals together you must: 1. Place them side by side. 2. Place them from the left to the right. ⟶ 3. Place them in order from the largest to the smallest.	CLXVI ⟶
The values of each of these numerals add together to make the total value of the new numeral.	CLXVI = 166 100 50 10 5 + 1 166

Text	Examples
Try adding another numeral from left to right.	III = I + I + I = 3 1 + 1 + 1 = 3
Is this numeral correct for adding, or is something wrong with the way the numerals are placed together?	? XLV
No, this numeral is incorrect. The X is smaller than the L, so the order should go like this; Now it is correct.	→Ⓧ L V LXV
Is this numeral correct for adding, or is something wrong with the order?	? VIII
It is correct because there are no larger numerals to the right of smaller numerals. All the Is are of the same value so they can be placed side by side. The Is must all be on the right side of the V because V is a larger numeral than I.	VIII

III. Student Participation

Practice	Feedback
1. Are the following numerals correct or incorrect for adding? Check your answers on page _____ .	1. The numerals must be placed from left to right, largest to smallest. largest ——→ smallest
1. IV	1. Wrong. It should be VI.
2. VI	2. Correct.
3. IXV	3. Wrong. It should be XVI.
4. XII	4. Correct.
5. XVI	5. Correct.
6. LC	6. Wrong. It should be CL.
7. CL	7. Correct
8. MDCL	8. Correct.
9. MDLCX	9. Wrong. It should be MDCLX.
10. CLVI	10. Correct.
2. Place the following numerals in the proper order for adding together. Check your answer on page _____ . IVXDMCL	2. The numerals should be placed left to right, largest to smallest. MDCLXVI

Text	Illustration/Cue
If you are going to arrange numerals to be added, you should always begin with the largest and end with the smallest. Place a circle around the numerals that are out of order. 1. XVI 5. IVII 2. XIV 6. VIII 3. DMC 7. VXI 4. MDC 8. XVI Check your answers on page _____ .	1. XVI 5. ⓘVII 2. XⓘV 6. VIII 3. ⓘMC 7. ⓥXI 4. MDC 8. XVI
You add Roman numerals the same way you add numbers. The only difference is that the + sign is left out.	$1 + 1 + 1 = 3$ III = 3 $5 + 1 + 1 = 7$ VII = 7
1. Add the following numerals together to find the total value of the numeral. Check your answers on page _____ . 1. II 6. XVI 2. III 7. XXI 3. VIII 8. XVIII 4. XII 9. XXVI 5. XV 10. LXVI	1. II = $1 + 1 = 2$ 2. III = $1 + 1 + 1 = 3$ 3. VIII = $5 + 1 + 1 + 1 = 8$ 4. XII = $10 + 1 + 1 = 12$ 5. XV = $10 + 5 = 15$ 6. XVI = $10 + 5 + 1 = 16$ 7. XXI = $10 + 10 + 1 = 21$ 8. XVIII = $10 + 5 + 1 + 1 + 1 = 18$ 9. XXVI = $10 + 10 + 5 + 1 = 26$ 10. LXVI = $50 + 10 + 5 + 1 = 66$

Embedded Test Items

Text	
Add the values within the following numerals to find the correct total value of each. Check your answers on page _____ . 1. II = _____ 2. III = _____ 3. VII = _____ 4. XVI = _____ 5. XXV = _____ 6. XVIII = _____ 7. LXXV = _____ 8. LXIII = _____ 9. CLXV = _____ 10. MIII = _____	

IV. Follow-Through Activities

A. Remediation

Text	Illustration/Cue
Roman numerals can be put together to form larger numerals. They should always be put together: 1. from the left to the right 2. from the largest numeral to the smallest numeral	$C \rightarrow L \rightarrow X \rightarrow V \rightarrow I$ $\uparrow \quad \uparrow \quad \uparrow \quad \uparrow \quad \uparrow$ 100 $\;$ 50 $\;$ 10 $\;$ 5 $\;$ 1

B. Enrichment

Text	Illustration/Cue
If you place numerals from left to right, and largest to smallest for adding, how do you think you place numerals for subtracting?	
Reorder the following numerals to show that they should be subtracted and record the total value. Check your answers on page _____ . $\quad\quad$ *reverse* $\quad\quad$ *order* $\quad\quad$ *value* 1. XI $=$ _____ $\;=$ _____ 2. VI $=$ _____ $\;=$ _____ 3. DL $=$ _____ $\;=$ _____ 4. LX $=$ _____ $\;=$ _____ 5. CL $=$ _____ $\;=$ _____	1. XI $=$ <u>IX</u> $\;=\;$ 9 2. VI $=$ <u>IV</u> $\;=\;$ <u>4</u> 3. DL $=$ <u>LD</u> $\;=\;$ <u>450</u> 4. LX $=$ <u>XL</u> $\;=\;$ <u>40</u> 5. CX $=$ <u>XC</u> $\;=\;$ <u>90</u> If you did not answer these questions correctly, don't worry. In lesson 5 you will learn to reorder numerals to show subtraction and to subtract using numerals.

V. Other Developmental Considerations

1. The four major components of an instructional package are:

   a. instructional manual
   b. instructional materials
   c. tests
   d. teachers' guide

2. Components intended for students are the instructional manual and the instructional materials. The component intended for instructors is the instructor's guide. The tests may be intended for use in evaluating students' performance or for students' use if included in a self-instructional, self-evaluation program. They fit into the category of being intended for both instructors and students.

3. The contents of the instructional manual will vary according to your instructional materials, your purpose, your needs, and your target population. Information you may want to consider includes:

   a. behaviorally stated objectives
   b. an overview
   c. motivational materials (historical, why do this anyway, overall goals, etc.)
   d. directions on how to use the instructional materials, any equipment needed, tests to be taken, and self-scoring procedures
   e. other references for remediation and enrichment purposes
   f. work schedules (what should be completed at what time)
   g. elaborations on any products or projects to be completed by students

4. Types of information you may be likely to include in instructional materials are:

   a. information that must be presented to students to enable them to achieve your objectives. This may include objectives and review materials as well as motivational materials and activities.
   b. examples and nonexamples of information, concepts, or skills which need to be learned
   c. performance activities that enable students to practice or to try out the concept or skills for themselves
   d. feedback on students' performance that enables them to reconsider their ideas or adjust their techniques
   e. follow-through instructions telling students what to do next

5. Types of materials you may want to include in an instructor's guide are:

   a. information about the target population for the materials
   b. suggestions on how to adapt materials for older, younger, brighter, or slower students
   c. an overview of the module
   d. intended learning outcomes of the module
   e. suggestions for using the materials in a certain context or sequence
   f. suggestions for materials management for individualized learning, small-group learning, learning-center activities, or classroom activities
   g. enrichment or remedial activities
   h. tests which can be used to evaluate students' performance on terminal objectives
   i. evidence of the effectiveness of the materials when used as suggested with the intended target populations
   j. suggestions for evaluating students' work and comparing progress
   k. an estimation of time required to use the materials properly
   l. any equipment or additional facilities needed for the materials

6. Major factors for deciding the most appropriate medium for an instructional module or unit are:

a. the type of learning expressed in the objective
b. the availability of equipment and facilities for certain media
c. the technical skills of the designer in designing materials for a specified medium
d. the flexibility, durability, and convenience of the materials using a specified medium
e. the cost effectiveness of a particular medium over the long run. It may be more expensive to develop some media than others (computer-managed instruction or videotape), but the costs of instruction using some media without the use, time, and constant supervision of a teacher over a period of time may defray developmental expenses and make it cheaper in the long run. A person on a videotape can repeat a lesson enthusiastically twenty-five times in one day. Few teachers could match that enthusiasm or energy.

7. A rigid pattern of development for the four components of a module, the instructional manual, instructional materials, tests, and instructor's guide, does not exist. The following order of events may serve as an example of how you might proceed. Constraints on your time, materials, and resources may cause you to deviate. The suggested order of development remains the same whether developing an instructional activity, a module, or a unit of instruction. It is:

a. tests
b. instructional materials
c. instructional manual
d. instructor's guide

IMPLEMENTATION

Activities required for developing an instructional package can be considered in terms of the input, process, and output model.

Input

Input for developing your package includes the evaluated design of your instruction which is made up of the instructional goal, instructional analysis, behavioral objectives, characteristics of target students, criterion-referenced tests, and your instructional strategy.

Process

At this point it may be beneficial to simply list all the steps the instructor takes in developing his or her instructional materials.

1. Select topic.
2. State instructional goal behaviorally.
3. Perform an instructional analysis based on the behaviorally stated instructional goal.
4. Describe the target population as specifically as possible and identify entry behaviors.
5. Write performance objectives and subobjectives.
6. Develop criterion-referenced tests for the objectives
   a. Determine whether your testing purpose is to diagnose students' entry behavior, to branch students, to evaluate students, to evaluate materials, or all of these.
   b. Determine whether a test on expected entry behaviors is necessary or advisable.
   c. Divide parallel questions written for each objective such that some can be included on a pretest (if a pretest is advisable), some can be used for embedded test questions, and some can be included on the posttest.
7. Develop the instructional strategy.
   a. Review the subskills included in the instructional analysis and determine which should be included in instructional materials and which should be included as expected entry behaviors. Order objectives in the sequence to be presented.
   b. Consider the target population relative to their attention span, work and study habits, responsibility, and motivation. Then estimate an average "best" time for each instructional objective.
   c. Consider the amount of time available for each instructional period. Using the estimated time required for each objective and the relationship among objectives (natural breaking points), cluster objectives into lessons.
8. Develop an instructional strategy for each objective in each lesson. Plan the strategy for preinstructional activities, presenting information and examples, practice and feedback activities, and follow-through activities for each objective and lesson.
9. Survey the literature and ask subject-matter experts to determine what instructional materials are already available.
10. Consider how you might adapt available materials by using a manual to guide students through the materials.
11. Determine whether new materials need to be designed. If so, proceed to 12. If not, begin organizing and adapting available materials, using the instructional strategy as a guide.
12. For each lesson, consider the best medium to present the materials, to monitor practice and feedback, to evaluate, and to pass students to the next instructional activity, whether enrichment, remediation, or the next activity in the sequence.
    a. Make decisions about the ideal media for the type of learning (stories for attitude, sound tape for language pronunciation, printed materials

for spelling and punctuation, relief maps for contouring or geography, etc.).

    b. The types of media required for a large set of materials may be many and varied. Cost effectiveness of developing materials using varied equipment and subskills should be considered.

    c. Availability of materials, portability of materials, availability and appropriateness of equipment should be considered.

    d. Tentative decisions about the best medium or media combinations should be made based on studying types of learning, activities required, physical and technical constraints, finances, facilities and the target population.

13. Determine the format and presentation procedures for each objective or cluster of objectives. Plan any general format or presentation pattern you believe is necessary or would be effective. Plan the actual script and illustrations for the instructional strategy.

14. Write the instructional materials based on the instructional strategy in rough form. A rough audiotape for a slide presentation may have the sound recorded on a simple cassette recorder with indicators for changing visuals, and the accompanying visuals can be magic-marker stick figures on 3-by 5 inch index cards. You will be amazed at how stick figures and rough illustrations can bring your ideas to life for a first trial. Printed, visual, or auditory materials in this rough form will allow you to check your sequence, flow of ideas, accuracy of illustration of ideas, completeness, pace, and so on. Make a rough set of materials as complete as possible for each instructional activity.

15. Consider each completed lesson or class session for clarity and flow of ideas. Does it go from easiest to most difficult, from the complete skill (instructional goal for that activity) back to the basic components or subskills, and so on?

16. Using one complete instructional unit (complete instructional diagram), write the student's manual or accompanying instructions to the students for that activity. This could include the objectives, directions, motivational materials, or assignments.

17. Using the materials developed in this first inexpensive, rough draft, you are ready to begin evaluation activities. Chapter 9 introduces and discusses procedures and activities for evaluating and revising instructional materials.

18. You may either develop materials for the instructor's manual as you go along, or you can take notes as you develop and revise the instructional presentations and activities. Using the notes, you can write the instructor's guide. If you wait until the end to complete the instructor's manual, you will surely want to design the manual and determine what types of information, suggestions, and tests you will want to include in it. By designing the manual early, you will know what information to collect and procedures to note to be included in the manual.

Output

The product you have as a result of your materials development is a set of draft materials.

We need to caution you on one important point: Do not feel that what you develop on the first attempt will stand for all time. It is extremely important that you consider the materials you develop as draft materials. These are materials that will be reviewed and revised based on feedback from students, instructors, and subject-matter experts. You should not begin engaging in elaborate and expensive production procedures. You *should* be considering the use of 3-by-5-inch cards instead of finely printed materials; the use of pictures as opposed to filmstrips; the use of videotapes as opposed to films. Delay the development of any mediated materials, particularly ones which will be expensive, until you have completed at least one revision of the instructional materials.

You can be assured that no matter how humble your materials may be at this point, there will be costs associated with them. Try to minimize the costs now in order to gather the data that you will need to make the correct decisions about the final version. We will have more to say about this in succeeding chapters.

REFERENCES

Briggs, L. J. *Handbook of procedures for the design of instruction.* Pittsburgh: American Institutes for Research, 1970, 93-162.

    The author provides a detailed procedure, with examples, for selecting appropriate media for learning outcomes.

Espich, J. E., & Williams, B. *Developing programmed instructional materials.* Palo Alto, Calif.: Fearon Publishers, 1967, 37-98.

    This reading describes various procedures which are used to develop effective programmed instruction materials. These procedures can also be used to develop an effective module.

Gagné, R. M. *Essentials of learning for instruction.* Hinsdale, Ill.: Dryden Press, 1974, 71-96.

    The conditions of learning are related to the types of learning outcomes which are desired.

Johnson, S. R., & Johnson, R. B. *Developing individualized instructional material.* Palo Alto, Calif.: Westinghouse Learning Press, 1970.

Russell, J. D. *Modular instruction.* Minneapolis: Burgess Publishing Co., 1974.

    This volume and the one just cited outline procedures which should be used in the systematic design of instruction. They present an orientation that differs somewhat from ours.

9 Designing and Conducting Formative Evaluations

OBJECTIVES

1. *You will be able to describe the purposes for and various stages of formative evaluation of instructor-developed materials, selected materials, and instructor-presented instruction.*

2. *You will be able to describe the instruments used in a formative evaluation.*

3. *You will be able to develop an appropriate formative evaluation plan and to construct instruments for a set of instructional materials or instructor presentation.*

4. *You will be able to collect data according to a formative evaluation plan concerning the effectiveness of a given set of instructional materials or instructor presentation.*

BACKGROUND

If you had been developing instructional materials ten to fifteen years ago, it is likely that your draft of those materials would have been put into final production and distributed to the target population. As a consequence, it is likely that many problems would occur in the classroom due to the limited effectiveness of instructional materials. Too often instructors and students have been blamed for poor learning when in fact the materials were insufficient to support the instructional effort.

The problem of untested materials was magnified in the 1960s with the advent of large curriculum development projects. At that time the concept of "evaluation" was defined as the determination of the effectiveness of a new product as compared with other existing products. When such studies were carried out, researchers often found a relatively low level of student achievement with the new curriculum materials. In reviewing this situation, Cronbach and Scriven concluded that we must expand our concept of evaluation. They proposed that developers conduct what has come to be called "formative evaluation"—gathering data on the effectiveness of instructional materials that provide feedback to the developer prior to final distribution of the materials.

Recent studies have shown that thousands of instructional products are distributed in the United States each year which have not been evaluated or revised prior to distribution. Other studies have demonstrated that simply trying out materials with a single learner and revising the materials on the basis of that data can make a significant difference in the effectiveness of materials. Therefore, this component of the instructional design model emphasizes the necessity of gathering data from members of the target population on the effectiveness of materials and using that information to make the materials more effective. You should note that all of the design and development concepts in the instructional design model are based upon theory, research, and some common sense. At this point, you are about to become a researcher in the sense that you will be collecting data about the effectiveness of your own instructional materials. Through the use of the instructional design model, you have, in essence, generated a hypothesis that states your instructional materials will produce significant learning gains for students who initially cannot perform your terminal objective. You are now at the point of testing that hypothesis.

A rather arbitrary partitioning of content has been made between this chapter and the next. Typically we think about formative evaluation and revision of instructional materials as one major step. However, for the sake of clarity of content presentation, and to emphasize the importance of re-examining the whole instructional design process when instructional materials are to be revised, we have separated the design and conduct of the formative evaluation study from the process of revising the instructional materials.

In this chapter we will discuss how to apply formative evaluation techniques to originally designed materials, to selected and adapted materials, to instructor-delivered instruction, and to combinations of these three presentation modes. We will also note how to apply these techniques to instructional procedures as well as to instructional materials to ensure that instruction, regardless of the presentation mode, is properly implemented and managed.

CONCEPTS

The major concept associated with this chapter is *formative evaluation.* Formative evaluation is the process used to obtain data for instructors to use to increase the efficiency and effectiveness of their instructional materials. The emphasis in formative evaluation is on the collection of data in order to *revise* the instructional materials, to make the materials as effective as possible. When they reach a final version, other people may collect data to determine whether the materials should be used in a particular setting or whether they are as effective as claimed. This latter type of evaluation is often referred to as *summative evaluation.*

There are three stages of formative evaluation. The first is *one-to-one* or clinical evaluation. In this initial phase the designer works with individual students to obtain data to revise the materials. The second stage of formative evaluation is a *small-group* evaluation. A group of ten to twenty students who are representative of the target population study the materials in an *approximate* "real-life" setting to collect the required data. The third stage of formative evaluation is usually referred to as a *field evaluation*. The number of students is not of particular consequence; often thirty are sufficient. The emphasis in the field evaluation is on the testing of the procedures required for the installation of the instruction in as real a situation as is possible. We will describe these three phases of formative evaluation in some detail.

One-to-One Evaluation

The first type of evaluation conducted by the instructor following the development of a draft set of the instructional materials is one-to-one. The term *one-to-one* refers to the fact that, at this stage in the evaluation, the instructor selects two or more students who are typical of the target population and actually sits at their side as each studies the materials.

Only the test and instructional materials are used with the student. The designer should pick at least one student from the target population who is slightly above average in general ability and at least one student who is below average, and work on an individual basis with each. After these evaluations the designer may wish to select more students from the target population to work in a one-to-one mode, although two is the minimum number of students to use.

The typical procedure in a one-to-one evaluation is to explain to the student that you are designing a new set of instructional materials and that you would like his or her reaction to them. You should say that any mistakes which students might make are probably due to deficiencies in the materials and not theirs. Encourage students to be relaxed and to talk about the materials. You should not only have the students go through the materials, but also have them take the test(s) provided with the materials. You might also note the amount of time it takes a student to complete the material.

Instructional designers have found this process to be invaluable in the preparation of materials. When students use the materials in this manner, they find typographical errors, omissions of content, missing pages, graphs that are improperly labeled, and other kinds of mechanical difficulties which will inevitably occur. Students are often able to describe difficulties they have with the learning sequence and the concepts being taught. They can critique the tests in terms of whether they think they measure your objectives. You can use all this information to revise your materials, both instruction and tests, through the correction of relatively gross problems as well as small errors.

You should avoid placing much importance on any posttest results that you obtain with the one-to-one evaluation method, because the score will obviously be the result of the teaching ability of both the materials and your own personal interventions with the learner. The score only indicates the best possible results you may obtain with this particular combination of learning resources. Similarly, the time required for the student to complete the material may be much longer than when the designer is absent.

Another possible source for one-to-one formative evaluation of your materials is the content expert. Content experts can often provide feedback information that you might otherwise overlook.

Small-Group Evaluation

After you have revised the materials on the basis of information obtained from the one-to-one evaluation, you should next select a group of approximately ten to twenty students. This number is not selected entirely arbitrarily. If the number of students is less than ten, then the data which you obtain will not be representative of the target population. On the other hand, if you obtain data on many more than twenty students, you will find that you have more information than you need, and that the data from additional students will not provide you with a great deal of additional information for careful evaluation and analysis in a small-group setting.

The selection of students to participate in your small group trial is a very important procedure. The students used to evaluate the materials should be as representative of your total target population as possible. In an ideal research setting, you would select the students randomly. This would ensure the generalizability of your findings to the entire target population. In real school, industrial and adult education, however, true randomization is often impossible.

When you cannot completely randomize your sample group, or when the group you have available to draw from is relatively small, you want to ensure that you include in your sample at least one representative of each type of subgroup that exists in your population. Examples of such subgroups might include (a) low-, average-, and high-achievement students; (b) students with various native languages; (c) students who are familiar with a particular procedure, such as computerized instruction, and students who are not; (d) boys and girls; and (e) younger or inexperienced learners as well as more mature learners. When your target group is homogeneous, then these subgroups are not a problem. When the target population is made up of persons with varied skills and backgrounds, however, then the designer must include representatives of each group in the small-group sample. For example, it is almost impossible to predict how a high-achievement student will perform on your materials based on the observed efforts of a low-achievement student. By selecting a representative target sample, you will be able to be more insightful about changes you may need to make in your instruction.

Small-group selections often reflect bias because they are the product of people who willingly participate in the group instead of being people who truly are a representative group. The instructor must be aware of this problem and obtain the most representative group possible, considering all the constraints usually present in obtaining participants for sample-group trials.

It is also important to note that while this stage is referred to as "small-group evaluation," the term refers to the number of students and not the setting in which the student actually uses the materials. For example, if your materials are intended for individual use at home or on the job, then you would attempt to obtain ten to twenty students who would use your materials in these settings. It is not necessary to get all the students together in one room at one time to conduct a small-group evaluation.

The basic procedures used in a small-group evaluation differ sharply from those used in a one-to-one. The evaluator (or the instructor) begins by explaining that the materials are in the formative stage of development and that it is necessary to obtain feedback on how they may be improved. Having said this, the instructor then administers the materials in the manner they are intended to be used when they are in final form. If an entry-behaviors test or a pretest is to be used, it should also be given. The students then study the instructional materials and all resources which are available to them and take the posttest after they complete the materials. The instructor should intervene as little as possible in the process. Only in those cases when equipment fails or when a student becomes bogged down in the learning process and cannot continue should the instructor intervene. The difficulty and the solution should certainly be noted as part of the revision data.

Additional steps in small group evaluation are the administration of an attitude questionnaire and, if possible, in-depth discussions with some of the students in the test group. The primary purpose for obtaining student reactions to the instruction is to identify, from their perceptions, weaknesses and strengths in the *implementation* of the instructional strategy. Therefore, the questions should reflect various components of the strategy. The following questions would usually be appropriate:

1. Was the instruction interesting?
2. Did you understand what you were supposed to learn?
3. Were the materials directly related to the stated objectives?
4. Were sufficient practice exercises included?
5. Were practice exercises appropriate?
6. Did the tests really measure your performance on the stated objectives?
7. Did you receive sufficient feedback on your practice exercises?

8. Did you receive sufficient feedback on your test results?
9. Were enrichment or remedial materials satisfactory?

These questions might be included in an attitude questionnaire, and then pursued at some depth in a discussion with students. By using questions directed at actual parts of the instructional strategy, such as those described above, it is possible to relate the students' responses directly to particular components of the instructional materials or procedures.

In the discussion with the student after the materials have been finished, the instructor can ask all types of questions about the pacing, interest, and difficulty of the materials. By providing cues to the student, the instructor may obtain a great deal of information about the relative effectiveness of the materials and areas of misinterpretation.

All the data from these various sources are summarized and decisions are made as to how to revise the materials. In the next chapter, we will show you how to summarize these data and determine the implications they have for the revision process. In this chapter, we will narrow our concern to the design of the formative evaluation study and the collection of data.

Field Evaluation

In the final stage of formative evaluation the instructor attempts to obtain a learning situation which is, or closely resembles that, intended for the instructional materials. All the materials, including tests and teacher's manual, should be revised and ready to go. If an instructor is involved in implementing the instruction, the designer should not play this role.

In picking the site for a field evaluation, you are likely to encounter one of two situations. First, if the material is tried out in the class which is presently using large-group, lockstep pacing, then using self-instructional materials may be a very new and different experience for the students. It will be important to lay the groundwork for the new procedures by explaining to students how the material is to be used and how it differs from their usual instruction. In all likelihood you will obtain an increase in interest, if not in performance, simply because of the break in the typical classroom instructional pattern. This is commonly called the "halo effect."

Second, if the materials are tried out in an individualized class, it may be quite difficult to find a large enough group of students who are ready for your instructional materials because students will be "spread out" in the materials they are studying. You do eliminate the possible halo effect in such a setting, however, and these students will be familiar with the type of materials you will be testing.

You should select a group of about thirty individuals to participate in your field trial. Again, the group selected should be selected in a manner to ensure that it is representative of the target population for which the materials are intended. Because a "typical" group is sometimes hard to locate, designers often include several different groups to participate in their field trial. This ensures they will obtain data on their materials under all intended conditions such as open classroom, traditional instruction, learning center, and so forth. Data obtained in a traditional classroom setting are difficult to generalize to a learning center setting.

Formative Evaluation of Selected Materials

The three phases of formative evaluation previously described are not totally applicable when the instructor has selected existing materials for tryout with a group of students. The kinds of editorial and content changes which are made as a result of one-to-one and small-group evaluations are typically not used when one uses existing materials. These procedures are avoided not because they would be unproductive in improving the instruction, but because in reality the instructor who selects existing materials seldom has the time or resources to conduct these phases. Therefore, the instructor should proceed directly to a field trial with a group of students. The primary purpose of formative evaluation with existing materials is to determine whether they are effective with a particular population, and to identify ways in which additions to or deletions from the materials or changes in instructional procedures might be made to improve the effectiveness of the materials. Therefore, the formative evaluation procedures for selected materials most nearly resemble those used in a field evaluation.

Preparations for the field evaluation of existing materials should be made as they would be for a field evaluation of original materials. An analysis should be made of existing documentation on the development of the materials, the effectiveness of materials with defined groups, and particularly any description of procedures used during field evaluations. Descriptions of how the materials are to be used should be studied, and any test instruments that accompany the materials should be examined for their relationship to the performance objectives. It should be determined if additional evaluations or attitude questionnaires are needed.

In the field evaluation study, the instructor should administer the entry-behavior test unless he or she knows that students already have these behaviors. The pretest should also be administered unless the instructor is certain that students lack this knowledge. A posttest and an attitude questionnaire should certainly be available to evaluate students' performance and their opinions of the materials.

The instructor who conducts a field evaluation is able to observe the progress and attitudes of students using a set of adopted or adapted materials. It is even possible to examine the performance of different groups of students using modified or unmodified materials to determine whether the changes increased the effectiveness of materials. The instructor should certainly take the time following the field evaluation to thoroughly debrief the students on their reactions to the instruction. Additional insights about materials or procedures used can be gained during debriefing sessions. After completing a field evaluation of selected materials, the instructor should have collected approximately the same types of data that would have been collected if original materials were being formatively evaluated.

Formative Evaluation of Instructor-Presented Instruction

If the instructor plans to deliver instruction according to the instructional strategy and a set of lecture notes, the purposes of formative evaluations are much the same as they are for the formative evaluation of independent instructional materials: The main purpose is to determine if all the instruction is effective and how to improve it further. Once again, the formative evaluation of an instructional plan most nearly approximates that of the field evaluation phase for instructional materials. In all likelihood, there will be little time for a one-to-one or even a small-group evaluation of a total lesson plan, and both will usually prove of little value.

In preparing for a field evaluation of instructor-presented instruction, the instructor should be concerned with the entry behaviors, the pretest knowledge, the posttest knowledge, and the attitudes of students. In addition, the instructor is in a unique position to provide interactive practice and feedback. Interactive practice and feedback should be included in the instructional plan, and will provide students with the opportunity to demonstrate specific skills they have acquired. These sessions also serve to identify those skills not yet acquired. This form of in-progress practice and assessment may be administered in one of two formats. It may be delivered orally by the instructor to a variety of students, and notes kept on students' performances. An alternative format is one in which various printed practice and feedback exercises are distributed periodically during the lesson. This latter approach provides concrete evidence of the students' learning as they progress.

The instructor can also use the field trial as an opportunity to evaluate the instructional procedures. Observation of the instructional process should indicate the suitability of grouping patterns, time allocations, and student interest in various class activities.

Many instructors already use these types of formative evaluation in their instruction. Our point is to stress that you thoroughly and systematically use these techniques to collect data to analyze and revise the lesson plan. To identify weak points in the lesson plan, and to provide clues to their correction, in-progress data can be compared to results obtained with the posttest, attitude questionnaire, and students' comments during debriefing sessions.

Very often, field testing of selected materials and the field testing of instructor-presented instruction are interwoven. Frequently, the use of selected materials will require an interactive role for the teacher and, likewise, the implementation of an instructional strategy may well involve the use of some prepared instructional materials. Therefore, under either of these circumstances, approximately the same types of field evaluation procedures should be employed and similar types of revisions carried out.

Data Collection

Here are some general guidelines that you should consider when planning the procedures for any stage of formative evaluation. The most important is that you gather all the data which you believe will help you make decisions about improving instruction. Any data which cannot stand up to this test, that is, data whose interpretation could not suggest ways the materials might be revised, should not be collected because they will be of only limited use to you, and may interfere with the collection of data you really need.

The types of data you will probably want to collect include the following:

1. Test data collected on entry behaviors, pretests, posttests and embedded tests. (The latter, embedded test data, is often overlooked as a rich source of information about students' performance.)
2. Comments or notations made by students to you or marked on the instructional materials about difficulties encountered at particular points in the materials.
3. Attitude questionnaires and/or debriefing comments in which students reveal their overall reactions to the instruction and their perceptions of where difficulties lie with the materials and instructional procedures in general.
4. Reactions of a subject-matter specialist are often appropriate. Provide the instructional materials to a person who is an acknowledged subject-matter expert in the area of the materials. It is the responsibility of this person to verify that the content of the module is accurate and current. You should be aware that the subject-matter expert may wish to critique the format or the general instructional strategy which you are employing. Our experience indicates that such suggestions often prove detrimental to the teaching effectiveness of the materials. Therefore, while the subject-matter expert may offer these kinds of comments, you should act upon them only after a great deal of consideration and perhaps additional formative testing.

The formative evaluation component in the instructional design model is what distinguishes this empirical procedure from a philosophical or theoretical approach. Rather than speculating about the instructional effectiveness of your materials, you will be testing them out with students. Therefore, you will want to do the best possible job of collecting data that truly reflects the effectiveness of your materials. There are several concerns the instructor should keep in mind when planning and implementing data collection procedures.

One concern in any evaluation of your materials is to ensure that the technical equipment is operating effectively. More than one instructor has been discouraged because when a new set of instructional materials was tried on a particular piece of equipment, the equipment failed to operate correctly. Therefore, the data from students was invalidated, and the instructor learned little more than that you need to have the audiovisual equipment operating effectively to try out materials.

It is also important that in the early stages of formative evaluation, especially in the one-to-one, that you work with students in a quiet setting—one in which you can command their full attention. At this point you are concerned about how the materials will work under the best possible conditions. As you move to the small-group and field evaluations you are increasingly concerned with how the materials will work under more normal settings. If the normal setting is an individualized classroom that has a relatively high noise level, then you will want to know if the materials work in that situation. But, you should not begin the formative evaluation under these conditions.

Another concern is the explanation which you provide to students who are participating in a formative evaluation. You will find that they are unaccustomed to criticizing instructional materials. They have been trained to believe that materials are correct, accurate, and effective, and if learning does not take place, it is the fault of the learner or the instructor or possibly both. You may find that you need to establish good rapport with students and encourage them to respond to derive critical information from the formative evaluation process. Do not take for granted that students are trained and accustomed to working in this type of setting.

Another caution with regard to the selection of students for participation in field studies is to avoid depending entirely upon the instructor to assess entry knowledge of the students. Whenever possible, administer entry-behavior tests or pretests to students to verify that they are in fact members of the target population for whom the materials are intended. Experience has shown that instructors, for whatever reason, make poor estimates of the readiness of students who are recommended for participation in formative evaluation studies.

A final word of caution: Be prepared to receive information that indicates that your materials are not as effective as you thought they would be after going through such an extensive instructional design process. It is common to become tremendously involved when putting a great deal of time and effort into any kind of project. It is just as common to be sharply disappointed when you find that your efforts have not been entirely satisfactory.

However, you should note that in the formative evaluation process, positive feedback from students provides you with little information about how you might proceed to change anything. Positive feedback only indicates that what you have is effective with the students who used the materials. You can then only make the limited inference that the materials would be effective with students who are of similar ability and motivation.

As you move through the formative evaluation process, it might be helpful to pretend that the materials were developed by another instructor and that you are merely carrying out the formative evaluation for that person. We do not suggest that you lie to the students about it, but rather that you adopt this noninvolved psychological set in order to listen to what students, instructors, and subject-matter experts might say. These kinds of feedback must be integrated into an objective assessment to the extent to which your materials are meeting the objectives you have set for them.

Data Collection for Selected Materials
and Instructor-Presented Instruction

Much of the information dealing with the collection of data in field evaluation of original instructional materials applies equally well to the data-collecting procedures used in the evaluation of selected materials and instructional procedures. For example, it is critically important that any equipment to be used during instruction be in good running order, and that the environment in which the field evaluation is conducted be conducive to learning.

When an instructor evaluates original materials, selected materials, or instructor-presented instruction, existing rapport with students can be a great advantage. It is important during the evaluation of materials and lessons that students understand the purpose of the evaluations and their role in them. They need to understand the critical nature of their participation in, and contributions to, the study. The instructor, in working with familiar students, also has knowledge of the students' entry behavior and, quite possibly, is able to predict accurately the pretest performance of students. However, the instructor should avoid relying entirely on such predictions. If there is any doubt at all concerning the students' performances, the students should be tested to verify the need for instruction in specified skills.

When the instructor selects materials to implement an instructional strategy, a number of unique concerns arise. Information can be gathered about these concerns by observation and the use of questionnaires. The major question will be, "Did the instruction have unity?" To answer this question, the instructor should determine the adequacy of the student guide in directing students to various resources. Redundancy and gaps in the instructional materials should be noted. Was sufficient repetition and review built into the strategy? If the instructor is presenting the instruction, events which reflect the same types of problems should be noted as the presentation progresses. The types of questions raised by students will provide a key to the strategy's inadequacies.

A final comment should be made about the psychological aspects of the field evaluations and instructor-presented instruction. While instructors may be completely unbiased about materials developed by someone else, it is difficult to avoid personal involvement in materials they have created, adapted, or prepared. The same applies to the actual delivery of instruction. If a field evaluation is to have any real significance for improving existing instruction, instructors must be prepared to accept, and even solicit, negative feedback. They must be prepared for the worst, but hope for the best!

EXAMPLES

The illustration below includes information you can use for planning a one-to-one, a small-group, and a field evaluation for instruction. While looking through these suggested procedures, assume you know your intended target population, but you are unsure whether they possess the required entry behaviors. The examples below are not offered as the only activities you should pursue in formative evaluation, but rather as a list of suggestions you can use to begin thinking about your own project. You may be able to identify other activities for your project.

Formative Evaluation Activities

I. **One-to-One Testing**
   A. Participation by students from the target population
      1. Identify students that are typical of those you believe will be found in the target population. (Include each type of student that can be found in the target population.)
      2. Arrange for the student(s) to participate.
      3. Discuss the process of a one-to-one test with the student.
      4. Evaluate the test you have constructed to measure entry behaviors.
         a. Can the student read the directions?
         b. Does the student understand the problems?
         c. Does the student have the required prerequisite skills?
      5. Sit with the student while he or she goes through the materials.
         a. Instruct the student to write on the materials to indicate where difficulty is encountered or to discuss verbally ideas and problems.
         b. If the student fails to understand an example, try another verbal example. Does this clarify the issue? Note in writing the changes and suggestions you make as you go through the materials.
         c. If the student fails to understand an explanation, elaborate by adding information or changing the order of presentation. Does this clarify the issue? Note the changes you make in writing.
         d. If the student appears to be bored or confused while going through the materials, you may want to change the presentation to include larger or smaller bits of information before practice and feedback. Record your ideas concerning the regrouping of materials as you go along.
         e. Keep notes on examples, illustrations, information you add, and changes in sequence during the evaluation process. Otherwise, you may forget an important decision or idea. Note taking should be quick and in rough form so the student is not distracted from the materials. Even changes that seem trivial should be included in a one-to-one evaluation report.
      6. You may choose to test another student from the target population before you make any changes or revisions in your materials in order to verify that the changes are necessary. If errors pointed out by your student "consultant" are obvious, you may want to

make revisions before testing the next student both to save testing time and to enable the next student to concentrate on other problems that may exist in the materials.

B. Participation by subject-matter experts
    1. You should provide the expert with (a) the instructional analysis, (b) behaviorally stated objectives, (c) the intended instruction, and (d) the tests. These materials should be in rough form, because major revisions could well be the outcome of this one-to-one testing. You may want to present your materials in the order described above.
    2. You should be looking for verification of the (a) objective statements; (b) instructional analysis; (c) accuracy and currency of the content; (d) appropriateness of the instructional materials in vocabulary, interest, sequence, chunk size, and student-participation activities; (e) clarity and appropriateness of test items and test situations; and (f) placement of this piece of instruction relative to prior instruction and follow-through instruction.
    3. The number of subject-matter experts you should approach for assistance will vary with the complexity of the information and skills covered in your materials. For some instruction, one expert will be sufficient while for others four may still seem inadequate. The nature of the teaching task will dictate the number and type of expert consultants you will need.

C. Outcomes of one-to-one formative evaluation
    1. Consider again the types of information you are looking for in the one-to-one testing. They include:
        a. Errors in judgment about entry behaviors of students in the target population
        b. Faulty instructional analysis
        c. Faulty wording or unclear passages
        d. Inadequate information presentation
           1) unclear examples
           2) examples or graphs which are too abstract
           3) too much or too little information at one time
           4) wrong sequence of information presented
        e. Unclear test questions, test situations, or test directions
        f. Unclear or inappropriate objectives and expected outcomes

II. Small-Group Testing
A. Participation by students from the target population
    1. Identify a small group of students that typifies your target population.
    2. Arrange for a student sample to participate.
        a. Adequate time should be arranged for required testing as well as instructional activities.

b. Students should be motivated to participate.

c. Students should be selected to represent the range of students expected in the target population. If a broad range of students is expected, you may want to include several students from each expected category in your sample.

3. During students' participation in the pretest, instruction, and post-test, you may want to make notes about suggestions for instructors who will use the materials or about changes you want to make in the instruction or procedures as a result of your observation of students interacting with the materials.

4. Administer the test of required entry behaviors if one is appropriate.

a. Check the directions, response patterns, and questions to ensure the wording is clear.

b. Instruct students to circle words they do not understand and place a check beside questions or directions that are unclear.

c. Do not stop and discuss unclear items with students during the test.

d. Record the time required for students to complete the entry test.

5. Administer the pretest of skills to be taught during instruction. This test and the test of required entry behaviors could be combined into one test if desirable.

a. Have students circle any vocabulary which is unclear to them.

b. Have students place a check beside any directions, questions, or response requirements that are unclear to them.

c. Have students write additional comments in the test if they desire.

d. Do not discuss problems during the test with students.

6. Administer the instructional materials. Have the instructional setting as close to reality as possible with all required equipment and materials present. Any instructional assistance required should also be available during the trial.

a. Train the needed instructional personnel to use the materials in the intended manner.

b. Instruct students whose help you will need in evaluating the materials.

c. Have students sign their work so you can compare their performance on the lesson with your expectancies of their performance based on their entry behaviors.

d. Instruct students to circle any unclear words and place a check beside any illustrations, examples, or explanations that are unclear in the instruction. Students should keep working through the materials to the end without stopping for discussions.

e. Record the time required for students to complete the instructional materials. Time required may be distorted if students require instruction on unfamiliar equipment or procedures.

7. Administer the posttest.
   a. Have students sign their posttest to enable comparisons with the pretest and embedded tests.
   b. Have students circle any unclear vocabulary and place a check beside any unclear directions, questions, or response requirements.
   c. Have students respond to as many items as they can whether they are sure of the answer or whether they are just guessing. Often incorrect guesses can provide clues to inadequate instruction. You may want them to indicate which answers elicited guessing.
   d. Record the time required for students to complete the posttest.
8. Administer an attitude questionnaire to students and/or to instructors administering the materials.
   a. You may want to ask questions like:
      1) Was the instruction too long or too short?
      2) Was the instruction too difficult or too easy?
      3) Did you have problems with any sections or parts of the instruction?
      4) Were the cartoons or illustrations appropriate or distracting?
      5) Was the use of color appealing or distracting?
      6) What did you like most?
      7) What did you like least?
      8) How would you change the instruction if you could?
      9) Did the tests measure the material that was presented?
      10) Would you prefer another medium?
9. Arrange for students to discuss the pretest, instruction, and/or posttest with you or their teacher after they have completed all the work.
   a. You may want to structure the discussion with planned questions.
   b. You may want to ask questions like, "Would you change the exercises in section X?" or, "Did you like the example in section X?"

III. Field Testing

A. Select an appropriate sample from the target population.
   1. Arrange for the selected group to try the materials.
      a. Ensure that there is an adequate number of students in the group. Thirty is an often-suggested number of students to participate in a field trial.
      b. Ensure that selected students reflect the range of abilities and skills of students in the target population.

      c. Ensure that there are adequate personnel, facilities, and equipment available for the trial.

  2. Distribute the instructional materials as well as the instructor's guide, if it is available, to the instructor conducting the field test.

  3. Discuss any instructions or special considerations which may be needed if the instruction is out of context.

  4. Stay away from the testing situation yourself as much as possible.

  5. Summarize the data you have collected. Summarized data may include (a) the report on the entry-behavior test, (b) the report on pretest and posttest scores, (c) the report on the time required for students to complete each test used, (d) the report on the time required for students to complete the instruction, (e) any remediation or enrichment needs that become apparent, (f) the report on the attitude survey for students as well as participating instructors, if possible.

IV. **Formative Evaluation of Selected Materials and Instructor-Delivered Instruction**

  A. Selected materials
      In addition to the formative suggestions for originally developed instruction, you should determine whether:

    1. All parts of the instructional strategy are accounted for in the selected materials or provided by the instructor.

    2. The transitions between sources are smooth.

    3. The flow of content in the various instructional resources is consistent and logical.

    4. The instructional manual or instructor adequately presents objectives.

    5. Directions for locating instruction within each source are adequate.

    6. Sections of the instructional strategy which must be supplied by the instructor are adequate.

    7. The vocabulary used in all the sources is appropriate.

    8. The illustrations and examples used are appropriate for the target group.

  B. Instructor-delivered instruction
      A major factor in evaluating instruction that you actually deliver yourself is that you are an interactive part of the instruction. Therefore, in addition to all the considerations we have mentioned previously, there are several important evaluation considerations unique to this type of instruction. You should determine whether:

    1. You are convincing, enthusiastic, helpful, and knowledgeable.

    2. You are able to avoid digressions to keep instruction and discussions on relevant topics and on schedule.

    3. You lecture in an interesting, clear manner.

    4. You use the chalkboard and other visual aids to help with examples and illustrations.

5. You provide good feedback to students' questions.
6. You provide adequate practice exercises and good feedback.
7. You record events that occur during instruction so that you can study them for what they imply about the effectiveness of instruction.

PRACTICE AND FEEDBACK

Practice

The following exercises are based on the instructional analysis of reading Roman numerals in Chapter 7. Again, the target population is sixth-grade students of varying math knowledge and skills. Below, for each type of formative evaluation (one-to-one, small-group, and field trial), you are to consider the questions and to determine decisions you would make based on the purpose for the evaluation, the nature of the instruction, and the target population.

I. **One-to-One Testing**
   1. Describe how many sixth-grade students you would select for a one-to-one evaluation of the Roman numerals instruction and explain why you included each student in your sample.
   2. Describe the kinds of information you would be seeking during the one-to-one evaluation with sixth-graders.
   3. Describe the appearance (typed, rough copy, polished copy, etc.) of your materials for one-to-one evaluation.

II. **Small-Group Testing**
   1. Describe the number and the achievement level of students that you would include in your small-group trial.
   2. Describe how you would determine whether one small-group evaluation session was sufficient.
   3. Describe the materials (level of completeness, rough copy, polished copy, etc.) you would use for a small-group evaluation session.
   4. Describe the information you would record to help evaluate the instruction on Roman numerals for sixth-grade students with varying backgrounds and levels of achievement.

III. **Field Evaluation**
   1. Why would you be interested in a field evaluation of the materials?
   2. What information would you collect during the field evaluation that you would not have collected during the small-group testing session?
   3. Describe an appropriate population and instructional setting that could be used to field evaluate the materials on interpreting Roman numerals.
   4. What materials would you include in the field evaluation?

IV. Formative Evaluation of Selected Materials and Instructor-Presented Instruction

1. How would your procedures differ if you were conducting a field evaluation of adapted or adopted materials, rather than a set of "original" materials?
2. Describe the major procedural differences between the field evaluation of selected materials and the field evaluation of instructor-implemented instruction and instructional management.

Feedback

I. One-to-One Evaluation

1. The exact number of students selected for one-to-one evaluation is arbitrary. The sample should include at least two students from different levels of arithmetic achievement in the sixth grade. If there are two, three, or four levels, then there should be at least one student from each of the levels. Should you discover that the instruction is inappropriate for the lowest achievers, you will need to decide whether to adapt the instruction to include these students, or to be more specific about required entry skills rather than reviewing entry skills.

   Students of average achievement should be included to check vocabulary, problem difficulty level, pacing, entry skills, clarity of examples, exercises, and feedback. Branching requirements could also be checked.

   You should also include high-achievement-level students to determine whether (a) some sections can be skipped, (b) examples are clear and exercises are challenging but clear, (c) exercises and feedback are appropriate, and (d) branching to enrichment materials is advisable. These students could help determine whether selected practice or enrichment activities appear to students to be interesting or busy work.

2. Types of information you should obtain during the one-to-one evaluation are:
   a. Can the student perform all the arithmetic skills identified in the entry-behaviors analysis?
   b. What review is necessary in entry behaviors?
   c. What instruction is necessary in entry behaviors?
   d. What skills from the instruction do the students already possess?
   e. Do the instructional materials provide adequate:
      1) vocabulary
      2) pacing
      3) size "chunk"
      4) clarity of descriptions
      5) clarity of examples
      6) adequacy of sequence of content and activities

7) interest level of exercises

8) student performance on embedded exercises

9) clarity of feedback information

10) motivation

f. Are the test instructions, vocabulary, questions, and response expectations clear to the students?

g. Are the objectives clear to the student, and do students understand why they are learning to interpret Roman numerals?

3. The appearance of materials is again arbitrary and rests on the judgment of the instructor. A set of materials to teach the interpretation of Roman numerals may consist of loose pages of instruction with directions typed and illustrations hand drawn.

Each new idea and any required student responses should be placed on one page, and feedback on a separate page. This way sequences can be changed easily. Another benefit of grouping instruction and student performances for one concept together is that it will help pinpoint concepts which have been inadequately explained or examples, illustrations, and feedback that confuse rather than clarify an idea.

Illustrations, graphs, and figures should be "roughed in" because students will "see" the idea whether you have stick figures or artistically drawn Romans.

Students should be encouraged to write on the materials (embedded questions, practice exercises), to circle unclear words, and place a check by unclear parts. Therefore, you will need as many copies of materials as students you intend to sample plus extra copies on which to tally your results and make revisions.

II. **Small-Group Evaluation**

1. You should include at least three or four students from each expected achievement level in your sample. This will help you avoid the error of assuming that all students at a particular achievement level will respond in the same manner. It will give you a basis for comparing students' responses who are at various achievement levels. Information of this type will help you determine the adequacy of remedial, review, and enrichment materials as well as the adequacy of the basic instruction for the entire target population. As a guideline you should have at least eight students, and probably not more than twenty.

2. One session of small-group evaluation may not be enough. A good way to judge is to consider the amount and types of revisions made in the materials as a result of the previous evaluation. If very few, slight revisions are made and you believe that similar students would react the same way to the instruction, then continued evaluation is not necessary. If, however, you make several revisions as a result of the previous evaluation, you will need another small-group session to

evaluate your new version of the materials. Some of your decisions may be improvements; others may not.

3. Your materials must be developed to the appropriate level of sophistication. If the lesson is to be on the computer, then it should be on the computer for the small-group evaluation. Problems resulting from the medium itself cannot be detected unless the instruction appears on that medium. If the instruction is a slide-tape and students are not allowed enough time to study the slide, this error will appear either in their performance test or on the attitude questionnaire.

Whether you chose computer-assisted instruction or individualized booklets to teach Roman numeral interpretation, you should have the materials plus instructions and directions for participating students as well as instructional assistants that might be required in either a classroom or a learning center. Tests used prior to and after instruction should also be complete and tested in their intended format.

If possible, the instructor's guide should be complete and tested at this time and necessary revisions could be made before the field evaluation. Information from the field evaluation session will probably be included in the information section of the teacher's guide, but it will be necessary to evaluate the clarity of instructions and suggestions for using the materials.

4. After the small-group evaluation, you may want to summarize the various types of information for the following groups:
   a. Divide the sample into low, average, and above-average achievement students.
   b. Record their responses on the pretest to:
      1) performance on each of the required entry skills 1 through 9.
      2) performance on each subskill required to reach the terminal objective.
      3) tally any vocabulary words circled as unclear.
      4) tally any questions checked as unclear.
      5) tally directions marked as unclear.
   c. Record their responses in the instructional package:
      1) tally any explanations marked unclear.
      2) tally any examples and illustrations marked unclear.
      3) tally vocabulary words circled or marked unclear.
      4) tally students' responses to embedded questions—both correct and incorrect.
      5) tally any feedback sections students mark as unclear.
      6) tally all students' comments directly on a blank form of the instructional materials.

d. Record their responses on the posttest.
   1) tally correct and incorrect answers.
   2) tally any questions marked unclear.
   3) tally any directions marked unclear.
   4) tally any response requirements marked unclear.
   5) tally any vocabulary circled or marked unclear.
e. Record time required for pretest, instruction, and posttest activities.

III. Field Evaluation

1. Materials are field tested to demonstrate their effectiveness on the specified target population when used under specified conditions. Field evaluation answers the question, "Do these materials actually work for given students?" It helps determine the instructional effectiveness of the materials in the absence of coaching by an instructor. It also aids in determining whether the materials are actually ready for use. The materials, tests, and instructions for both students and teachers should be examined during the field evaluation. Have the materials had enough revision, or is more revision required? Revision at this point can be either in the materials themselves or in suggestions for using the materials.

2. You would probably want to collect all the information which was collected during the small-group evaluation. Other information might include students' attitudes concerning (a) their interest in the instruction; (b) whether they thought instruction was too easy, too difficult, or just right; (c) whether they thought instruction was too fast, too slow, or just right; and (d) whether they thought the materials were easy to use or too complicated.

   You might also want to include instructors' attitudinal information about whether the materials are easy to use, complicated, or just right and why the instructors hold these opinions.

3. An appropriate population to field test the instruction on Roman numerals would be a regular sixth-grade class that includes above-average, average, and below-average achievers in arithmetic, a class of approximately twenty-five to thirty-five students. This would enable the instructor to use individualized techniques in a regular classroom and evaluate whether enrichment and remedial and review instruction, as well as basic instruction was effective. It would provide information about both performance and learning time when materials are used in normal classroom conditions.

4. All materials developed should be included and evaluated in the field evaluation. This may include the students' manual, instructional materials, audiovisual equipment required for materials, tests, and the teacher's guide.

IV. Formative Evaluation of Selected Materials and Instructor-Delivered Instruction

The major difference between the field evaluation of selected materials and original materials is that the instructor is present during the evaluation of selected existing materials. This provides the instructor with the opportunity to observe the use of the materials and to determine the adequacy of the various components of the instructional strategy.

IMPLEMENTATION

The ideas presented here can be put into the input, process, and output model.

Input

The input for a formative evaluation is a draft set of materials that can be used with students on a trial-revise basis. These materials include any tests to be used, the instructions, and any special student directions or guides as needed. Under special circumstances, a lesson plan may replace the instructional materials.

Process

The procedures require the instructor to design and carry out one-to-one, small-group, and field-trial formative evaluation studies in order to collect data concerning the effectiveness of the materials.

Output

The products of this component are the data from the one-to-one, small-group, and field-trial evaluations.

REFERENCES

Baker, E. L., & Alkin, M. C. Formative evaluation of instructional development. *Audio Visual Communication Review*, Vol. 21, No. 4, 1973, 389-418.

   The authors describe in depth the formative evaluation process and some of the research on formative evaluation.

Cronbach, L. J. Course improvement through evaluation. Reprinted in Payne, D. A., & McMorris, R. F. (Eds.) *Educational and Psychological Measurement.* Morristown, N. J.: General Learning Press, 1975, 243-256.

This is the original article on the need for formative evaluation of instructional materials.

Komoski, K. P. An imbalance of product quantity and instructional quality: The imperative of empiricism. *Audio Visual Communication Review,* Vol. 4, 1974, 357-386.

Komoski documents the number of instructional materials being commercially produced and the lack of formative evaluation prior to sale.

Scott, R. O., & Yelon, S. R. The student as a coauthor—The first step in formative evaluation. *Education Technology*, October, 1969, 76-78. √

This is one of the few articles which describes procedures to be used in one-to-one formative evaluation with students.

Scriven, M., Tyler, R., & Gagné, R. *Perspectives of curriculum evaluation.* AERA Monograph Series on Curriculum Evaluation, Chicago: Rand McNally, 1967.

In this article the authors made the first functional distinction between formative and summative evaluation.

10 Revising Instructional Materials

OBJECTIVES

1. *You will be able to describe various methods for summarizing data obtained from formative evaluation studies.*

2. *You will be able to summarize data obtained from formative evaluation studies.*

3. *You will be able to use summarized formative evaluation data to identify weaknesses in instructional materials and instructor-delivered instruction.*

4. *Given formative evaluation data for a set of instructional materials, you will be able to identify problems in the materials, suggest revisions for the materials, and revise them appropriately.*

BACKGROUND

The area about which we know the least in the entire instructional design, development, and evaluation process is that of revising instructional materials. If you examine almost any instructional design model, you will find major emphasis on the concept of formative evaluation, that is, on collecting data to determine the effectiveness of instructional materials. The model will then indicate that after data have been collected and summarized, you should revise the materials "appropriately." Although a number of studies have indicated the benefit of revising instructional materials, they have not proposed any theories around which to gather the data. In effect, we interpret the data in the most reasonable way possible and then make changes which seem to be indicated by the data.

There are two basic types of revisions you will consider with your materials. The first is changes that need to be made in the content or substance of the materials to make them more accurate or more effective as a learning tool. The second type of change is related to the procedures employed in using your materials.

In this chapter, we will point out how data from various formative evaluation sources can be summarized and used to identify portions of your materials that need to be revised. You need not be concerned about statistics in this step of the instructional design process. For the most part, simplistic descriptive summaries of the data are sufficient. Elaborate statistical tests are seldom employed in the formative evaluation and revision process.

CONCEPTS

There are many different ways in which the data collected in the formative evaluation may be summarized to point to areas of student difficulties. The methods we describe here are merely suggestive. As you begin to work with your own data, you may find other techniques that will help you to derive more insight from them.

Perhaps the most basic data table is one which lists the entry-behavior scores, pretest scores, and the posttest scores for each student who participated in the small group or field trial formative evaluations. Often these scores are represented in terms of percentage of the total possible points on each instrument or as a percentage of the objectives which students mastered. Table 10.1 indicates how these data might be displayed. Notice that the two comparisons in Table 10.1 differ only in terms of the heading.

What criterion for mastery?

Table 10.1
**Entry Behavior, Pretest, and Posttest Data Summarized
by the Percent of Total Possible Scores
and by the Percent of Total Possible Objectives**

Student Performance as a Percent of Total Possible Score				Student Performance as a Percent of Total Possible Objectives			
Student Number	Entry Behavior	Pretest	Posttest	Student Number	Entry Behavior	Pretest	Posttest
1	90	15	85	1	90	15	85
2	90	25	92	2	90	25	92
3	100	20	87	3	100	20	87
4	90	10	98	4	90	10	98
5	60	0	65	5	60	0	65
6	90	10	82	6	90	10	82
7	95	15	87	7	95	15	87
8	100	20	93	8	100	20	93

A more detailed analysis can be provided by displaying the performance of each individual student in the formative evaluation for each objective. This is most often done by devising one chart for the pretest and another for the posttest. Typically an X in the box for a particular objective and a particular student indicates whether the student successfully achieved that objective. Such a chart, as in the example shown in Table 10.2, indicates the pattern of responses and can be summarized to show the total score for each student, and, more importantly, the percentage of students achieving each objective.

Table 10.2
Student Performance on the Posttest
(X indicates objective was achieved)

Students	Objectives 1	2	3	4	5	Percent
1	X	X	X	X		80
2	X		X	X	X	80
3	X	X	X	X	X	100
4	X	X	X	X		80
5	X		X	X	X	80
6	X	X		X	X	80
7	X	X				40
8	X	X	X			60
	100	75	75	75	50	$\overline{X} = 75$

Percent of Students Achieving
Each Objective

A source of data sometimes overlooked by the instructional designer, but of great importance for pinpointing students who have problems working through instructional materials, is embedded test items. It is very helpful to summarize the performance of students on these test items and to cluster the item data in terms of the objectives to which they relate. A sample of this type of data summary is shown in Table 10.3. Of major interest is the average performance on the items for each objective.

Table 10.3
Percentage Correct on Embedded Test Items, Clustered by Objective

Student	Objective 1	2	3	4	5
1	100	100	100	100	90
2	90	80	90	95	100
3	70	85	80	65	60
4	100	100	90	100	80
5	100	90	100	90	90
6	80	80	70	60	70
7	90	80	85	75	70
8	100	100	90	100	95
Average percent	91	89	88	84	82

Another way to display data is through the use of various graphing techniques. A graph may show the pretest and posttest performance for each objective in the formative evaluation study. You might also want to graph the amount of time required to complete the instructional materials as well as amount of time required for the entry-behaviors test and posttest. An example of a pretest/posttest graph appears in Figure 10.1.

Researchers have found that the best way to summarize data from an attitude questionnaire is to indicate on a blank copy of the attitude questionnaire the percent of students who chose each alternative to the various questions. If you request open-ended, general responses from the students, you can summarize them at the end of the questionnaire.

An important type of data is comments obtained from students, other instructors involved in the formative evaluation, and subject-matter experts who react to the material. It is almost impossible to summarize these comments in tabular or graphic form. It is better to try to relate each of these comments back to the instructional materials themselves, or to the objective in the materials to which they refer. These comments can be written directly on a copy of the materials.

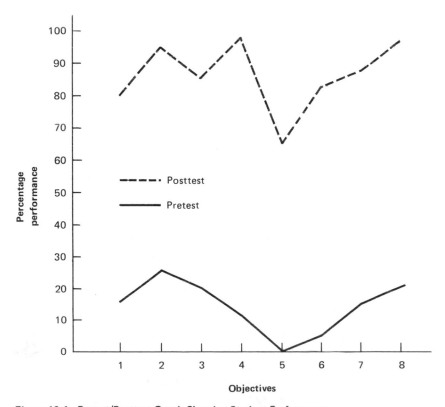

Figure 10.1 Pretest/Posttest Graph Showing Student Performance

The final technique for summarizing formative evaluation data involves the instructional analysis chart. This procedure requires the determination of the average pretest and posttest performance of students participating in the formative evaluation on each of the skills indicated on the instructional analysis chart. The designer draws a copy of the instructional analysis chart but omits the statement of skills. See Figure 10.4 for an example of this technique. The pretest and posttest scores for each objective are entered in the appropriate boxes. This provides an interesting display of the inter-relationships of the scores on the various skills in the instructional materials. It will become apparent if students' performance declines as they reach the top of the hierarchy. You may also find that a skill which is not mastered seems to have little effect on the mastery of related skills.

As you prepare summaries of your data, you will quickly begin to get an overall picture of the general effectiveness of your instructional materials and the extent of revisions you may need to make. After generally examining the data, we suggest that you examine the data in the sequence described below.

First, you should examine the data with regard to the entry behaviors of students. Did the students in the formative evaluation have the entry behaviors you anticipated? If so, did they succeed with the instructional materials? If they did succeed, but did not have the required entry behavior, you must question whether you identified critical entry behaviors.

The second step is to review the pretest and posttest data as displayed on the instructional analysis chart. If you sequenced the materials appropriately and if you identified skills which are hierarchically dependent upon each other, then decrements in student performance should increase as you move upward through the hierarchy—that is, there should be poorer student performance on the final terminal objective than on the early tasks. These data will help you to identify exactly where problems exist and perhaps even suggest a change in the instructional sequence for certain skills.

Third, you might examine the pretest scores to determine the extent to which individual students, and the group as a whole, already have acquired the skills which you were to teach. If they have the majority of skills, then you know you will receive relatively little information about any of the instruction that might need improvement. If they lack these skills, then you will have more confidence in the analyses that follow.

By comparing pretest with posttest scores by objective, which is usually what is done when you examine the instructional analysis chart, you can assess students' performance on each particular objective and begin to focus on specific objectives which appear to need revision.

As you identify objectives on which the students performed poorly, examine the exact wording of the objective and the associated test items. Prior to undertaking a major revision of the instructional materials, look to see if it was poor test items, rather than the materials, which resulted in poor student performance. All that may be needed is revised test items to bring them in line with the objectives and the instruction, rather than a revision of the instructional materials.

The next step is to reexamine the instructional strategy associated with various objectives with which students had difficulty. Was the planned strategy actually used in the instructional materials? Are there alternative strategies that might be employed? The final step is to examine the materials themselves to evaluate the comments made by students, teachers, and subject-matter experts with regard to problem areas.

An important concern in any formative evaluation is to determine the amount of time required by students to complete the instructional materials. It may be necessary for you to revise the materials to make them fit within a particular time period. This is an extremely difficult task and it must be done with great care. With individualized materials it is not unusual for the slowest student to take two or three times longer than the fastest student. Knowing what to remove from the materials without interfering with performance is very difficult to determine. Often the decision can be made only after a trial/revise/trial/revise process with target students.

Data that relate to the implementation of the instructional materials must also be examined. We suggested earlier that you may gather misleading data simply due to the faulty operations of some media equipment. There may also have been disruptions in the classroom, a break to go to lunch, or any one of a million other kinds of activities which are common in various instructional settings. Some of these activities and disruptions cannot be controlled and simply must be noted and accounted for.

On the other hand, there are procedural concerns that *can* be controlled. Were students hindered by the logistics required to use the materials; were there questions about how to proceed from one step to the next; were there long delays in getting test scores? These are the kinds of problems with implementation procedures often identified in questionnaires and debriefing discussions. Solutions to such problems must be found and incorporated into the instructor's manual to make the instructional activity run more smoothly.

We suggest that as you begin the revision process, you summarize your data as suggested in this chapter. We recognize that the needs of instructional designers will differ according to the type of materials with which they are working. However, the strategy suggested here should apply to almost any instructional design effort.

One caution: Avoid responding too quickly to any single piece of data, whether it is the performance of students on a particular objective, a comment from an individual student, or an observation by a subject-matter expert. They are all valuable pieces of information, but you should attempt to corroborate these data with other data. Look for performance as well as observational data which will help to focus on particular deficiencies in the instructional materials.

An additional suggestion is that when summarizing data from the field evaluation, you should be particularly careful to summarize it in an accurate and attractive fashion. You will probably find that these data will be of interest not only to you as the instructional designer, but will also serve as an effective vehicle to show others how students performed with this mode of instruction. The table and graphs can provide both a general and a detailed description of the overall performance of the students on the materials.

Revising Selected Materials and Instructor-Presented Instruction

The data summary and revision procedures described above are equally appropriate when the instructor develops original instructional materials, uses a variety of selected materials, or works from lecture or presentation notes. The types of data which are collected, the ways in which they are summarized, and the ways in which they are used to direct the revision process are all similar. When working with selected materials, however, there is little opportunity to revise the materials directly, especially if they are commercially produced and copyrighted. Therefore, the instructor can consider the following: In the future, delete portions of the instruction, add other materials, or simply develop supplementary instruction. Procedures for the use of the materials and the student guide in the use of the materials should also be reconsidered in light of formative evaluation data.

Instructors working from lecture notes or an outline have the same flexibility as the developer for changing instruction. A pretest, embedded tests, and a posttest, together with an attitude questionnaire, should provide you with data for a thorough analysis of the instruction. Summary tables that indicate performance on each objective and performance on each item in the hierarchy should be prepared. Examine the objectives and test items before the instructional analysis.

The instructor has class notes that should reflect questions raised by students and responses to those questions. Students' questions should be examined to determine if basic misunderstandings have developed. Were the responses to the questions sufficient to provide adequate performance by students on the related test items?

An instructor who uses lecture notes is also likely to obtain a greater "spread" in the scores on tests and reactions on attitude questionnaires. Research data indicate that by the very nature of group-paced, interactive instruction, some students are unlikely to understand the concepts as rapidly as others during a given class period. Since there are typically no embedded remedial strategies in group instruction, such students learn progressively less during a series of lessons, receive progressively poorer scores, and feel left out, and their attitudes will likely reflect this situation. In this interactive, group-paced mode, students' performance is likely to resemble a bell curve distribution (i.e., a few high scores, a few low scores, and mostly average scores). This indicates that as instruction progressed, increasing numbers of students performed poorly.

Identifying students who are performing poorly, and inserting appropriate activities are important components of the revision process for the instructor who is using an interactive instructional approach. Unlike in the use of instructional materials, the instructor can revise the presentation during instruction and note the reasons for the change, as well as make changes after the instruction has been completed.

One final observation needs to be made. You must recall that we have stressed that you are working with a systems approach and that you are, in fact, building a system. We have also noted that when you change one component of the system, you are changing the whole system. You need to be aware, therefore, that when you make changes through the revision process, you cannot assume that the rest of the instruction which remains unchanged will have the same effectiveness. If the parts do interact with each other, there will be changes. You may hope that these will be changes for the better, but you cannot always assume that this will be the case.

EXAMPLES

The hypothetical data below are based on the instructional analysis of the Roman numerals example from chapter 7. The data are summarized from a field trial of the student's manual, the instructional materials, the tests, and the teacher's guide. The instructor who selects instructional materials or has presented the instruction should be familiar with the total process that follows, but may, in fact, only use portions which are most appropriate for a particular learning activity.

Thirty students from a typical sixth-grade arithmetic class participated in the field test, and the data are summarized in Table 10.4.

The scores reported for sixth-grade students have been further divided into scores for those students who are below average, average, and above average on a measure of general aptitude. This breakdown will be helpful in analyzing students' scores and identifying additional instruction that might be required for the three groups.

If general aptitude scores are unavailable for students, as they often are not, then test scores from appropriate achievement tests may be substituted. A less desirable alternative is to use a general classification of the students as determined by their present instructor. In some situations there will simply be no desirable way to distinguish among students, either on the basis of their aptitudes or test scores, and therefore the data from students should simply be treated as a single group of scores. In the discussion that follows, the term "low scores" can be substituted for "low achievers" without changing the intent of the analysis as it is described.

The posttest scores for the low achievers indicate they failed to answer an adequate number of questions. Their entry skills test scores are also low. Perhaps there was inadequate review and remediation for this group. By

Table 10.4
Summary of Entry Behavior, Pretest, and Posttest Scores

	Student Number	Entry-Behavior Test	Pretest	Posttest
Low Achievers	1	.50*	.00	.60
	2	.40	.10	.60
	3	.40	.10	.50
	4	.50	.00	.60
	5	.70	.00	.80
	6	.60	.20	.80
	7	.50	.00	.60
	8	.50	.00	.60
	9	.40	.00	.50
	10	.15	.00	.20
Average Achievers	11	.50	.00	.80
	12	.70	.10	.90
	13	.70	.00	.85
	14	.60	.20	.70
	15	.80	.30	.80
	16	.75	.20	.85
	17	.65	.00	.85
	18	.95	.00	.90
	19	.85	.10	.85
	20	.75	.20	.75
Above-Average Achievers	21	.75	.50	1.00
	22	.80	.60	1.00
	23	.80	.40	.95
	24	.85	.10	.90
	25	.95	1.00	1.00
	26	.95	1.00	1.00
	27	1.00	1.00	1.00
	28	.90	.25	.90
	29	.95	.50	.90
	30	1.00	.55	1.00

*Scores reported are the percent of items answered correctly on each test.

comparing their pretest and posttest scores, you can see that they did make gains as a result of instruction, but their gains were not adequate for mastery.

The average group scored low on the entry skills section, low on the pretest, and, for the most part, adequately on the posttest. The review and remediation in the instruction appears to be more appropriate for this group.

The high achievers scored well on the entry skills test: some were low and some were high on the pretest, and all were high on the posttest. This table illustrates that students 25, 26, and 27 did not need the instruction and could have been directed to another activity. The review and remediation instruction was sufficient for students 21 and 24. All high-achieving students scored at mastery levels on the posttest.

To make a generalization, it appears the instruction is adequate for above-average achievers. Could it be made more challenging and interesting? This may be answered through collected attitude information. The instruction is adequate for average achievers, but can it be made more efficient or more interesting? Can the posttest scores be improved?

The instruction appears to be inadequate for low achievers, but it is impossible to determine why simply on the basis of this general analysis.

Table 10.5 contains a comparison of the total group's performance for each objective on both the pretest and the posttest. By comparing performance in this way, specific objectives which may need revision can be located. Objectives 5 through 8, 10 through 12, and 14 all appear to be taught adequately. However, objectives 9 and 13 need some revision, and objectives 15 through 20 definitely need major revision.

Table 10.5
Summary of Pretest and Posttest Scores by Objective

Objective	Pretest	Posttest	Objective	Pretest	Posttest
1	100	———	11	50	100
2	100	———	12	30	100
3	100	———	13	10	67
4	100	———	14	10	93
5	70	100	15	10	53
6	60	100	16	10	57
7	60	100	17	10	53
8	27	100	18	10	53
9	17	70	19	10	53
10	63	100	20	10	50

By comparing the pretest summary by objective in Table 10.6 and the posttest summary by objective in Table 10.7, you can observe the patterns of student responses by objective for the three different groups. Note that on the posttest, Table 10.7, test questions for objectives 1 through 4 were dropped, because, based on student performance on the pretest, the entire population already seemed to have these skills. Entry-behavior objectives 5 through 9 remain on the posttest, because instruction for remediation and review purposes is needed in the instructional materials.

All students in the above-average group mastered all twenty objectives. Students in the average group achieved all entry-behavior objectives, but several missed objectives toward the end of the instruction. Almost all students in the below-average group missed questions on objectives 9, 13, 15, 16, 17, 18, 19, and 20, while they generally answered questions 10, 11, 12, and 14 correctly. As you can observe, when response patterns exist they can be detected if results are summarized in this fashion.

A summary of student responses to the embedded test items appears in Table 10.8.

Table 10.6
Pretest Summary of Objectives

Student	Entry-Behavior Objectives									Instructional Objectives (X = pass)										
	1	2	3	4	5	6	7	8	9	10	11	12	13	14	15	16	17	18	19	20
Below Average																				
1	x	x	x	x																
2	x	x	x	x						x	x									
3	x	x	x	x																
4	x	x	x	x																
5	x	x	x	x	x															
6	x	x	x	x	x					x	x									
7	x	x	x	x						x										
8	x	x	x	x																
9	x	x	x	x																
10	x	x	x	x																
Average																				
11	x	x	x	x						x	x									
12	x	x	x	x	x	x	x													
13	x	x	x	x	x	x	x													
14	x	x	x	x	x					x	x									
15	x	x	x	x	x	x	x			x	x	x								
16	x	x	x	x	x	x	x			x										
17	x	x	x	x	x	x	x													
18	x	x	x	x	x	x	x	x												
19	x	x	x	x	x	x	x			x										
20	x	x	x	x	x	x	x			x	x									
Above Average																				
21	x	x	x	x	x	x	x			x	x	x								
22	x	x	x	x	x	x	x			x	x	x								
23	x	x	x	x	x	x	x			x	x	x								
24	x	x	x	x	x	x	x	x		x										
25	x	x	x	x	x	x	x	x	x	x	x	x	x	x	x	x	x	x	x	x
26	x	x	x	x	x	x	x	x	x	x	x	x	x	x	x	x	x	x	x	x
27	x	x	x	x	x	x	x	x	x	x	x	x	x	x	x	x	x	x	x	x
28	x	x	x	x	x	x	x	x		x	x									
29	x	x	x	x	x	x	x	x	x	x	x	x								
30	x	x	x	x	x	x	x	x	x	x	x	x								

By displaying students' performance on embedded test questions, the designer can observe patterns of responses and quickly identify examples of presentations which are unclear as well as identify members of student groups who failed to receive enough instruction. For example, note question 16 under objective 13 in Table 10.8. Only four students out of thirty answered that question correctly, three of which were in the top group. The objective is related to the introduction of rules for subtraction. Perhaps something was left out of the instruction, the example was unclear, or the question was too confusing. A careful study of the test items and the instruction at that point will probably reveal the problem.

Table 10.7
Posttest Summary of Objectives

Student	Entry-Behavior Objectives									Instructional Objectives (X = pass)										
	1	2	3	4	5	6	7	8	9	10	11	12	13	14	15	16	17	18	19	20
Below Average																				
1					x	x	x	x		x	x	x		x						
2					x	x	x	x		x	x	x		x						
3					x	x	x	x		x	x	x		x						
4					x	x	x	x		x	x	x		x						
5					x	x	x	x	x	x	x	x	x	x						
6					x	x	x	x	x	x	x	x	x	x						
7					x	x	x	x		x	x	x		x						
8					x	x	x	x		x	x	x		x						
9					x	x	x	x		x	x	x								
10					x	x				x	x	x								
Average																				
11					x	x	x	x	x	x	x	x		x						
12					x	x	x	x	x	x	x	x	x	x	x	x	x	x	x	x
13					x	x	x	x	x	x	x	x	x	x	x	x				
14					x	x	x	x	x	x	x	x	x	x		x	x	x	x	
15					x	x	x	x	x	x	x	x	x	x						
16					x	x	x	x	x	x	x	x	x	x	x	x	x	x	x	x
17					x	x	x	x		x	x	x	x	x	x	x	x	x	x	x
18					x	x	x	x	x	x	x	x	x	x	x	x	x	x	x	x
19					x	x	x	x	x	x	x	x	x	x						
20					x	x	x	x	x	x	x	x		x	x	x	x	x	x	x
Above Average																				
21					x	x	x	x	x	x	x	x	x	x	x	x	x	x	x	x
22					x	x	x	x	x	x	x	x	x	x	x	x	x	x	x	x
23					x	x	x	x	x	x	x	x	x	x	x	x	x	x	x	x
24					x	x	x	x	x	x	x	x	x	x	x	x	x	x	x	x
25					x	x	x	x	x	x	x	x	x	x	x	x	x	x	x	x
26					x	x	x	x	x	x	x	x	x	x	x	x	x	x	x	x
27					x	x	x	x	x	x	x	x	x	x	x	x	x	x	x	x
28					x	x	x	x	x	x	x	x	x	x	x	x	x	x	x	x
29					x	x	x	x	x	x	x	x	x	x	x	x	x	x	x	x
30					x	x	x	x	x	x	x	x	x	x	x	x	x	x	x	x

The instructor can also compare at a glance the performance of students with different entry skills and achievement levels. It will become obvious where slower students should be branched to additional examples for practice.

Students' test results as well as the time required to complete their instruction can be graphed to illustrate their performance on the various measures. Figure 10.2 is a graph of the average time required on each objective for low, average, and above-average math students. Figure 10.3 is a graph of the average scores for the below-average, average, and above-average groups on the entry-skills test, pretest, and posttest.

Table 10.8
Student Responses on Embedded Items

Objectives	8			9			10			11			12			13		14				15			16			17			18			19			20		
Embedded Items	1	2	3	4	5	6	7	8	9	10	11	12	13	14	15	16	17	18	19	20	21	22	23	24	25	26	27	28	29	30	31	32	33	34	35	36	37	38	39
Students Below Average																																							
1	x	x	x	x			x	x	x	x	x	x		x	x		x		x	x	x				x														
2		x	x							x	x		x	x	x	x	x		x	x					x														
3			x	x	x					x	x	x	x	x			x								x														
4	x	x	x	x	x					x	x		x	x		x	x						x																
5		x	x	x	x	x	x	x	x	x	x	x	x	x	x		x		x	x	x	x	x		x	x		x											
6		x	x	x	x	x	x	x	x	x	x	x	x	x	x		x		x	x	x	x	x		x	x		x											
7		x	x				x			x	x		x	x	x	x	x						x	x		x													
8										x	x		x				x					x	x	x	x														
9	x	x	x	x						x	x		x		x		x		x																				
10			x	x			x	x	x				x	x	x	x	x		x						x														
Average																																							
11	x	x	x	x	x	x	x	x	x	x	x	x	x	x	x				x	x	x	x	x	x	x	x	x		x										
12	x	x	x				x	x	x								x	x	x	x	x	x	x	x	x	x	x	x		x	x	x	x	x		x	x	x	x
13		x	x	x	x	x	x	x	x	x	x	x	x	x	x	x	x			x	x	x		x	x		x	x											
14		x	x				x	x	x	x	x	x	x	x	x	x	x	x	x	x	x	x	x	x		x		x	x			x	x		x		x		x
15	x	x	x	x	x	x	x	x	x	x	x	x		x	x		x		x	x	x	x	x			x			x		x								
16		x	x				x	x	x	x	x			x	x		x	x		x	x	x	x	x	x		x		x			x		x	x	x	x		x	x
17	x			x	x	x	x	x	x	x	x	x	x	x	x	x	x		x	x	x	x	x	x	x	x	x		x		x			x	x	x	x	x	x
18	x	x	x				x	x	x	x	x	x	x	x	x	x	x		x	x	x	x	x	x		x	x	x		x		x	x	x	x	x	x	x	x
19	x	x	x	x	x	x	x	x	x	x	x	x	x	x	x				x	x	x	x	x	x		x			x				x	x	x	x	x	x	x
20		x	x	x	x	x	x	x	x	x	x	x	x	x					x	x	x	x	x	x	x	x	x		x	x		x	x	x	x	x	x	x	x
Above Average																																							
21	x	x	x	x	x	x	x	x	x	x	x	x	x	x	x				x	x	x	x	x	x	x	x	x		x	x		x	x		x	x	x	x	x
22	x	x	x	x	x	x	x	x	x	x	x	x	x	x	x		x	x	x	x	x	x	x		x	x	x	x	x	x	x	x	x	x	x	x	x	x	x
23	x	x	x	x	x	x	x	x	x	x	x	x	x	x	x		x	x	x	x	x	x		x	x	x	x	x	x	x		x	x	x	x	x	x	x	x
24	x	x	x	x	x	x	x	x	x	x	x	x	x	x	x	x	x	x	x	x	x		x	x	x	x	x		x	x		x	x	x	x	x	x	x	x
25	x	x	x	x	x	x	x	x	x	x	x	x	x	x	x		x	x	x	x	x	x	x	x	x	x	x	x	x	x		x	x	x	x	x	x	x	x
26	x	x	x	x	x	x	x	x	x	x	x	x	x	x	x		x	x	x	x	x	x	x		x	x	x	x	x	x		x	x	x	x	x	x	x	x
27	x	x	x	x	x	x	x	x	x	x	x	x	x	x	x		x	x	x	x	x		x	x	x	x	x		x	x		x	x	x	x	x	x	x	x
28	x	x	x	x	x	x	x	x	x	x	x	x	x	x	x	x		x	x	x	x	x	x		x	x	x	x		x	x		x	x	x	x	x	x	x
29	x	x	x	x	x	x	x	x	x	x	x	x	x	x	x		x	x	x	x	x	x	x	x	x	x	x		x	x		x	x	x	x	x	x	x	x
30	x	x	x	x	x	x	x	x	x	x	x	x	x	x	x		x	x	x	x	x		x	x	x	x	x		x	x		x	x	x	x	x	x	x	x

By observing your students' performance on the time graph in Figure 10.2 you can determine which lessons meet your expectations of thirty minutes per lesson. You can also determine which objectives could be clustered to better meet the thirty-minute time frame. For example, observe the line for above-average students on objectives 8, 9, and 10. It required only thirty minutes for these students to complete the review of these skills; therefore clustering objectives 8, 9, and 10 into the first instructional activity for the above-average students would be advisable. The average achievers required sixty-five minutes and the below-average achievers required one hundred minutes to complete the same instruction. The graph in Figure 10.2 illustrates the error of making the same clustering decisions for all sixth-graders.

Another interesting phenomena illustrated on the time graph is the narrowing of time requirements between the average and below-average achievers on objectives 17 through 20. If you consider the time graph alone, it would appear that below-average students are catching up. Using other summary tables, you can see that this is *not* the case. The below-average students

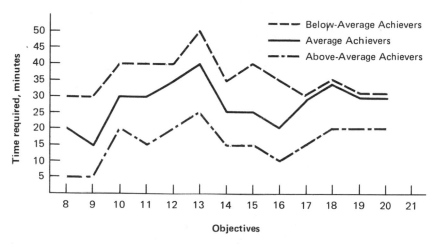

Figure 10.2 Average Time Required to Complete the Module for Below-Average, Average, and Above-Average Achievers

missed all the test items on objectives 17 through 20. It appears from these combined sources of information that the low achievers have given up. The time graph helps explain students' performance on objectives as well, because the instructor may think students are spending a great deal of extra time on objectives they miss, when in fact they may be completing the instruction along with their friends. A combination of displays of performance will help answer some questions about students' performance which might otherwise appear mysterious.

The graph in Figure 10.3, which compares students' performance, illustrates that students in the three different achievement groups enter the instruction with very different capabilities. It appears that either three different versions of the instruction are needed, or a pretest/branching model should be used to move higher-achieving students through instruction they already know.

Table 10.9 summarizes students' responses on an attitude questionnaire.

Table 10.9
Sample Questions from an Attitude Questionnaire

	Percent Responding "Yes"		
	Below Average	Average	Above Average
1. Did you enjoy the discussion about ancient Rome?	90	90	90
2. Were the examples clear and easy to follow?	20	70	90
3. Was the instruction interesting?	60	80	90
4. Was the instruction too long?	10	60	90

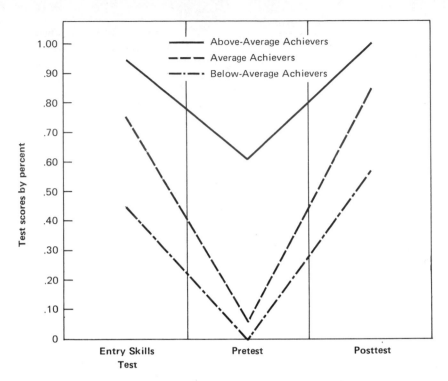

Figure 10.3   Average Scores on the Entry Skills Test, Pretest, and Posttest for Below-Average, Average, and Above-Average Achievers

From this example you can see that students from different groups had very different reactions to the instruction. If students in the target population had not been identified and blocked, the responses the designers received would have been averaged across all students. For example, average the students' responses to question 4. Fifty-three percent of the total group of students thought the instruction was too long. This information is not nearly as useful to the designer as the fact that 90 percent of the high achievers and 10 percent of the low achievers thought the instruction was too long.

Likewise, if the designer records students' checks and comments they have made in an instructional packet, confusing areas will soon become obvious. Note words students have circled as unclear, and a pattern of inadequate vocabulary may appear.

A summary chart of pretest and posttest scores which is related to the instructional analysis is very useful. The chart in Figure 10.4 shows such an analysis for the hypothetical data on Roman numerals. (The specific skills represented in the hierarchy can be seen in Figure 3.5.)

The instruction designed for sixth-grade students does not appear to be effective for all members of the target population. Careful analysis of the objectives where students were and were not successful will help locate where revisions are needed in the instruction.

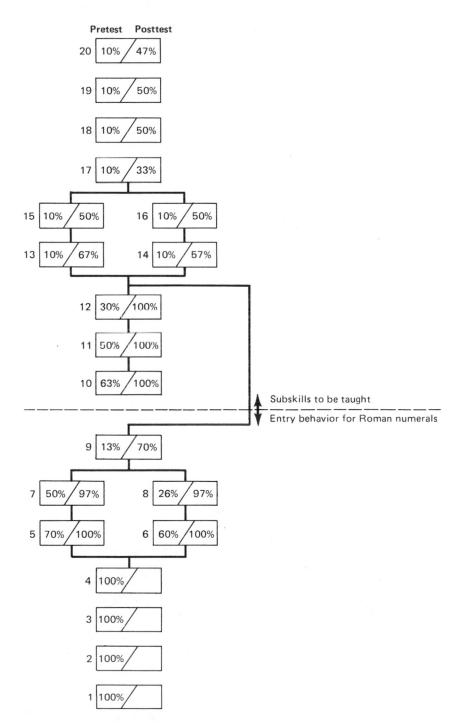

Pretest Posttest

20	10%	47%
19	10%	50%
18	10%	50%
17	10%	33%
15	10% / 50%	16	10% / 50%
13	10% / 67%	14	10% / 57%
12	30%	100%
11	50%	100%
10	63%	100%

Subskills to be taught

Entry behavior for Roman numerals

9	13%	70%
7	50% / 97%	8	26% / 97%
5	70% / 100%	6	60% / 100%
4	100%
3	100%
2	100%
1	100%

Figure 10.4 Summary of Pretest and Posttest Scores for Each Objective in the Instructional Analysis

(Numbers represent percent students achieved on pretest and posttest)

PRACTICE AND FEEDBACK

Practice

A. Examine student performance on entry-behavior objectives.
    1. Examine the performance of students on the entry-behavior skills shown in Table 10.6. Did all the sixth-grade students have the entry behaviors identified (objectives 1 through 9) in the instructional analysis chart?
    2. What are two possible solutions to adequate instruction for sixth-graders who do not have appropriate entry behaviors?

B. Review the pretest and posttest data in the instructional analysis chart in Figure 10.4.
    1. Does instruction appear to be sequenced properly?
    2. In the instruction, do students have an increasingly difficult time working toward the terminal objective? Why might this have occurred?
    3. Can you locate the objectives where students begin to fall behind?

C. Examine pretest scores in Table 10.6 to determine whether students possess some or all of the subskills.
    1. What students in the above-average achievement group do not need this instruction?
    2. Compare the above-average achievers' performance with below-average achievers' performance on the entry behaviors.

D. Compare pretest with posttest scores by objective in Table 10.5.
    1. Determine which specific objectives may need revision.

E. Compare students' performance on embedded questions with instruction in Table 10.8.
    1. For objectives 13 through 20, can you locate any questions which were missed by a majority of the students?
    2. Can you make generalizations about students' performance relative to their math achievement level?

F. Review the amount of time required for students to complete the instruction in Figure 10.2.
    1. How would you cluster objectives for the low-achieving students if instruction had to fit into a thirty-minute period?
    2. What kinds of information would you hope to gain using a procedure to summarize students', teachers', and content experts' comments on the instructional package?

Feedback

A. Student performance on entry-behavior objectives.
    1. No. Many students did not have the entry behaviors the designer

judged they would have. Most of the above-average achievers had the prerequisite skills, as did many of the average achievers. However, the below-average achievers did not have more than half the prescribed entry skills.

2. Two possible solutions would be:

    a. to declare the instruction inappropriate for low-achieving sixth-grade students.

    b. to include instruction and review exercises for needed entry sub-skills in the instructional materials.

B. Pretest and posttest data in instructional chart.

1. Yes. The instruction does appear to be sequenced properly. Though students perform better on the pretest on instructional objectives 10, 11, and 12 than on entry behavior objectives 5, 6, 7, and 8, it is un-derstandable. Objectives for those entry skills are not subordinate to instructional objectives 10, 11, and 12, but rather to objectives 13 and 14.

2. Yes. Students do appear to have an increasingly difficult time working toward the terminal objective. More students were unable to perform the terminal objective, because they appear to lack some subordinate skills.

3. Students begin to fall behind on objectives 13 and 14, which require rules for addition and subtraction of numerals.

C. Pretest scores

1. Students 25, 26, and 27 do not appear to need the instruction. They could correctly answer questions on the terminal objective on the pretest.

2. The above-average achievers had all the prerequisite skills through objective 7; however, they need either review or instruction on ob-jectives 8 and 9. The below-average achievers only have entry skills through objective 4 and will need either review or instruction on objectives 5 through 9. The below-average group will require more instruction on entry skills than will the above-average group.

D. Pretest and posttest scores by objective

1. From the analysis of the pretest and posttest data, it appears that revisions in instruction may be necessary for objectives 9, 13, 15, 16, 17, 18, 19, and 20. This is a large portion of the instruction.

E. Performance on embedded questions

1. It appears that most students had difficulty with question 16 in ob-jective 13, question 24 in objective 15, question 26 in objective 16, question 27 in objective 16, question 29 in objective 17, question 32 in objective 18, and question 37 in objective 20. They had most difficulty with questions 16, 29, 32, and 37. Careful observation of the wording in test questions, directions, instruction, and examples leading to these various questions should pinpoint some problems.

2. The pattern of student responses does allow some generalizations about students' math achievement and their performance in the instruction. The instruction appears very good for high achievers as it is, but it is less appropriate for average achievers, and it is inappropriate for low achievers. Average achievers probably could use more examples and more practice. Low achievers may need simpler examples or smaller steps as well as more practice and feedback.

F. Time required to complete instruction.
1. Perhaps the cluster, presented in Table 10.10, would work to meet the thirty-minute time requirement. So far there are seventeen thirty-minute lessons based on the time chart. It is difficult to determine a time strategy for objectives 16, 17, 18, 19, and 20, because the low-achieving students did not perform well on either the embedded tests or the posttests. Therefore, their performance times are misleading. From this point you could only guess based on their pace in prior objectives.

Table 10.10
Suggested Objective Cluster for Feedback Item Number

Thirty-Minute Periods	Objectives
1	8
2	9
3	Review 8 and 9, introduce 10
4	Complete 10
5	Review 8, 9, 10, introduce 11
6	Complete 11
7	Review 8, 9, 10, 11, and introduce 12
8	Complete 12
9	Introduce 13
10	Complete 13
11	Review 13, introduce 15
12	Complete 15
13	Review 13, 15, introduce 14
14	Complete 14
15	Review 14, introduce 16
16	Complete 16
17	Introduce and complete 17

2. There are several types of information to be gained. Some of these types are:

a. clusters of comments in a given area
b. clusters of checks indicating unclear wording
c. clusters of inappropriate vocabulary
d. directions that are unclear
e. students' incorrect responses which may help determine what confused them
f. comments about procedures, the number, and type of exercises
g. comments about the adequacy of feedback

IMPLEMENTATION

The revision of instructional materials can be summarized in an input, process, output model.

Input

The input for this component is data collected prior to, during, and after the administration of your instructional materials.

Process

1. You should, based on the type of data you have collected, summarize the data to enable you to identify weakness in your materials. (This will include performance as well as attitudinal measures.)
2. Examine the summarized data relative to entry behaviors and draw implications about the entry behaviors of students in your target sample group.
3. Review summarized pretest, embedded test, and posttest data both for total performance, and objective by objective, and superimpose it on your instructional analysis chart. Draw inferences about your sample group's performance on each test and each objective. You may want to compare data obtained from entry-behavior tests with pretest and posttest data as well.
4. Examine the objectives, test items, and instructional strategy for those objectives for which student performance failed to meet your established criteria. Check the objectives, test items, vocabulary, sequence, and instructional strategy for those objectives prior to making direct changes in the instructional materials.
5. Revise the materials based on any faults you find in your original materials. Often these revisions are guided by students' errors, but sometimes they must be made by a careful reanalysis of the instructional strategy, sequence, or time allotted to the learning task.
6. Check procedural and implementation directions as well as equipment required for instruction for possible guides to revision.
7. Revise instruction according to your reanalysis of your tests, materials, directions, procedures, and equipment.

Output

The product you have after this revision should be one that is, we hope, more effective in bringing about intended learning with your target students.

If you made major changes and revisions, another field trial is advisable to check the effectiveness of your revisions.

At this point, with revised, effective materials, you are ready to have a good, professional set of materials produced. You may even want to seek a publisher! Good luck.

REFERENCES

Baker, E. L. *Evaluating instructional programs*. National Institute for Education Researcher Training Task Force, University of California, Los Angeles, 1974.

This book describes the various stages of formative evaluation, the types of data that can be collected, and the types of revisions that may be made.

Singer, R. M., & Dick, W. *Teaching physical education: A systems approach.* Boston: Houghton Mifflin, 1974, 258-275.

The authors stress both content and procedural revisions, with specific reference to the use of instructional analysis charts.

Wolf, R. M. Data analysis and reporting considerations in evaluation. In Popham, W. J. (Ed.), *Evaluation in education, current applications.* Berkeley, Calif.: McCutchan Publishing Corp., 1974, 205-242.

This chapter suggests various ways of setting up evaluation studies, how to analyze data, and how to display data.

11 Summative Evaluation and Grading

OBJECTIVES

1. *You will be able to describe the purpose of summative evaluation and the various types of data and information included in a summative evaluation.*

2. *You will be able to describe several grading methods and relate each method to instructional design and grading philosophy considerations.*

3. *Given a set of test scores, you will be able to assign grades to each student, using at least three different grading methods.*

BACKGROUND

In previous chapters, we described the role of the designer in formative evaluation. The major function of formative evaluation is to collect data and information for the purpose of improving an instructional product or activity. Formative evaluation is conducted as a positive, constructive, nonjudgmental process. At some point, however, you must decide whether the instructional materials are effective. In order to reach that decision, a *summative* evaluation must be conducted. Likewise, at some point an instructor must evaluate a student's performance in instruction and report some type of grade.

The purpose of this chapter is not to teach you how to conduct a summative evaluation of a set of instructional materials, but rather to describe the purpose and procedures used by an instructional designer in the summative evaluation. In addition, we will describe the relationship between these procedures and those used in various grading practices. Several grading methods will be described, along with their implications for the instructor and the student.

CONCEPTS

Summative evaluation may be defined as the design, collection, and interpretation of data and information for a given set of instructional materials for the purpose of determining the value or worth of those materials. In order to undertake a summative evaluation of instructional materials, evaluators must have the materials available to them. In addition, they must also have a set of criterion-referenced assessment instruments for the materials. Evaluators analyze the materials in terms of content coverage, statements of objectives, and the relationship of the test instruments to the objectives. It is likely that an instructor's manual will also be available for examination. The evaluator then makes arrangements for instructors not involved in the design process to use the instructional materials in their classrooms with groups of students from the target population.

Following the analysis of the materials, the next step in a summative evaluation is a pretest of the students in the study. This will determine their entry-skills level for the intended instruction. As the students use the materials, the evaluator observes the instructional process to determine whether the materials are being used by students in the manner in which they were intended to be used. If the instructor has a role in the delivery of the instruction, such as discussion leader or demonstrator of particular examples, the evaluator verifies that the instructor appropriately carries out this role.

After the instruction has been completed, a posttest is administered to determine the students' level of achievement of the various instructional objectives. Typically, an attitude questionnaire is administered to measure the students' reactions to the content, the instructional materials, and the instructional process used for instruction.

The procedures described above closely resemble the techniques undertaken during the field-trial phase of a formative evaluation. Sometimes it is almost impossible to distinguish between a formative evaluation field trial and a summative evaluation. There are two important differences, however. First, the purpose of the formative field trial is to provide data for further revision of the instruction, while a summative evaluation deals with materials which will typically undergo no further revision. Second, the purpose of the formative field trial is to collect data which will facilitate the revision of the instruction. The purpose of a summative evaluation is to determine the value of the present materials for a defined target group.

The summative evaluation procedures already described are basic steps for the evaluator to determine the effectiveness of the instruction and to gather data for a decision about its continued use. There is, however, another important consideration. The question may be raised, "Is this instruction better than . . . ?" In other words, an instructor is often interested in comparing the effectiveness of two or more sets of instructional materials. In order to answer this question, it is necessary to set up an experimental study that includes several different groups of students. At least one group of students must study the newly developed instructional materials, while another group studies other materials or experiences other types of instruction based on the same content.

It is extremely difficult to set up such experimental studies in a manner which satisfactorily meets all the conditions of a scientifically controlled study. Often a number of compromises must be made in terms of the random assignment of students to various instructional activities (i.e., students must often be treated as intact classroom groups), time of day in which instruction is provided, and so forth. Regardless of the difficulties, however, it is necessary to conduct such studies not only to determine which set of instructional materials is more effective (at least with a given set of students), but also to answer such questions as the following:

1. What are the comparative costs of the two sets of materials?
2. How much time do students spend studying the materials?
3. Is any special teacher training required for either set of materials?
4. What are the side effects of using any of the materials (e.g., development of new student interests, increased reading scores)?
5. What are the long-term effects of using the materials?
6. Will the materials be quickly out-of-date or has a system been established for updating them?

These are the types of questions an evaluator must consider when designing a summative evaluation study. Various procedures and techniques can help answer these questions and provide comparisons between two or more instructional products. The purpose of such investigations is to determine the cumulative value of instruction, and to allow a decision maker using this data together with its interpretation to determine which particular set or sets of materials to use. Because of the relative difficulty of replication, however, these techniques are seldom applied to teacher-selected materials and almost never to instructor presentations.

The designer of the materials in question may or may not be involved in a summative evaluation study. The evaluator may wish to work with the designer in obtaining information about the background and development of the materials and in determining the exact process to use in implementing the materials. However, the actual evaluation of the materials usually takes place in a normal classroom setting with regular instructors. The instructional designers are typically absent during the instruction and they have no responsibility for the summary and analysis of collected data.

Summative Evaluation and the Process of Grading

The rationale behind most grading systems is that something has been taught to a group of students, and an assessment of their learning of the content has taken place. Based on the outcome of that assessment a label or grade is assigned to each student. Typically, a certain amount of instruction takes place for a day, a week, or longer, and students are given a test on the instruction. Quite often there are two or more tests given during any grading period. These test scores are accumulated in some fashion and a distribution of the students' scores is determined. The instructor examines the scores and looks for natural gaps between clusters of scores, and, based on the natural gaps that appear, assigns a grade. A variation of this procedure is simply to assign a percentage score to each student on each test and then to compute the average of those tests. Grades are then determined on some basis, such as 90 to 100 percent is an A, 80 to 89 percent is a B, and so on.

What are the implications for the grading process when an instructor uses systematic design procedures? If the instructor follows the procedures described in this text, students will receive well-designed instruction in self-instructional, small-group, or, at times, in large-class formats. Time and materials will be provided for remediation and attempts will be made to provide each student with the instruction needed. At the end of various units of instruction, criterion-referenced posttests directly related to the objectives for the instruction will be administered. If the instruction has been effective, many students should reach mastery on the desired objectives, and relatively few students should obtain poor scores. Then a grade must be assigned.

This, in essence, is a replication of the summative evaluation procedures previously described. It is the responsibility of the instructor to use the data collected to assign students grades which reflect their degree of success in accomplishing the objectives. The instructor's position is similar to that of the decision maker who receives the data from a summative evaluation study. Both can use the data in two different ways. It may be used in an absolute sense, that is, to determine the level of performance achieved on a given set of instructional materials by a given student. The evaluation and decision are made based upon the absolute level of performance. The alternative approach is to make a decision based on relative comparisons. The instructional materials decision maker can determine which is the better of two sets of materials and act accordingly. The instructor can look at the scores of a number of students and decide which students will receive the highest grade in comparison to the other students (regardless of how good or how poor the performance was of the total group).

It may be surprising to find that the use of criterion-referenced tests does not facilitate the grading process or make it automatic. Consider for a moment the writing of an instructional objective. It is the responsibility of the designer to state the performance level expected from the student. This criterion is based on the professional judgment of the designer, which in turn is based upon the designer's experience in teaching the content in the past. While good instructional designers will set reasonable criteria, it must be recognized that, in fact, the criteria are arbitrary.

Another type of evaluation decision is to determine the number of objectives that a student must successfully complete before moving to the next unit. Students may be required to achieve at least eight of the ten objectives in a unit before progressing to the next unit. Such a requirement, while perhaps professionally sound, is relatively arbitrary. Experience with students in the instructional unit can, in the future, lead to changes. The instructor must employ this same type of judgment when determining the grade for a student in a course. There is no automatic system, based on systematic design principles, for assigning grades. Deciding the purpose and intent of grades must be made more from a philosophical point of view than on any type of instructional theory.

Those who struggled with the problem of grading within the context of systematically designed instruction first attempted to describe performance as either meeting the goal of mastery or not. This resulted in a grading system which consisted simply of "pass" or "fail" or, in some situations, "pass" and "incomplete." Students who failed to meet a preset criterion level at the end of a grading period repeated the instruction until they achieved mastery. Upon doing so, they were assigned a grade of "pass" and continued on to the next unit of instruction. Instructors who used this system, however, soon found that there were relatively large gradations in the performance of those students who achieved mastery and were assigned a grade of "pass." There was seemingly a strong urge on the part of the instructors to use a system such as "honors," "pass," and "incomplete" in order to reflect the range of performance exhibited by students. While a few institutions still use this system, grades on a scale of "A" to "F" are more typically used. Given this situation, what methods of assigning student grades are available to the instructor?

Method 1. After considering all the factors involved in the grading process, the instructor may decide that, although criterion-referenced tests have been employed to assess student performance on systematically designed instruction, a comparative or norm-referenced standard will be employed for grading. For example, during a grading period an instructor may use three fifty-item multiple-choice tests to assess student performance. At the end of the grading period, the scores on the three tests may be totaled for each student and the student's rank ordered from the highest to the lowest total score. The instructor will look for natural breaks in the distribution of total scores and assign grades accordingly. This would be considered a relative grading system in which the grade assigned to any particular student depends upon the performance of other students. Using Method 1 could result in a problem: It is possible for most students to score very low on all three tests, but the students with the highest scores would still obtain a grade of "A." The opposite situation may also occur; that is, nearly all students perform very well, but some receive poor grades.

Method 2. If instructors wish to avoid any problems that might exist with Method 1, they may wish to use a fixed-percentage grading method. This is usually reported to the students in advance.

For example, the instructor may wish to announce that the test scores will be converted to percentages and an average percentage of 90 to 100 will be required in order to obtain an A, 80 to 90 for a B, and so forth. This is considered an absolute grading system. The criterion level for achieving a grade is fixed in advance and the grade achieved by any one student does not depend upon the performance of any other student.

Method 3. Some instructors may prefer to relate the grading system more directly to their instructional objectives. Therefore, they may determine in advance how many objectives students must obtain during a given grading period in order to achieve a stated grade. The instructor may announce that, in order for students to achieve a grade of "A," they must achieve mastery on nine or more of the ten objectives covered during the grading period; a grade of B will be assigned to students achieving seven or eight of the objectives; and a grade of C will be assigned to students achieving five or six of the objectives. This method is also an absolute grading system in that students' grades depend on the number of objectives they achieve during a given time period, and do not depend in any way upon the performance of other students.

Method 4. The final grading method is tied directly to the entry ability of students. With Method 4, the grade is based on the amount of material learned during a given time period rather than on the absolute level of achievement at the end of that time. For example, the instructor could negotiate with each student on the number of objectives required to achieve a particular grade. If there is a wide range of individual differences within a group of students, the effort required by one student to achieve three objectives might be equivalent to the effort required by another to achieve ten. Therefore, it might seem reasonable that they should each obtain the same grade. This method would also be considered an absolute method of grading in that a student's grade is based on a predetermined scale negotiated by the instructor and the student. In theory, a student's grade would in no way depend upon the performance of other students in the class.

Today, grading practices in public schools and universities reflect all four of these methods. Most often, elementary schools tend to use Method 4. Students are rewarded and evaluated on the basis of their effort as well as the level of performance they achieve. While this may serve to motivate students, the purpose of a grade (namely, to convey information about the performance level of a student) is obscured. If such a system is used, it is important that parents also receive information on the student's actual level of performance on tests as well as scores on standardized tests in such areas as reading, language, and mathematics.

In middle schools and high schools, there is a tendency to grade on the absolute achievement of students, regardless of the entry ability or effort exerted in the course. Perhaps the most predominant method is the relative performance comparisons among students as identified in Method 1. Methods 2 and 3 are used less frequently. College grading appears to be based predominantly on the relative performance of students described in Method 1.

While traditional grading practices tend to prevail in most institutional settings, a number of instructors use methods that make use of objectives and criterion-referenced testing. Some school systems actually list the major skills and objectives for each curriculum area and provide the parents with a summary of student assessments. This method does not attempt to determine value, but simply indicates achievement or nonachievement of particular skills and objectives.

Instructors have encountered several grading problems that still do not have satisfactory solutions. Consider, for example, the problem of assigning grades to a homogenous group of students, especially if that homogeneity involves very high or very low intellectual ability. Examples of such situations would be an elementary special-education class or a college-equivalent high-school English class. Students in these classes differ greatly from their "average" peers and instructors can therefore expect that regardless of the type of instruction, students' performance will not distribute itself in any type of "normal" fashion. The question must then be raised whether any type of relative grading system is appropriate. For example, should a certain percentage of these students in these classes receive As, Bs, Cs, Ds, and Fs? The answer may vary.

A student who works hard in a college-equivalent English course but does less well than other students in the class might receive a grade of C. If the same student had taken the regular English course, the grade received for the same level of effort would have been an A. This situation does not have an easy resolution. Assigning either an A or a C to the student will result in problems. Seemingly, the best solution is to establish some type of absolute standard of performance in each course. If the student achieves that standard, he or she receives the corresponding grade. If all students reach the standard for an A, they would all receive a grade of A.

The introduction of objective-referenced grading systems and the consideration of absolute standards of performance has occurred at the same time that education is experiencing what has been termed "grade inflation." Colleges and universities in particular have noted dramatic increases in the number of higher grades received by students in the various courses, and some evidence of this is also apparent in high schools. At the same time, standardized achievement test scores have declined. Much of this grade inflation has been attributed to lower grading standards being set by instructors, and such may be the case.

It is important, however, to consider the situation in which an instructor has used systematically designed instruction and criterion-referenced tests designed not to trick, deceive, or create a spread in students' scores. These practices will certainly tend to raise the overall level of performance of a group of students, particularly by raising the grades of students who formerly would have failed or done quite poorly. The instructor who assigns a large percentage of high grades to a group of students under these conditions may be accused of contributing to grade inflation. If students are in fact achieving a clearly defined set of criteria, however, they should be graded accordingly.

If the instructor finds that a group of students is reaching mastery with relative ease, then the criteria for the next group of students may be changed.

Steps for Assigning Grades

The following list contains the steps for collecting data for assigning grades.

1. Prepare and administer the evaluation instruments which will be used to determine student achievement. These instruments may include paper and pencil tests, written reports, oral reports, or other indicators of student performance.

2. Record the scores for all students and summarize the scores. If the tests have different numbers of items or points (such as one test having fifty items and another seventy-five), it may be desirable to convert the scores to percentages of total possible scores, or to simply record the number of objectives achieved or the number of points earned.

3. Based upon the method for assigning grades, the scores should be treated in the following ways:

   a. If Method 1 is used, in which the instructor looks for gaps in the distribution of scores, it is only necessary to total the points or percentages, rank order the students, and look for the natural breaks in the distribution. A letter grade is then assigned to each cluster of scores.

   b. If Method 2 is used, in which absolute standards are set, it is only necessary to total the scores and determine the average percentage for each student. A letter grade can then be assigned based on each student's average percentage.

   c. If Method 3 is used, in which the basic data indicates the number of objectives obtained, it is only necessary to total the number of objectives achieved by each student and then apply the predetermined scale to each total to determine the grade that should be assigned to each student.

   d. If Method 4 is used, in which an individual contract is made with each student indicating the number of objectives that must be achieved during a given grading period, then the number of objectives completed by the student is compared with the original contract and an appropriate grade is assigned.

EXAMPLES

Consider the data shown in Table 11.1. Assume there is a score for each student on a test for each of five objectives. The scores can either be considered as point totals or percentage of items answered correctly. What grades might an instructor assign these six students? How would different grades be assigned if other grading methods were used?

If Method 1 were used, the instructor would look at the total scores or average scores for the students and look for natural breaks or clusters. In rank order they are 95, 91, 86, 82, 80 and 73. The instructor might decide to assign a grade of A to the 95 and 91, B to the 86, C to the 82 and 80, and D to the 73. However, with such a small number of students it is almost impossible to look for clusters of scores in the manner suggested by Method 1.

With Method 2, in which a percentage grading scale is applied to the average test score, it would be possible to determine that the students with average percentage grades of 95 and 91 would receive an A, students with scores of 86, 82, and 80 would receive a B, and the student with a grade of 73 would receive a C.

In order to use Methods 3 and 4, it is necessary to convert the scores as shown in Table 11.1 to indications of pass or fail. Therefore, in Table 11.2 the percentage scores have been converted to 1s or 0s on the basis of whether the student achieved a score of 80 or above on the objective. It should be noted that this 80 percent criterion level is completely arbitrary.

If Method 3 is applied to the data in Table 11.2, and if a predetermined scale had indicated that five correct objectives were needed for an A, four for a B, three for a C, and so on, then two of the students would receive As, one a B, one a C, and two a D.

In Method 4, the instructor would need to have established individual contracts with students in order to determine their grades. Let us assume that

Table 11.1
Assessment Scores on Five Objectives
for Six Students

Student	Objectives					Total	Average
	1	2	3	4	5		
1	85	75	83	87	78	408	82
2	53	88	66	75	82	364	73
3	93	97	100	94	91	475	95
4	87	83	78	95	88	431	86
5	78	74	76	88	83	399	80
6	92	95	83	88	97	455	91

Table 11.2
Scores from Table 11.1 Converted to 1 or 0
Based on 80 Percent Criterion for Each Objective

Student	Objectives					Objectives Achieved
	1	2	3	4	5	
1	1	0	1	1	0	3
2	0	1	0	0	1	2
3	1	1	1	1	1	5
4	1	1	0	1	1	4
5	0	0	0	1	1	2
6	1	1	1	1	1	5

for the first three students the contract indicated that three objectives had to be met in order to get an A, two for a B, and one for a C. But, for the last three students, five objectives had to be obtained in order to get an A, four a B, three a C, two a D, and one an F. It is apparent that, with this small number of objectives, it would be impossible for a student in the first group to achieve anything lower than a D. This would be a problem the instructor would have to deal with. On the other hand, if the contracts described above were applied to students one, two, and three, there would be two As and a B, and the grades for students four, five, and six would be one A, one B, and one D.

It can be seen that a student's grade for a given level of performance can vary depending on the method used to determine the grade—either in comparison with the performance of other students being assessed at the same time, or in comparison with a predetermined standard. Table 11.3 lists each of the six students and the grade each would receive with the four grading methods.

Table 11.3
Grades Which Would Be Assigned to the Six Students Based
on the Four Grading Methods

Student	Grading Methods			
	1	2	3	4
1	C	B	C	A
2	D	C	D	B
3	A	A	A	A
4	B	B	B	B
5	C	B	D	D
6	A	A	A	A

PRACTICE AND FEEDBACK

Practice

Use Table 11.4 to determine the grades which would be assigned to the eight students, based on their performance on the five objectives. Assume that on each assessment a student has received a score of 20 or 0, depending on whether he or she achieved the objective. You may also make the following assumptions when using the various methods:

1. When using Method 2, assume that 90 to 100 is an A, 80 to 89 a B, 70 to 79 a C, and so on.
2. When using Method 3, assume that achievement of four or five objectives is an A, three a B, two a C, one a D, and zero an F.
3. When using Method 4, assume that students one through four must meet criterion for five objectives to get an A, four for a B, and so on. Students five through eight must obtain three for an A, two for a B, one for a C, and zero for an F.

Table 11.4
Scores for Eight Students on Five Assignments*
Using a Pass/Fail Strategy

Student	Objectives					Total
	1	2	3	4	5	
1	20	20	20	0	0	60
2	20	0	20	20	20	80
3	20	20	20	20	20	100
4	20	20	20	20	0	80
5	20	0	20	20	20	80
6	20	20	0	20	20	80
7	20	20	0	0	0	40
8	20	20	20	0	0	60

*20 = pass and 0 = fail on the objective

After you have applied the scales suggested above, create a table like that illustrated in Table 11.3 and indicate the various grades students would receive when the various grading methods are employed. You might also want to apply standards other than those which have been suggested and see what effect those have on the distribution of grades.

Feedback

You should compare the grades you obtained with those shown in Table 11.5. You probably will have noted that, regardless of the scale you use, the top students will nearly always obtain grades of A or B and that the scales most influence the grades of students receiving lower point totals or achieving mastery on fewer objectives.

Table 11.5
Grades Which Would Have Been Assigned to the Eight Students
in Table 11.4 Based on the Four Grading Methods

Student	Grading Methods			
	1	2	3	4
1	C	F	B	C
2	B	B	A	B
3	A	A	A	A
4	B	B	A	B
5	B	B	A	A
6	B	B	A	A
7	D	F	C	B
8	C	F	B	A

IMPLEMENTATION

This chapter has drawn an analogy between the summative evaluation process and the task of assigning grades. The instructional designer's major input into a summative evaluation is a set of instructional materials and evaluation instruments. Various instruments are administered and the resulting data is summarized and interpreted by the evaluator. The output is a report that describes the summative evaluation study and includes an interpretation of the data. A report is issued to a decision maker (not the instructional designer) who must determine the value of the instruction.

There is a direct analogy between this process and that of grading students. The instructor has an obligation to collect data on student performance in order to assign a grade. Therefore, the following three phases have been considered:

Input

Instruments for assessing student performance and a predetermined plan for grading that performance. This grading plan is usually shared with students prior to the instruction.

Process

Students are observed during instruction and are tested with several assessment instruments. The scores on the tests are summarized and pre-established grading scales are applied.

Output

Grades are assigned to students which reflect their performance following instruction.

REFERENCES

Dick, W. Summative evaluation. In L. J. Briggs (Ed.), *Instructional design*. Englewood Cliffs, N. J.: Educational Technology Publications, Inc., 1977.
    The major models of summative evaluation are presented together with a step-by-step description of the process.
Gagné, R. M., & Briggs, L. J. *Principles of instructional design*. New York: Holt, Rinehart, and Winston, Inc., 1974, 236-238.
    This reference includes a brief description of the summative evaluation process from the instructional designer's point of view.
Payne D. A. *The specification and measurement of learning outcomes*. Waltham, Mass.: Blaisdell Publishing Company, 1968.
    This book includes an excellent description and implications of the various grading options available to instructors.

Index